D0783751

The Fox Boy

The Fox Boy

THE STORY OF AN ABDUCTED CHILD

Peter Walker

BLOOMSBURY

First published in Great Britain 2001

Copyright © Peter Walker 2001

The moral right of the author has been asserted

Bloomsbury Publishing Plc, 38 Soho Square, London W1D 3HB

A CIP catalogue record for this book
is available from the British Library

ISBN 0 7475 5347 5

10 9 8 7 6 5 4 3 2 1

Typeset by Hewer Text Ltd, Edinburgh
Printed in England by Clays Ltd, St Ives plc

For Miri Rangi

Contents

List of Illustrations

Acknowledgements

With thanks to Amiria Rangi, Raukura Coffey, Huriana Raven, Piripi Walker, Oriwa Solomon, Te Miringa Hohaia, Jim Vivieaere, Jane Campion, Richard McArley, Sue Hancock, Sandy and Lorna Parata, Te Rapa Broughton, Rauru Broughton, Melissa Collow, Brian Tracy, Kathy Walker, John and Nan Fogarty, Griz Park, Mary and Andrew Collow, Jimmy and Eve Wallace, Samantha Russell and Dan Witters; and in memory of the late Matthew Pohio Timms who three times came along for the ride.

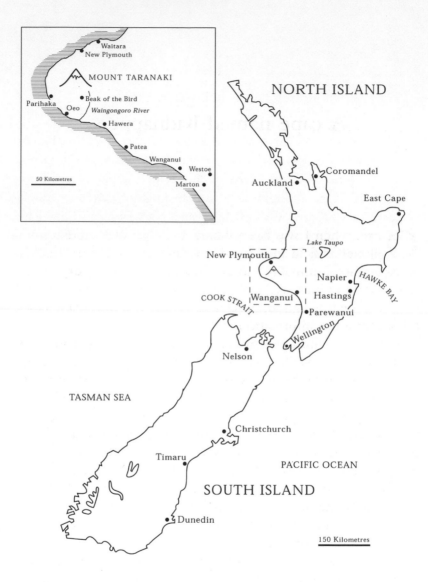

Waitara
New Plymouth

MOUNT TARANAKI

Parihaka
Oeo
Beak of the Bird
Waingongoro River
Hawera

Patea
Wanganui
Westoe
Marton

50 Kilometres

NORTH ISLAND

Coromandel

Auckland

East Cape

Lake Taupo

New Plymouth

Napier
HAWKE BAY

COOK STRAIT
Wanganui
Hastings

Parewanui

Wellington

Nelson

TASMAN SEA

Christchurch

Timaru

PACIFIC OCEAN

SOUTH ISLAND

Dunedin

150 Kilometres

1

A cape named Kidnappers

Once, when I was twenty-two, I stood in the middle of a ploughed field and listened to a farmer tell a ghost story. It was a bright autumn day and the furrows gave off the dry, dusty smell of old upholstery. The farmer spoke in a laconic tone, to show that he was a good, sensible man, and not to be blamed for transmitting the information to hand.

There was a third person standing a few feet away from us. I wasn't sure if he was listening or not. He had a smile on his face, which might have been one of embarrassment or approval; on the other hand, he could have been miles away, thinking of something else. Or perhaps he was just squinting at the sun. He was the farmhand who lived with his wife and children in a paintless house down the road near the coast. He was a Maori. As, apparently, was the ghost.

This was the story Gordon told me. For a long time, almost from the day he moved on to his land – one of the new blocks the government gave soldiers after the Second World War – there was a series of disasters in one part of the farm, which was the field we were now in. Tractors broke down; fencing-wire snapped, lashing the fencer across his face; sheep struggled through barbed wire in order to cast themselves over a precipice. I forget the full catalogue of rural mishaps. One day, the top-dresser pilot came in to land and announced that his engine

1

had kept cutting out while he was flying over this particular spot.

'Finally,' said Gordon, pointing his thumb at the farm hand, 'one of these fellas told me what the problem was. He said there was a Maori spirit up here who didn't like me on his territory. He said I had to *talk* to it and, you know, mend fences.

'So I came up here one day, and I looked around, and I said: "Now, listen: I didn't mean to do any harm. I'm sorry if I've disturbed you. I'm only trying to make a living, and if you leave me alone I'd be grateful.'

'And since then,' said Gordon, 'there hasn't been a peep out of the old bugger.'

This wasn't, clearly, one of the great ghost stories. It lacked suspense, and the degree of obstinacy one expects of the dark powers. At first I thought that it might be just another excuse to add to the list of reasons why Gordon's farm was something of a failure and a reproach to the district. The property was too small – only eight hundred acres of hill country. The soil was poor. The price of fertiliser was high. Then there was Gordon's wife who had taken herself off to live in an expensive hotel on the Marine Parade in Napier. And there were also the bottles of Scotch on the sideboard, towards which, on that farm, thoughts turned lightly at the close of day.

But I was pleased to hear the story all the same. It added a dimension to the matter-of-fact landscape and even to Gordon, who was the father of an old school friend. I liked the thought of him reluctantly plugging up the hill on his tractor to commune with a spirit in this field beside the Mohaka Gorge.

The most interesting thing, however, about the tale escaped my attention for several years.

Even with the thistles in the paddocks and the empty bottles at the back door it was a lovely place, the farm at Kotemaori. It had the blackest night sky I had ever looked up into, with stars like

Van Gogh's shining above the house and shearing-shed; behind the farm, hills rose towards a dark line, the edge of the Urewera forest, the home of the Tuhoe, the least-assimilated Maori tribe in New Zealand.

From a hilltop nearer the road you could see, in the other direction, the wide sweep of Hawke Bay, sixty miles across, always empty, always azure. With binoculars you could sometimes just make out, in the middle of the bay, plumes of white spray rising where the gannets dived. It was like watching a far-off battle, Iwo Jima or Midway, where the ships are invisible to one another and the explosions rise among them, random, white, dreamlike.

At least one naval battle, a real one, has been fought in Hawke Bay. This took place not far from the southern end of the bay, a headland called Cape Kidnappers, and it was this engagement which gave the headland its name. If anyone in the month of October 1769 had happened to be equipped with binoculars and standing on the hill where Gordon's house now stands they might have watched a curious series of ancounters between a three-masted English ship – a Whitby collier equipped for a global voyage – and a fleet of Maori canoes. For two days, the ship had been zigzagging around the bay, skirmishing with Maori, whose pugnacity surprised the English. 'This Reine of courage is unparrelled' wrote one sailor, 'these People was so far from shewing any kind of fear . . .' Both races were utterly strange to each other. Here is a Maori account of a first contact:

It was during the nights of Tangaroa [23rd to 26th nights of the moon] on the night called Whatitiri Papa [Crashing Thunder]. The seas were calm and there was no wind. Before dawn when everything was still, the canoes floated, waiting to catch the land breeze. They sailed out and as dawn came they reached the fishing grounds. Then a great boat full of *turehu* [fairy people], *purehurehu* [misty-looking], *ma* [fair], pale like

3

albinos, came paddling towards us. This is what their language sounded like:

Pakepakeha pakepakeha
Hoi hoi hii, hoi hoi hii
hihi hii, hihi hii

In no time their boat seemed to rise up out of the sea, it looked as if they were paddling in misty air and finally they were lost in the clouds.

There is no 's' in the Maori language. That *hihi hii* was a way of reproducing the sibilance of English. The English sailors would have been surprised to know that that was the main impression they made. They *hissed*. To put it simply, there is a gap between two races which have never met before. Neither would recognise themselves as they are seen across that space. Time – the thousands or tens of thousands of years lived apart – is suddenly compacted. There might, for example, be a peculiar hissing sound in the air. History becomes denser and denser and normal rules of behaviour do not apply.

One of the strangest phenomena in the gap is what happens to children who wander or fall into it. Abduction is carried out without compunction and even with the sense of conferring benefit.

In the climacteric encounter near Cape Kidnappers, a skirmish broke out while both sides were bartering for fish and pieces of cloth. A boy on board the ship was seized, the marines fired at the abductors, the Maori holding the boy was killed, the child leapt into the sea, a canoe came after him, the cannon was fired, canoes shot this way and that, more Maori were killed, then the canoe fleet made off at high speed and the engagement was over.

The contact between Maori and English was at that point only one week long, but this was not the first interracial kidnapping that had taken place. A few days before, a hundred miles north, the English had seized three Maori boys. The plan

4

was to capture some locals, take them aboard and treat them kindly in an attempt to gain their friendship.

The three boys ate heartily, danced, fell asleep, woke in the middle of the night, wept, and in the dark sang a song 'like a Psalm tune, containing many notes and semitones' to comfort themselves.

In the process of seizing these strangers, the English had had to kill two men and wound two others. They did not name a headland after this.

The kidnappings between Maori and English during that one week in 1769 were the first of a series that were carried out, by both sides, in New Zealand. And of course those are only a small part of a very old theme, of removal and transformation – as old, as a Jewish friend said to me, as the story of Moses. For three centuries Ottoman Turks made the abduction of Greek and Serbian Christian children a state policy. In living memory, thousands of Polish youngsters were taken by the Nazis and an unknown number of Aboriginals were taken from their parents by a white government, in order, it was said, to give them a better life.

Whatever the motive, the real impulse, the zest in the performance, comes from the idea of transformation.

This is worth examining for a moment. The child wanders into the gap, but the gap is not a real place, it exists only in the mind. In other words it is not so much that the child is in the gap, as that the gap is in the child. And there it can be reduced, erased, or turned into its exact opposite, so that the child's native race become the aliens. There is a paradox here: the greater the apparent distance between two peoples, the greater their hostility to each other – between Poles and Germans, for instance, or Aborigines and Australian whites – the more readily the experiment of transformation is undertaken.

A hundred years after the events at Cape Kidnappers, another child, a Maori boy aged five or six, was captured in a forest, and was then adopted by the Prime Minister of the day, educated to become a lawyer and an 'English gentleman'.

There was one distinction in his case. In all the thousands of instances of children being carried across no man's land into the possession of strangers, there have been few photographers standing by to record the moment. A few days after this kidnapping, however, the boy was photographed in a studio in the town of Wanganui.

He is wearing an Eton suit and good English boots. There is a vase of flowers and a book – let's say a Bible – on an ebony table with a spiral stand. There is a painted classical landscape as backdrop. Someone has combed the boy's hair and made him put one hand in his trouser pocket. He looks as if he has seen a ghost.

Only one original print of the photograph exists. It is in the National Library in Wellington. Who deposited it there, and when, are not known. On its back, in careful, faint handwriting, are a number of inaccuracies. It is in the nature of images to change their efficacy, and this photograph of a kidnapped child – the image of powerlessness – has now accquired, more than a hundred years later, an unexpected potency. Now, for example, it waylaid me. I saw a copy of the picture a few months before I was to go to New Zealand to write a travel book. Well, I thought, looking at this child's expression, I wonder what happened to *you*.

I knew he had been adopted by Sir William Fox, and was trained up as the 'first Maori lawyer.' I also knew from brief published references that, at the age of nineteen, he went back to his own people, which, it was said, 'greatly displeased Sir William and Lady Fox'. And I thought it would be interesting to track his progress out of a Maori forest, into the palms and ferns of drawing rooms in Wellington and London, and then beyond. Knowing what I did of New Zealand and the Maori, a notably memorious people, I also thought: I bet I can find out.

About thirty miles around the coast from Gordon's farm a smudge like a grey thumbprint is visible – the town of Napier, where I lived from the age of fifteen to eighteen. Behind that on the plains is its twin city, Hastings, where I had gone to school. At the far end of the bay, beyond both cities, stands a line of saw-tooth cliffs ending in a cape where the gannets nested. The final tooth is the one named Cape Kidnappers, and the birds have coloured it a dirty off-white.

One year when I was still at high school, I made a trip out to Cape Kidnappers. We rode along the shingle beach on a tractor-trailer and at the cape climbed a few hundred feet to see the birds. I later wrote a school essay about that trip. I was rather proud of a sentence stating that the waves rose 'from green hells' of the sea – I can't remember from where I stole this lurid phrase, although I have run into it again, which means I have now forgotten the source twice. Our English teacher, a calm, idle man named Gill, every week marked all the essays of all boys in all his classes with the word *Good*, so no one ever discovered what he thought of green hells or of anything else for that matter.

It did not occur to me, while writing the essay, to mention the most important thing that happened on the outing – that I nearly lost my life. After reaching the colonies where the gannets lived, I had wandered off around the cliffs before remembering that I had no head for heights. This is what teenagers die of – absent-mindedness. I ended up on a ledge with no room to turn around, and no way forward, unless – perhaps – I could hold on to a niche in the rock just in front of me, and reach a higher ledge.

The niche, however, was occupied. There was a gannet in it. The gannet is about the size of a goose, has dashing yellow pilots' stripes and a long, sharp beak, with which it strikes the sea's

7

surface at about 80kph. If it slashed at my hands or face with that beak, I thought, I would fall. The cliff was not far off the vertical. At the base, a long way down, big, blue, well-behaved waves could be seen but not heard.

In fact, I was not in much danger. The gannet is a peaceable bird and generally doesn't resent intruders to its colonies. But I didn't know that at the time. The gannet and I looked at each other. I put my hand towards the rock. A beak slanted, a grey-irised eye tilted thoughtfully. It is an odd sensation to imagine, even wrongly, that your life is in the hands, so to speak, of a sea-bird the size of a goose.

Then the bird slowly, deliberately, turned its head away, as if I was simply not there. Perhaps, in a sense, I did *not* exist to it, or had no more existence than a puff of wind or a cloud shadow. After all, our species' paths had separated hundreds of millions of years ago, no two creatures could be less connected to each other. But to me, knowing nothing about that and with no head for heights, the creature had seemed to turn its head away as if offended, *sadly* in fact, as if – as if what? As if I had doubted the intentions, the good taste, the fellow-feeling, of an elderly relative.

None of this, of course, might appear in a fifth-form essay written for Father Gill, even though it was widely suspected that he did not read them. By convention, the school essay was not a place where anything of importance was to be mentioned. We regarded our teachers as, above all, deeply ignorant, not just about the Rolling Stones or the brassiere-strap, but about *us*, the atmosphere in which we were living – each generation inde-pendently and rightly reaching the conclusion that they and the world are coeval, that everything is now new and different. It seemed wise not to disturb their ignorance, for you could never tell the consequences. Even Fr. Gill, a languid, placid man, who was also rector of the school, was capable of sudden bizarre outbursts.

'I will not have boys from this college going around the town wearing *Chinese COOKS' pants*!' he thundered one morning in assembly. No one had any idea what he was talking about, but we all were deeply interested: it was the first time we had ever seen him excited.

I was once summoned to his office, after a prefect reported that I had been seen in the XL on Friday night. The XL was a milkbar on the main street, with old-fashioned high-backed booths and a juke box. It was run by a Greek couple who demonstrated a kind of menacing disinterest in their customers and the whole business. I used to go there with the tough guys of the fourth form, Fly Kennedy and Terry Pullen, to watch and sometimes even talk to the girls who came in. Perhaps that Friday night we were wearing Chinese cooks' pants – by then believed to be the cotton-drill trousers worn by about half the male population.

Fr. Gill sat behind his desk in a room crammed with furniture, every surface covered with geological layers of papers and chimneys of books, lightly mantled with dust and pipe-ash. Beside him, on his desk, in a bell-shaped wire cage, sat a harrier hawk, the native hawk, that is, the *kahu*, with its rust-coloured feathery breeches and incredulous cruel stare.

'Ah,' said the rector when I came in. 'Ah. Yes.' He snuffled at his pipe, put it down, picked it up, scratched around inside the blackened bowl with a shiny blade, then looked away, with rapt blue eyes, towards the playing fields. He looked out the window for a long time. Finally he spoke.

'Well,' he said, 'let us all *fervently* hope that this doesn't happen again.' That, I understood, was it. I was free to go, and so I went.

Throughout the interview, the hawk, as if gazing over a desert waste, watched my every move. The English harrier has a series of faint markings on its feathers like the high cirrus of summer, but the cloud-pattern on the feathers of the native hawk looks like a black band of storm-cloud on its way.

Where this fierce visitor had come from, why the rector sat communing with it in his office for a day or two, and where it vanished to thereafter were not things ever made known to us. Fr. Gill was not a man who fraternised with his pupils. He had no nickname: he was above that. The notion – which some of his pupils had – that he actually read our weekly writing was ridiculous. *Good*! on the bottom of the essays when they were returned to us – exercise books sent whirling across the room like Frisbees – meant it was good we'd written them and good that he hadn't read them.

If I make the school sound eccentric, it was. It was one of the smallest of a number of Marist colleges around the country and the suspicion was abroad that the oddballs in the order, the misfits, had been sent to Hawke's Bay★ where they could do less damage than in the big and important Marist colleges competing with the Protestant and state schools in Wellington and Christchurch. There was the chemistry teacher, a tiny, furious man who had no wristwatch but instead carried at all times a brown suitcase with an alarm clock ticking inside it. The Master of Discipline was a stout, pink-faced friendly soul whose glasses misted over when he had to use the cane. The Christian Doctrine teacher had suffered some war injury that had affected his nervous system. Often he spent his full hour with us in silence, simply staring at the class, holding a handkerchief, occasionally dabbing his eyes.

The text book for this class was called *Living The Truth*. Many boys, during these periods of mute suspense, covertly amended the title to *Living With Ruth*. Oddly enough, although we did not much like him, no one ever ridiculed or persecuted him or even misbehaved badly, which would have been easy.

The school was near the centre of the town of Hastings, a flat country town of about 30,000 people where the main industry

★ The body of water is known as Hawke Bay. The province itself, for some reason, was given an apostrophe 's'.

10

was canning food. From a hundred square miles around Hastings came apples, peaches, tomatoes, peas, maize, all of which disappeared into the ovens of Watties Canneries. Then also, one morning, just before the noon whistle, came catastrophe. The cannery caught fire. During the lunch hour, an immense pillar of black smoke, a mile high and as thick as a giant's waist, roiled up above the town.

After a while, we saw that this column was *glinting*. Here and there, appearing in its dark depths, were thousands of points of light.

It was not long before the explanation for this began to arrive around us. The canning section itself, where the tins were manufactured, had gone up in smoke, and the heat was enough to waft into the sky thousands of shining tin lids. One by one, they began to fall to earth. I cannot quite explain the elation that I felt as these silver discs, returning from the sky, landed around us on the grass of the football field. *Ping* . . . silence . . . *ping* . . . silence . . . *ping*.

At the same time they were falling all over the dull, provincial town of Hastings, over its rooftops and rose beds and roadways and petrol-station forecourts. Monotony and conformity were, of course, things we were always aware of, accepted, scarcely noticed even. In a small provincial town these things were like the weather. Yet there also seemed to be an element of fraud involved, as if this was not the real weather, but had been imposed artificially from above, and then strictly and grimly enforced. 'The *anger* and monotony of our suburbs,' New Zealand's only great poet, James K. Baxter, once wrote.

The gannet-moment on the cliff, the rector and his hawk, the silvery discs dropping on the grass, even Gordon and his ghost (though that story came later) were like gaps in this fabric revealing something else above us, old and real, like a glimpse of rock seen through a cloud that has been hiding a mountain.

11

One day, our school idyll ended. The rector was sent away to another school. Into assembly one morning, in his place, strode a new master. He fixed us with a look of distaste and icy reproval which for the next two years never left his features. We were a disgrace, the school a sump of idleness. Iron discipline, respect, hard work, fear . . . the younger boys shivered in their shoes, but my friends and I were by then in the senior class and we felt we were beyond all that. At most, the new man, whose name was Davenport, was a bore. But we underestimated him. He had the light of battle in his eyes. One morning, for instance, I was caught in his radar.

The school at that time had a staff of about twelve priests and one or two lay-teachers who were, of course, at the bottom of the staff pecking order. One was a man named Mr Karaitiana, who taught the lower grades and therefore had little contact with us. But precisely because he was not a priest, and he even caught the school-bus home with us, hopping off half way back to Napier in the town of Clive (Hawke's Bay place-names were slanted heavily towards the Indian Raj) and disappearing down a side road to his house, wife and children, he seemed more approachable, reasonable and peaceable than the men in cassocks marshalled under the new Davenport regime. There was not even a great difference in age between us: in short, we felt friendly towards him, greeted him casually, and imagined that he felt the same as we did about the new headmaster with his grim bass voice and high, well-lit fore-head.

On the morning in question I was going into the teachers' staffroom to drop off a paper when I met Mr Karaitiana.

'Hi,' I said.

'Hi,' he said.

We passed and went our separate ways.

About thirty seconds later there was a roar.

'*You!*'

For some reason you always know when 'you' means you. I turned to face a furious grey face.

'*In* my office,' the rector said. I followed him, in a mood of jaunty curiosity.

'I heard that,' he said. 'I heard the whole thing.'

'But what?' I said.

'Your deplorable manners to Mr Karaitiana. He may be a – layman –' (or did he say 'Maori'? I think so, but I cannot bring myself to believe it; in any case, the issue of the junior teacher's race was heavy in the air). 'That is no reason to show him anything less than the ordinary respect owing to a member of my staff.'

'But I think you must have made a mistake, Father,' I said. 'I have far more respect for Mr Karaitiana than any other teacher in the school.'

This was quite off-the-cuff, probably not even true, and knowingly insolent as well. But I felt on reasonably safe ground: he could hardly veer in the same moment from one accusation – that I had too little respect for a certain teacher – to its opposite, no matter how insulting that was to himself.

The rector sat with his palms flat on the desk in front of him. After a pause, he inclined his head towards the wood grain.

'Out,' he said, very grim, very low-voiced.

It was the last word he ever spoke to me. That, in fact, was our sole sublunary conversation. The advantage of my remark was that the breach between us was total. Since it was my final year at the school, I came and went as I pleased. I spent much of my time studying at home or down on Napier beach, reading, swimming in the dangerous surf, or just looking out across the bay towards Cape Kidnappers, waiting, in a sense, for a few more months to pass and the day to come when I would leave Napier for good. And that was what happened. I went away · to university, my parents moved from the town and I did not see the place again for years, until I stood on the hill by Gordon's

13

farm and looked at a smudge on the coast which had once been my home.

The most interesting thing about Gordon's ghost story, as I said, was not that he believed it – which he did – but that he believed in it only because the ghost was Maori, and that, furthermore, ghosts in New Zealand always *are* Maori. The English, while sailing out to a new life in the South Pacific in the nineteenth century, had somehow misplaced the ability or desire to haunt one another after death, rather in the same way as they had changed their accents and lost certain words, some facial expressions and the more extreme aspects of the class system overboard. The notion of exclusive Maori rights in this area did not strike me for several years, until one night on the side of a road on the opposite coast of the North Island.

I had just returned from a trip to Europe and America and now I was back in one of the places I liked most in the world – in the draughty cab of an old Chev truck, circa 1947, painted green – *forest*-green, its owner stipulated – with the owner at the wheel.

This was Richard, who had been my best friend since I was twenty-one. We had met at university and, at first, we had not got on well. I liked parties, arguments, words, city life, and I knew nothing much about rifles or what was under the hood of a truck. He was musical, taciturn, liked animals, his Winchester 22 and his Chevrolet. Yet slowly we became friends; it was the companionable road that brought us together. Again and again we headed for the wild country of the North Island, sleeping out on hilltops, climbing through the Moehau forest, hiking the great empty dunes inland from Ninety Mile Beach.

When I found him after my two years abroad, he was living on the Coromandel Peninsula and something of a hero in the district. A few weeks before, with two or three neat punches, he had knocked down the local bully, a Maori bulldozer-driver

14

named Camp Potae, a giant of a man who was, the locals agreed, as quiet as a lamb all week and a roaring menace from Friday night to early Sunday morning. 'Keep away from Camp once he's had a few beers' was the received wisdom in Coromandel.

The trouble broke out over Richard's girlfriend. She was a great beauty who had been to school in Paris (her father was ambassador there), met the Pope, busked in Washington Square and, long before the fashion swept the world, wore a diamond stud in her nose.

It was the arrival of this nose-stud, twenty years early, in the Coromandel pub which caused the fracas. Camp Potae came jeering and pawing towards her, casually elbowing Richard aside. A minute or two later he was lying dazed on the floor of the bar. Richard, who was wearing his cricket boots, then kicked him in the groin.

'Not too terrific, I know,' he told me cheerfully. 'But Camp was a maniac. I think he would have killed me if he ever got up again.' Camp lay mumbling on the floor, his reputation in ruins. Richard became famous for a radius of twenty miles around the town, out on the farms and out to sea where the fishing trawlers and the scallop-boats rode.

As for me, I thought, I could have no more knocked Camp Potae over than fly to the moon.

So there we were again, back in the cab of the Chev, with its skinny, dancing gear stick and friendly reek of engine oil. Richard and his girlfriend had recently split up and he had driven to Wellington to deliver her loom to her – a huge hand-loom the size of a piano which she had left behind when she departed from Coromandel. Loom and weaver reunited, we were on the way north again, driving via the western province of Taranaki, which was rather off the beaten track and new territory for us both.

I had, in point of fact, lived in Taranaki once, but as a very young child. All that remained from that long ago era were a few simple memories – a race of grasshoppers, tawny and gifted, living among the stems of long grass behind the house; big bumble bees creeping into the red or orange gladioli by the side of the house; a bull with an evil reputation standing in a paddock at the end of the street.

Those sunny patches of fresco bore no connection to the cold, dark Taranaki we were now entering. It was the start of winter. Every so often a shower of rain slashed at the windshield. We went through a number of small towns all shut up for the night. At about eleven we stopped at the side of the road to spend the night. Never, in all our travels, had it occurred to us to check into a motel: they were for a quite different sort of traveller, salesmen, retired couples, Canadian schoolteachers on tour, checking that the soap was virginal and the sachets of complimentary instant coffee were in their proper place on the shelf above the fridge. We preferred on principle to be roughing it, to be out miles away like kings of the dark. And so that night it was the usual system: some plastic sheeting and a couple of old down sleeping bags under the tray of the truck, where the two dogs, which during the day rode on the back, came creeping in to spend the night as well. We all fell asleep.

Some time later a hand touched my shoulder.

This might have frightened me, but I was already in a state of terror. I was in a nightmare from which I could not escape.

I must have been groaning, because I had woken Richard and, eventually, he reached out under the axle and shook my shoulder.

'You OK?'

I was not OK. I was not OK at all. Lengthy descriptions of dreams are generally frowned on by readers, but even if one was wanted here I could not oblige. There was virtually nothing to see. This nightmare consisted solely of a crowd of men, women and children coming through the dark, pleading and full of hatred at the same time and then . . . nothing. Three times, four

16

times, five times . . . the same crowd, whom I could scarcely discern in a wretched darkness, rising at me, then disappearing.

Generally a very vivid dream is a signal for a sleeper to wake, in order, as it were, to remember it, but in this instance I could not escape. It was Richard who, from the other side of the truck, played the part of the invisible watchman who wakes us so that dreams are not lost in thin air. And of all the minor benefits casually conferred by friendship, it was this one – shaking me awake – for which I was most grateful to him. Once, years later, I asked him where we had stopped that night but he had no recollection of the occasion. The trip south with his girlfriend's loom, and his first sight of the great solitary mountain in Taranaki, those things he remembered, but everything else had dropped from his view.

After I woke, I lay there in a state of shock. What was *that* all about? Dreams generally have an internal logic and while they are under way, at least, you believe them and even think that you understand them. In this case, I had been puzzled *during* the dream and afterwards, seeing those antagonistic and hopeless figures, men, women and children, I felt that I had been unfairly attacked. I felt affronted, like a motorist hit by a rock thrown off an overpass, or a golfer chased down the fairway by an electric storm.

In the morning we were up early and got ready to drive on. We had stopped, I could now see, in a small valley with a few rows of trees and a paddock or two on the hillsides. As we were packing up, I saw there was a semi-derelict Maori house with a carved gable standing in the grey light about fifty yards away, across a paddock. As soon as I saw it, I decided that my dream had 'come from' there. This was so easy to do. Without any hesitation I joined the list of people like Gordon who, while never believing in any such phenomena from their own world, were quite ready to ascribe it to the Maori background, dark and atmospheric, that rises in so many places behind ordinary rural

New Zealand. The dream, I thought, was associated with this place. It would never have got me if, for instance, we'd slept a few miles down the road, and in that sense it was not 'mine' at all, for it was not even really a dream, but a kind of haunting. I looked at the building again: it was just an old Maori meeting-house standing in a field of docks in the rainy daylight – the perfect address, in other words, to consign a nightmare when the morning came. By that time of my life I had heard several other whites – more Hawke's Bay farmers, a senior government lawyer, a group of road engineers – describe 'their' stories of Maori ghosts and things *tapu*. I cannot account for the suspension of disbelief among these severely practical people. It may be that the Maori world provided a kind of outlet from precisely the constraints of the world they had constructed. Or perhaps there was a hidden acknowledgement that between whites and Maori there was much unfinished business, that the accounts have not yet been balanced and until they are such anomalies in the force field between the races are only to be expected.

I knew nothing about the place where Richard and I had woken up, nothing at all about the district, which in any case did not appeal to me. It looked like dull country, farmland stripped to bare basics, barbed-wire fences, a few blocks of conifers here and there. We drove away.

But for one piece of serendipity, I would never have been able to locate the place again. All I knew was that we had stopped somewhere between the city of Wanganui and New Plymouth – a hundred and fifty miles of country road. We drove on that morning, went through a couple of hamlets which were still asleep, had coffee in a small town and then, a few miles on, the mist lifted off the road and above the power-lines, the sun shone and ahead of us rose the mountain, Mt. Egmont as it was then named. (It has now reverted to its old name, Taranaki.)

'*There she is!*' said Richard, in the same tone, I suppose, that people used to yell 'There she blows!' He had never before seen Mt. Egmont. The peak, 8,000 ft. high, solitary and symmetrical, hung above a thousand square miles of hazy paddocks. The Chevy's hood was pointing down the white centre line. The road was running straight towards the mountain. Behind us, on each side of the cab, the two dogs, father and son, both grave and hypocritical grey terriers, pointed their muzzles forward.

For half a minute, the light of the rising sun struck through the rear-window, lit the dashboard, and fixed the moment as if on silver nitrate. We had not turned into cameras. We had turned into a photograph.

'*There she is!*'

Because of that memory alone I was able to reconstruct our route years afterwards and find the place where we had slept out. Driving west into Taranaki, I found there are only one or two places where the road points directly at the peak. Working back from there, I found the sleepy town where we stopped for coffee, and a few miles back from there, past a corner hamlet or

two, I found on the left-hand side of the road, fifty yards beyond the fence, a dilapidated Maori meeting-house – though less dilapidated than I remembered – it had a new coat of bright green paint and a toilet-block had sprung up beside it – standing in a paddock in a shallow valley.

When I saw the photograph of the kidnapped boy, I remembered this incident and that was another reason why I was attracted to his story. I knew that he had been kidnapped in roughly the same district and I thought that his story, whatever it was, would throw some light over that whole locality which to me at least – since everyone has a private map of their own country – had always seemed problematic, uncomfortable, even benighted.

What I did not expect to find was evidence of a series of hidden crimes, both victims and perpetrators having close connections with the child. Nor did I expect to discover that this boy, about whom perhaps five or ten lines have ever been published in history books, went on to play a crucial role in one of the most perplexing, and yet redemptive, events in the history of European colonial expansion. He was to lead the country into the heart of its greatest moral drama and then, just as it reached its climax, he removed himself with the modesty of a guide who knows he is no more than a minor figure. Thereafter he was lost from view.

The place where we slept out was called Whenuakura. The little town where we stopped for coffee was Patea. The road leads on to the larger country town of Hawera. And it was down this same road, through Patea County to Hawera, that the story I was now following, of a boy abducted in the forest, first led.

Hawera – 'the burnt-down place' or 'the breath of fire' is what the name means – a prosperous, bustling town of eight thousand people on the plains of south Taranaki, has always turned its back on the mountain; the snowy peak may be glimpsed from the town only by accident, by planners' oversight as it were – from the car park outside the Price Chopper supermarket, or down an alley by the public toilets or over the washing line in someone's back garden. The town's major landmark is a huge concrete water tower, sketchily embellished as a Norman keep, which dominates the main street and is visible much further away out in the country on the main roads that approach Hawera from north, east and west. There used to be another route into town, on the railway, but the station is now closed to human traffic; the only things that arrive in or depart from Hawera by rail today are dairy products. Just outside the town is the largest dairy factory in the country or in the universe, I forget which, and it is that which has made the town prosperous and rather smug compared to other country towns in the area. The plant is closed to visitors for security reasons, although who, you wonder, would want to bomb a nearly infinite Cheddar cheese? There is, however, a Visitor Centre, named Dairyland.

Outside Dairyland stands a fibreglass black-and-white cow, at least twenty feet high from hooves to ear-tips.

Inside, behind a desk, a beautiful young woman with striking blue eyes and Maori features awaits the public.

'How tall is the cow?' I asked when we went in.

'Wouldn't have a clue.'

'Have you got any postcards of it?'

'Run out.'

Just the missing 'we've' made it plain that I at least was the wrong type of Visitor. I leaned back and checked the sign above her glossy head. Yep: *Information*. Disdain on the part of the beautiful and informed always depresses me and I lost heart at the idea of a tour of Dairyland, even though there were a lot more fibreglass cows inside, as I could tell from photographs in the brochure. 'Enjoy our simulated tanker ride as we take you on a journey to collect milk from the surrounding dairy farms . . .' said the brochure.

We went outside and stood under the cow. Above its

21

horizontal fibreglass ears the sun shone on the snowy peak and lit up, variously, roads, rivulets, tankers on the move, smoke from factories, green farms, and, here and there, small, tardy late-morning fogs still rising out of gullies.

It was September 1998. I was visiting Hawera with my sister, brother-in-law and niece. My brother-in-law, Dene, who is Maori, had a distant cousin in Hawera who thought he might be able to help me find some details about the child kidnapped a century before. We left Dairyland, drove into town and parked in the main street. It was a hot morning with an iridescent blue sky like that in a Kodak advertisement. The centre of town was being revamped with brick paving and curly lampstands. I went into the White Hart Hotel, on the main intersection, the only street corner which had the faint skirl of downtown to it. Inside, it was dark, beery, half-friendly, interrogative. A Maori, thin, elderly, ill-looking, wearing a lady's red V-necked jumper, and his companion, a plump white woman wearing a man's tweed jacket, and with blue eyes as hard as pebbles, began to tell me about their triumphs at the races. The barman looked on sceptically and after a while observed that, unlike some people he could name, he had once actually owned a share in a racehorse. The old man and his girlfriend were untouched by this rebuke; they began to dance in an automatic way, as if it was not so much that they remembered the Twist as that the Twist remembered them. It was noon.

Outside, along the street, I found my sister buying chips for my niece at the Bonanza Burger Bar. The woman behind the counter was about sixty-five, with a face like granite; she was formidable, the dam of All Black forwards and prison guards. A teenaged girl came in, and the woman shouted, to no one in particular: 'What does *she* want?'

The menu behind her read:

Paua fritters Not/Available
Oysters N/A
Whitebait N/A
Fish
Chips
Mussels
Kumara chips N/A
Sauce Extra.

'I've got pains in my legs and pains in my side and a pain in my shoulder,' the woman said to my sister, 'and I'm in here all day standing over hot fat.'

'Oh, you *poor* thing,' my sister said. 'I don't know how you can stand it.'

'To tell you the truth,' said the woman. 'I don't know if I *can* stand it.'

A Maori girl, about fourteen, sitting cross-legged on a post-box, watched us with keen if disguised attention from the other side of the road. A shirtless Maori youth, very dark, about eighteen, wearing a red turban, Bette Davis sunglasses and Bermuda shorts went bopping past listening to headphones. As soon as this exotic personage had departed, a second Maori about the same age appeared from the same direction, very sombre and thoughtful. Dressed entirely in dingy grey denim, he gave the impression of having been sent out, having been *issued*, to erase the impression left by the first. He looked as if he was thinking about the interior physics of the stars. A white family – father, mother, two children – browsed along the street and stopped for a long time to look, in silence, at a row of motor-mowers in a store window. A young white man came along, about twenty-five, heavy-set, wearing a slouch hat and black windcheater with a kind of sheriff's badge pinned on it.

He stopped and looked at us.

'Do you know what we're doing here?' he said.

'Gee, that's a big question,' said my brother-in-law.

The man gave him a look, but went on: 'Today our company is offering a special reduction etching your registration number on your windshield. And today only we can offer you a twenty per cent reduction.'

'Which reduces it to?' I asked.

'The price, with today's reduction, is $25.99, plus GST.'

'Maybe some other time,' I said.

'Well, that's bloody lovely, isn't it?' he said, and strode off, looking left and right.

At the far end of the main street, there is a large, beautiful and secretive park hidden behind very high hedges. Inside are several smaller walled gardens, one with a moon gate, opened, according to a plaque, by the Chinese Ambassador, His Excellency, Hong Sin C. Shah, in 1968. But for whom exactly was this series of paradises (OED. f. Gk *paradeisos* royal park, fr. *pairi* around + *diz* to form) intended? At 1 p.m., a single jogger ran through. Two blonde teenage girls, langorously not at school, were killing time on the children's swings, but they got up and departed. The cedars, the palms, the pines, deciduous and evergreen, trees from every page of the atlas, stood waiting under the Taranaki sky.

At dusk that day we were on a high ridge on the north side of town overlooking the countryside. I was with Dene and his cousin, Sandy Parata, who knew the town well. Things were very good in Hawera, he said. Plenty of jobs. Race relations? Excellent. The police and local authorities and farmers were all well-disposed to the *iwi* – the local tribe. 'They're our friends. They're my *mates*. They look out for our kids. When our *marae* [meeting place] burned down, we took the hat around and they filled that hat – *lots* of money!'

The ridge was once the site of the greatest *pa* – fortified settlement – of Maori Taranaki. It was a long and sinuous hill and on the summit grew a row of immense and venerable

24

cabbage-trees – not actually trees but rough-barked members of the lily family which grow to forty or fifty feet and look like primitive palms. The ancient terracing of the *pa* was still visible in the dusk. Sandy told Dene what had happened here on this hill. It was a horrible story, strangely like the tale in Genesis, early in the wanderings of Israel, when the goatish inhabitants of Shechem had allowed themselves to be circumcised, and then, a day or two later, while they were 'still smarting', were easily slaughtered by the ruthless sons of Jacob.

In the Polynesian version it had not been religion and the circumcision knife which had undone the local people but vanity and the tattoo chisel. Their neighbours and rivals had kindly sent over one of the most sought-after tattooing artists of the land. He was wildly popular. He paid special attention to two tattoos named *rape* and *puhoro* on the hips and thighs, which were extremely painful men often fainted from the pain – and took a long time to heal. And then, a few days later, while the men were still smarting . . . The slaughter was terrific.

The hill, in fact, had lost its original name. No one remembered it. All those living there had been killed. Ever since, the place had been called Turuturu-mokai after the innumerable human heads, beautifully tattooed, which were left staring from stakes on the summit.

This story, only about three hundred years old, seemed incredibly distant – as old as Genesis – and yet also rather close, like the rough bark of the cabbage-trees that stood in a line stretching away to the left and right in the darkness. It was, I thought, the first time I had ever heard, unmediated by whites, an account from the Maori past of the country, a period five times longer than the white history of the country.

Sandy also knew a little about the story of the boy who had been kidnapped. He was able to point in the direction of the battlefield, down there in the farmlands below, where this had happened. A tiny orange flame, the flare-off from a natural-gas plant, marked the spot where I should go next.

That night we stayed in the Rembrandt Motel on the main road out of town. Our quarters were actually an old villa that we had to ourselves, behind the motel units. I switched on the television, then quickly turned it off. After a decade of free-market reforms, TV in New Zealand has become unwatchably bad – a blizzard of ads, soaps, cheap movies and news lists in which every story is about money.

'All toothpastes are the same, right?' a pearly-mouthed woman was shouting. '*Wrong*!'

We left the motel and went out for pizza. Near the entrance to the motel was a Shell gas station; a lit-up Kentucky Fried Chicken bucket; trucks rolled by. Hawera in the daylight had been a place of marked character. By night it turned into anywhere, one of a million towns in the West. For the first time since I had started thinking about the story of the kidnapped boy, I sensed the powerful indifference of the present for the past, especially the unstated past, the lost past, the past which did not win.

When we came back, my niece, aged eight, began to write a novel. On the wall of the motel sitting room I read a framed poster:

Fair Play Sport Charter of New Zealand
We at our school agree when playing sport we will *enjoy ourselves *respect the referee *respect the opposition and their supporters *be gracious winners and dignified losers *play hard but play fair.

PLAY HARD. PLAY FAIR
Signed:
Wilson Whineray.
Chairman
Hillary Commission.

Wilson Whineray was a captain of the All Blacks in the long-lost early sixties. Hillary was Sir Edmund Hillary, the first man to climb Everest.

At nine, my niece went to bed. Her novel was already four pages long. The text was crammed in the top left-hand corner of each sheet – the rest of the space, she explained, being needed for last-minute changes:

Once upon a
time there lived
a kind old
Woman who
lived in a
small village

in Russia.
She had two
Daughters who

were both married.
One married a fisherman and
the other married

a merchant.
One had a baby,
while the other had Luxury.

From the south, during the night, came the whistle of the trains heading for the dairy factory, and every now and then the house shook as giant road tankers went past. Somewhere out there to the west was the place now surrounded by dairy farms where a boy had been snatched and taken away on a great journey that led him to Wanganui, to Wellington and – although I didn't know it at this point – San Francisco, Yosemite, London, Beirut

27

and the Pyramids of Giza. And then finally back to Hawera. A few of his relatives, his lateral descendants, were now scattered about the town and the plains.

The house shook occasionally. We were surrounded as we slept by streams, by rivers of milk, on the move in the night.

2

The Beak of the Bird

The next day I drove across the plains to a place called Te Ngutu O Te Manu, the site of a battle between Maori and colonial forces in 1868. It was particularly peaceful, as, I suppose, former battlefields always are: your head is full of the din of the history book and yet there in front of you is . . . nothing: green grass, a bird calling, in the distance the sound of traffic. A bee zoomed above the turf. The wind dropped in the trees but a cloud sailed on and a shadow moved over us. Then the sun shone again on the few acres of clipped lawn and a tall stone cross, put up to mark the spot where one of the British commanders fell, although experts say the cross is in the wrong place.

There was a caretaker's bungalow in one corner of the field, with a radio playing through a window. A padlocked public toilet with the word *Closed* daubed in black paint on the door. Around the park, a thin screen of native trees remains, through which, here and there, the farmland can be seen beyond: black-and-white cows, a red tractor, and the orange flame of the natural gas flare-off.

Te Ngutu O Te Manu means The Beak of the Bird and is one of those names on the old maps (Owl's Nest, Million-Leaves) which give a hint of an incomparable lowland forest that has entirely vanished.

It is possible today to drive for hour after hour through New Zealand without passing a remnant of the great forest which covered the land a hundred and fifty years ago. Everywhere there are belts of black pines, of course, and lines of poplars; there are English oaks and Australian gums; a line of Californian cypresses with their grey, disordered hearts stands behind every cowshed. But of the ancient lowland bush, Te Wao Nui a Tane, the Great Forest of Tane, scarcely a leaf remains.

There is something eerie about this. For the first ninety years of European presence in the country, the wooded antipodean landscape was painted and praised to the skies. It was both picturesque (crags and snowy peaks, strange new creatures, none dangerous) and romantic (wild, variegated, filled with *energy* – with waterfalls and the songs of infinite flocks of birds). The timber was, moreover, extremely valuable. It was an ideal Victorian prospect.

Then something changed. First, the forest began to fall silent. The infinite flocks of birds dwindled with the arrival of new predators and competitors – dogs, cats, the weasel and the stoat, the rat, men with guns, and even, according to Maori observers, the European bee. Many of the native birds were nectar-sippers and the immigrant honeybee swarmed into the forests stripping the flowers.

Having fallen silent the forest then, as in a fairy tale, began to grow dark as well. Colonial New Zealand was full of amateur landscape painters and it is easy to see in their paintings how the bush changed in front of their eyes. The sylvan glades and dappled foliage narrow and darken, the trees lean in closer and the Maori slips away suspiciously into the shadows.

By the 1870s, picnickers on a Sunday ramble out of town would find the biggest totara or rata tree they could, and set fire to it. The fire might smoulder on for six months. In 1881, the police in Wellington banned shopkeepers from using nikau palms and native tree ferns or punga to decorate their verandas at Christmas time. This simply seems mad, but it must be agreed that policemen, even the youngest constable, have a delicate eye for a symbol. The punga and the nikau, emissaries from the native wilderness, were not wanted in lower Cuba Street: they were, the police said, an 'obstruction'. It is impossible to imagine the same charge being laid against the holly and the ivy. In short, the bush had become an enemy. It was no longer wild, romantic and safe, but shockheaded, dark and dangerous. Above all, it had become the ally of the Maori. The fate of the forest and the state of relations between the races were tied together.

It was at about two in the afternoon one day in September 1868, at the Battle of the Beak of the Bird, that the native trees and the Maori fused together in the European mind, and became a single enemy.

New Zealand had become a British colony in 1840 and for the first twenty years the two races lived together in comparative peace, or at least on better relations than in other colonies of the Western powers. A treaty, the Treaty of Waitangi, guaranteed Maori rights and full citizenship. Intermarriage, the fusion of the races, was seen as an ideal. The government was determined to prevent aggression and theft of Maori land by settlers. The Maori for their part enjoyed many of the benefits of British law and civilization. By 1860, however, war broke out.

Much has been written about the origins of the conflict. The underlying cause was simple: many settlers, especially those in Taranaki led by 'the Mob', as they called themselves, a group of intermarried families, Richmonds, Atkinsons and Hursthouses, who ran things in the province, had lost patience with the founding principle of the colony – the equality between Maori and European. The Maori were not equal, they argued, they were a barbaric race who were 'absurdly petted', 'precious niggers' who 'ought to be kicked'; they had been allowed to hold up settlement and progress for twenty years. All else having

31

failed, war was a necessity to establish dominance. 'A few lines on our great shadow, the Maories . . .' an Atkinson wrote musingly to a Richmond. 'We are to have the land. But how?'

The war began in 1860 with a dispute over a few hundred acres of land; in 1863 the government decided to confiscate millions of acres to punish the Maori who had been deemed rebellious. The tribes who were to lose their property were not necessarily those who had fought against the Crown. What was declared confiscated was simply the most desirable property in Maori hands. The province of Taranaki, a great cape of rolling plains surmounted by its single snowy mountain, seemed to many settlers not just the most beautiful part of the country but the most beautiful place in the world. They named it the 'Garden of New Zealand'. When the Premier, Alfred Domett, dreamed up confiscation, one of his main aims was to steal this garden from its owners. A great semi-circle of land to the north, west and south of the mountain was declared confiscate.

When the hostilities died away in 1866, however, the colonists had not occupied much of this territory. The tribes were still in possession and did not imagine that the wartime legislation would ever be enforced. But then, nibble by nibble, the Maori said, like a cow cropping the grass, the surveyors and armed police came on and on. This seemed both cowardly and dishonest to the Maori, who refused to accept that land not won from them in open battle could be taken later by proclamation.

It was this 'creeping confiscation', not far from Hawera, which sparked a new war between the colonists and a local chief named Titokowaru, one of the formidable characters whom Maoridom threw up to deal with the crisis of colonisation. He was a man of many parts. As a youth he was noted for his passionate love affairs and strong theological bent. He immersed himself in both the ancient Maori and the new Christian teachings. He was about five foot nine, dark-skinned, sinewy; his most remarkable physical attribute was an incredibly powerful voice. When roused to anger, it was said, he could be heard two miles away, his voice was like the raging of a lion.

In his twenties he was converted by the Wesleyans and baptised under the now somewhat unlikely name of Joe Orton.

As the surveyors came closer and closer, Christianity receded among the Maori. They found it impossible to reconcile the teachings of the Gospel with the actions of the English or alternatively with the requirements of war, and various forms of a spiritual tradition, under the general name of *Pai Marire* or 'Good and Peaceful', sprang up combining elements of the Old Testament and ancient Maori beliefs. The adherents to the new religion were often known as Hau Hau; a name taken from one of their chants. By 1868, the Wesleyan lay-teacher Joe Orton no longer existed – Titokowaru was back, as war lord and as the priest of *Uenuku*, god of the rainbow, a divinity known across Polynesia, but who in New Zealand had evolved into a terrifying spirit called 'the man-eater'.

Titokowaru began his war in mid–1868 with the murder of three settlers clearing Maori land which had been declared confiscated by the government. In September, his headquarters, The Beak of the Bird, was attacked by a crack force of about four hundred men, the finest troops in the colony.

The colonial forces were led by two officers both famous at the time, one of whom is completely forgotten, the other still visible in a faint web of legend. The commanding officer was Thomas McDonnell, a ridiculous figure, brave, self-aggrandising and self-pitying, with a walrus moustache and an air of outraged innocence.

On the day he approached The Beak of the Bird, it was the refuge for a large number of non-combatants from other villages who remembered a night massacre led by McDonnell on a settlement named Pokaikai, whose name translates roughly as 'Feast of Darkness'. Here is a young Londoner, Charlie Money, describing the assault on Pokaikai:

A sudden uprising of ghostly figures, a creeping along the narrow track, the word 'Charge!' and a mad, shouting, leaping host of dark forms . . . firing into wharries [native huts] crammed with niggers . . .

It was to avoid another such 'uprising of ghostly figures' that neutral and even some friendly Maori took refuge at The Beak of the Bird, although they knew the war would one day come there too.

McDonnell's second-in-command was Gustavus Von Tempsky, ruthless and handsome and popular with his men and in the country at large. A Polish aristocrat who had once been aide-de-camp to the Prince of Lichtenstein, he had emigrated to the Mosquito Coast and there formed an irregular force of Indians against the Spanish. He travelled through Mexico and wrote a book, *Mitla* (1858), about it – now unreadable but nicely illustrated with his own paintings. He was nearly murdered in San Francisco for his gold and only escaped by jumping into the harbour and swimming for his life.

He appeared early in the New Zealand wars, engaged in 'bloody sprees' in the Hunua forests, from which he emerged 'loaded with potatoes and Maori clubs', one obituarist wrote.

During that campaign he found the place he wanted to settle with his new wife – a sweep of plain below the forested slopes of Mt. Pirongia. With its descending paths and rivers and blue illimitable plain, Pirongia has that exemplary look of some landscapes by Brueghel which seem to depict not just one place but the wide world.

Pirongia and the surrounding country had also been confiscated. The mountain was one of only three or four places in the country which the Maori believed to be haunted by *patupareihe*, a race of pale-skinned people who were never seen but who could sometimes be heard talking and laughing in the forest, always at night, and always receding as one approached.

It was there that Von Tempsky's thoughts were now turning. He intended this expedition to The Beak of the Bird to be his last military adventure, which it turned out to be.

The force attacking The Beak consisted of some regular army units and various settler militias and volunteer forces and about a hundred Maori allies or *kupapa* from different tribes. British imperial troops meanwhile were chafing in town, seventy miles away, under strict orders from London not to get involved in any fighting. Britain had long been suspicious of the settlers' policies. '*Generally*,' Gladstone wrote to an old school-friend, Bishop Selwyn, in New Zealand, 'I share with all my heart in your dislike of the arbitrement of force to which we Englishmen are as much too prone in our dealings abroad with other races, as we are noted for a salutary tardiness in resorting to it for the settlement of our own affairs.'

But the real reason for Gladstone's horror of war in New Zealand was the cost. He wrote another letter to the Secretary of State, Lord Lyttleton:

Dear George,
The colonists have been so long carried in a nurse's arms that they cannot stand on their own feet. My belief is that this war against some 2,000 Aboriginals has cost poor John Bull the best part of 3 millions . . . The command of colonial ministers over the money of the English for injustice and absurdity has no parallel on earth.

Well before dawn on the day of the battle, the colonial force left camp, crossed the breast-deep Waingongoro River at 4 a.m., and were in the forest before the sun rose.

They got lost for an hour or two but had found themselves on a forest track by midday.

At two in the afternoon, the main body of the forces were

looking across a shallow stream into a clearing where they could see a lightly fortified *pa*. They were at The Beak of the Bird.

Almost immediately, something peculiar happened. Men began screaming and falling down. From inside the *pa*, a familiar voice kept ringing out.

'*Whakawhiria! Whakawhiria!*' – 'Surround them! Surround them!'

It was a terrific voice like the raging of a lion. And soldiers were now dropping everywhere. 'The firing was something awful,' a soldier later wrote, 'men were being knocked over like ninepins,' yet no one had seen a single Maori. The enemy were all around them but they were quite invisible, hidden in treetops, inside hollow or loop-holed tree-trunks, in pits dug between the roots and under the humus of the forest floor.

It was at this moment that the forest itself and the Maori became a single dark enemy. I remember sitting in a sunny classroom when I was ten years old and looking at a contemporary illustration of the battle which was still being used in the schoolbooks of the 1950s.

The soldiers are slightly lit up, in a glade. They are firing in all directions, but blindly, upwards, into the trees, out of which nearly naked warriors are falling headfirst like the damned. The sky has the imperial gloom of all Victorian etchings. All around, immense trees loom in closely, looped with vines like hangmen's nooses. It is a forest as dark – and of the same vintage, almost to the month – as the dreadful wood out of which Tenniel's Jabberwock comes screeching, or that in which Tweedledum and Tweedledee agreed to have a battle.

This picture was roughly accurate, except for one thing: hardly a single Maori lost his life in the engagement. It was the colonial force that was shattered into pieces. Whether the men tried to advance, to take cover or to retreat, death came to them through the leaves. There were too many wounded to carry and some were left behind to be killed by the victors. The retreat was a disaster. The men ran off in all directions, some, it was said, not stopping until they reached the Rangitikei river, a hundred miles away. Others went north and wandered in circles for days before being found and killed or simply dying of hunger.

Von Tempsky was one of the first officers to fall. In his last battle he was described as 'curiously listless. He was cutting away with his sword at a hanging bush vine . . . cutting shavings from it' and muttered to one young soldier: 'I am disgusted. If I get out of this scrape I will wash my hands clean of the business.'

Killer and mercenary as he was, pitiless, and even slightly mad some said, there was something oddly graceful about Von Tempsky. When he spoke to the soldier he had minutes left to live. He would never see his young wife Emilia again, or look out at the world from a veranda on the slopes of Mt. Pirongia. But there was a certain style to his exit from life. In his last minutes, he turns his back on himself, he washes his hands of his profession. It is rather like a deathbed conversion but in one sense it is also finer than that: he had no intention of dying and did not know the scale of the disaster about to overwhelm the army.

Then he was killed by a bullet through the forehead. His curved sword, which fell from his hand as he pitched into the humus, was the great trophy of the wars and it is still hidden away somewhere in Taranaki. From time to time treasure-hunters and amateur historians turn up knocking at Maori doors enquiring after it. I have talked to one wise and well-informed Maori who knows where it is, though of course he did not tell me, nor did I ask. But he did say that Titokowaru himself took possession of the sword and, before he himself died, he buried it with these words:

'Let war return to the great nations of the North.'

The sword was buried without a scabbard so that it would rust away more rapidly. A mild little myth has grown up that if it is ever seen in the light of day again, war will return between the 'two tribes' of New Zealand, Maori and English.

The Battle of the Beak of the Bird was worse than a military defeat. It was a national calamity. The core of the colonial army had been broken. At the same time, another insurrection had broken out on the East Coast. If all the Maori tribes had risen at that moment, there was a real possibility that the North Island would have to be abandoned, which would have been the greatest retrenchment in British power since the loss of the American colonies. There was talk among the settlers of leaving the British Empire in any case – the colonists were furious with Britain not only for failing to come to their aid but for kindly pointing out that they had brought their troubles on themselves by their greed, injustice and clumsiness.

Even greater journalistic energy was expended against the Maori victors. The newspapers vied with one another to demonise the Maori. The rules of war between civilised nations did not apply to them. They were not human at all, but 'anthropophagi', and 'wild beasts which must be hunted down and slain'. They were 'infuriated devils in human form', and even 'bird-fiends as are read of in books of *diablerie*'. And the Beak of the Bird itself because a terrible place in the colonial imagination, as this letter in the *Wanganui Chronicle* shows: 'The bones of the gallant Von Tempsky lie bleaching . . . and the eyeless heads of his comrades – brave men every one – are peering out of that dismal bush of the Beak of the Bird, the bird that pecked the life out of New Zealand's bloodiest war – but I must stop or this page will be blurred with tears.'

On the ground, the effects of the defeat were immediate. Six military posts in Taranaki were abandoned; Von Tempsky's Forest Rangers mutinied and were disbanded. The garrison town of Patea was, according to the newspapers, 'abandoned to Bacchus'. Settlers abandoned their farms and streamed into town.

This had been the infant state's first military expedition unaided and alone.

One of the newspapers that week printed a map of the engagement. It looked like this:

The army camp was the point at the bottom. The heavy line to the right marks the line of advance, and the broken lines to the left the various paths of retreat. The line running east to west is the river, the Waingongoro. The map is not at all accurate, but I think it was quite unintentional on the part of the artist that he made it look like a broken heart. The cross at the top, within that poignant indentation which can be seen on subway walls all over the world, was the site of The Beak of the Bird itself.

That night, back at the camp – a terrible place on the night of 7 September, with dribs and drabs of men wandering in, with 'cheering, and shaking of hands and crying in turn which was rather a queer sight among strong bearded men' – it took a while for anyone to notice that one of the men had returned with a trophy. It was a boy aged five or six.

This is what happened.

While the army column was still stumbling around in the forest about midday looking for The Beak of the Bird, the scouts

39

in the vanguard heard voices. They could see nothing but at that point the column cautiously rearranged itself, the Maori allies going to the rear and Von Tempsky with a few Maori scouts taking the lead.

They went forward and found a clearing with a couple of bark huts and a tent. This was the 'hospital' for Titokowaru's people. A woman came out, saw the strangers, screamed and ran away down a track. She was never seen again.

Then a man emerged from a hut and fired a single shot. He was shot dead. Inside the huts, the soldiers found only two patients – a very sick little girl and a crippled boy aged about nine. In the meantime, more and more men arrived, while Von Tempsky and McDonnell conferred.

While they did so, a Maori scout named Pirimona arrived in the clearing. With him was a third child, a boy he had found wandering through the bush. This boy was named Ngatau Omahuru, a child from the village of Mawhitiwhiti whose people had come to The Beak of the Bird for safety.

It was at this point that something bestial occurred. The murder of children commenced. The crippled boy was seized and his brains were 'dashed out', because 'he would not stop crying'.

Titokowaru's forces had already been alerted to the arrival of the enemy by the sound of two gunshots.

As to the little girl, no two accounts agree: She was very sick and left alone. She was killed by 'being thrown up and spitted in mid-air on a bayonet'. She was 'taken' (McDonnell). She was 'left' (a Captain Newland). She was 'taken out and killed by our Maoris because she would not keep quiet' (a settler named Livingstone). 'There was no suggestion that she . . . should be killed' (Omahuru himself, forty years later). Whatever happened to her that day, she vanishes from the story.

In all the written accounts, the blame for the murder or murders was put on the Maori, though some doubt must also be allowed here. It seems unlikely that one or two Maori scouts could have carried out the act on their own initiative or without the consent of their European officers at their side. Von Tempsky was there and he did nothing to stop it.

At this point, whatever he himself thought forty years later, Ngatau Omahuru was in great danger. Murder like anything else is contagious. In a wood, during a war, a moral darkness can set in. That noon in the hospital clearing it already had.

But the boy was lucky. Pirimona was a rather pedestrian character. He was a scout: he had snatched up the child and brought him back without much caring what happened to him, like a policeman who collars a shoplifter. But when he reached the clearing he gave the boy into the care of a man named Herewini who was a very different character. The Maori allies or *kupapa* came from several different tribes: both Pirimona and his friend Herewini were outsiders from a small but 'virile and bellicose' tribe named the Ngati Te Upokoiri which was based in Hawke's Bay. Quite what wafted these two young men into this distant campaign is unclear. It may simply have been the three shillings and sixpence a day the government paid both Maori and white soldiers.

In any event, it was into Herewini's hands that he delivered the boy. Herewini was a fatherly, one might even say a motherly, figure aged about twenty-five. He and his wife loved children, but it seems they were themselves childless. Herewini instantly saw the danger the boy was in, like a fallen nestling. At least one child had just been murdered for making the mistake of crying. Perhaps Herewini bent down, grasped the newcomer by both arms and hissed a fierce warning.

'*Don't make a sound.*'

The boy turned into a block of wood. Or, as a Christchurch newspaper put it, with a kind of insouciant brutality: 'He was an attractive child and did not blubber, so he did not get "brained".'

The danger then lifted – to an extent. The army moved on,

41

and split roughly into three parts. The Maori allies took the left wing and when the withering gunfire began from the surrounding forest, they instantly took cover. Throughout the massacre by the unseen defenders, they suffered scarcely any casualties and when the retreat began, they moved off in good order, came through the forest, crossed the river and reached the camp by eight o'clock that night.

The small captive, Ngatau Omahuru, spent the battle and the retreat strapped across Herewini's back. Was he being kidnapped? Or did Herewini just think that the forest was a death-zone, that if he let the boy down to run off on his own, he could easily have been killed by someone in a murderous frame of mind, or by a bullet with no mind at all?

There is one other sighting of the boy during the battle. At some stage of the six-hour engagement, he was baptised.

This surprising event was the work of a Fr. Jean-Baptiste Rolland, a French priest who frequently accompanied the British forces in the wars in Taranaki. At The Beak of the Bird he is reported as rushing here and there through the gunfire and among the trees, with 'black hair, blue eyes, active gait, wearing a frock-coat and black leggings'. He gave the last rites to several men and came out of the forest with his hat full of bullet holes. He later told the *Wanganui Evening Herald* that he had 'sprinkled the boy lest he should be killed and die a Hau–Hau'.

Later, curious tendrils of invention curled out of this incident. In one, the priest was said to have baptised the child, who thereupon was immediately murdered, by the *kupapa*, on the grounds that the child was *now* a Christian and would go to heaven, but in a month or two – who knows? – he might return to the Hau Hau and his soul would be lost.

In the second, the priest went to baptise the boy but then realised that he had no water. He had come into battle to bless the dying but was not equipped for baptism. Being French, however, he was naturally carrying a supply of wine. He

42

uncorked a bottle, prayed over it, it turned into water, and he was able to proceed with the sacrament. Reports of this reverse miracle-of-Cana were still circulating as late as the 1930s in pious Catholic magazines.

Just north of the clearing at The Beak of the Bird, a small stream still runs through the trees where the army first encountered the deadly fusillade. On my visit there one afternoon in 1998 I went down through the bush to the water. The stream was a few inches deep, running over brown stones. An empty Coke can lay in the water. Down there on the bank the poignant smell of forest decay hit me. Now and again a *tui* called, always the same seven notes, although its song varies from district to district. This is one of the few songbirds in the world said to suffer from sound pollution. The tui is a great mimic and over the years it has been said that its songs have become contaminated by noises of the modern world – car horns, sirens, railway whistles, the popping of gunfire and so on. One of the seven notes, among the flute-like others, was exactly like a cork being pulled from a bottle. The bird is unique in another respect, according to a correspondent to *Forest and Bird* magazine of November 1944: 'When our family settled in bush country fifty years ago, we always noticed that the tui changed or varied his song every month, about the time of the new moon.'

The *tui* I heard, hidden somewhere above the stream, was singing a song that, in this thin grove of trees, had undergone 1,560 variations – twelve a year for a hundred and thirty years – since 1868.

A few miles from the Beak of the Bird is the small settlement of Mawhitiwhiti where the kidnapped boy came from. It was here, Sandy and Lorna Parata advised me, that I could find a lady named Amiria Rangi, who was his closest living relation and who would know more about his story than anyone else. There was no difficulty in finding Mawhitiwhiti; the problem was pinning down Aunty Miri, as everyone called her. She is now retired, in her seventies, and therefore leads a life of unexampled velocity – for several weeks I felt I was constantly watching plumes of dust as Aunty Miri disappeared over the horizon to meetings and funerals and symposiums on Maori health, youth, smoking, culture, song, museum policy, and so on.

On the phone, when we did speak, she was rather guarded. *What* did I say I wanted? Why? *Who* was I again? But eventually she agreed to meet me.

Mawhitiwhiti was not even a village, just a row of wooden 1950s bungalows beside a T-junction among fields and hedge-rows and a country golf course. One of the houses was sur-rounded by a small army of plaster gnomes, some painted, and some simply white, like gnomes that have been caught out naked in public; among them were also plaster flamingos, plaster ducks and one rare species – a solitary white plaster hen.

'My house is the one with the plaster ducks,' Miri said on the phone.

We arrived one afternoon about a month after my visit to Hawera. I found the house with the plaster ducks. At the end of the road, Mt. Taranaki glistened loftily in the sun. Miri Rangi was very short, neat, droll and that day she was rather on her dignity. She wore large fluffy slippers, and, I sensed, she was slightly hostile towards me. I was glad that my brother-in-law was there.

We sat down in a sitting room crammed with cabinets, mirrors, pot-plants, curios, cushions, vases. There on a wall, among dozens of other photographs, portraits, landscapes on velvet, was that now familiar photograph of the boy standing by the table with its ebony helix pedestal.

Miri Rangi knew his story better than anyone else, starting from the very beginning. What, for example, was he doing wandering about in the forest on the very day that an attack by the *Pakeha* (the whites) was expected?

44

'Oh, he was a *tutu* kid. He was a mischief boy, that one.

'He had *taringa maro* – hard ears, starched ears. *Cloth* ears, you would say in English,' she went on.

'He never listened, he took no notice. His mother, Hinewai – poor Hinewai, she was pretty, but she had asthma. She was never very well. She couldn't control that boy. And so that day – off he went . . . and he never came back.

'No one knew what had happened to him. They thought, "*Where's Ngatau?*" His older brother, Ake Ake, was eighteen or so. The little one, he tried to follow him around everywhere. After the fighting, Ake Ake hunted for him in the bush. They couldn't find a body, but they thought: "The boy is dead."'

But before she told me this – and a great many other things – something else took place. There was a slightly strained atmosphere. Maori and whites meet easily and pleasantly on many occasions, but when the *past* is brought up, the atmosphere often changes. There is immediately a little electricity in the air. Something must be said; there is a hint of a storm on the way.

Curious tales are reported arising out of this atmosphere. Already, after only a week or two visiting Taranaki, I had heard some of these. In the 1970s, for instance, an elderly white man, the son of a man who fought at The Beak of the Bird, decided that the time had come for him to make a personal reconciliation with his Maori neighbours, whom he had seen in the distance all his life but had never got to know.

He sought out an extremely ancient lady, 103 years old in fact, who had been an infant at The Beak when the battle took place. He went to her house somewhere on the South Taranaki plains. He knocked on the door, was told to him come in. He told her his business and she understood it.

'Sit down. Have some *kai* [food],' she said.

She gave him some Maori (unleavened) bread.

'If we eat this together, then we will have peace.'

45

A few days later, he decided to go and see her again. He drove across the county to her house. He knocked at the door.

No answer. He tapped at a window. He peered around the garden. The property had suddenly acquired an air of neglect. A Maori neighbour came over and asked what he wanted.

'I came to see the old lady.'

'Oh, we've lost her.'

'*Lost* her?'

'Yes, she died three months ago.'

Well . . . but the fact such a tale even has currency says a little about the atmosphere in the matter-of-fact sunlight of bi-racial and rural Taranaki.

The electricity at my meeting with Miri Rangi was less sensational.

We sat in armchairs in her sitting room; her slippered feet nearly touched the floor. She straightened her back and said decisively:

'You know . . . I want to say one thing to you before we talk about anything else. I have to say one thing: I don't like what you Pakehas . . . *did.*'

This cost her some effort. It went against her instinct for hospitality (she had prepared a huge afternoon tea for three complete strangers). But it was said, and there was a silence.

And what was I to say in reply? What, in fact, did she refer to? What had we done? There are rather a high number of candidates among the offences.

Perhaps it was simplest just to think of those sunlit green fields stretching away for miles beyond Aunt Miri's house. They were one sign of a great wrong – a broken promise, a broken treaty of which it was said (by Gladstone) in the House of Commons in 1847: 'As far as England is concerned, there is not a more . . . rigorously binding treaty in existence than that of Waitangi.'

All that land, from Miri's front gate as far as the mountain, was just one of the tracts taken in breach of the covenant. It was an

46

immense loss to the owners of course, but also to ourselves. 'Do not do this,' some settlers had pleaded with those in power. 'The Maori will say we are a *nation of liars*.'

But in the end it was done, and the cost was too high. Sometimes it is impossible not to notice the poverty of speech, the woodenness of expression, among New Zealanders – unlike, for instance, the loquacious Australians just across the sea. Was this an ingenious judgement on us? We broke our word, and, since then, have had oddly broken words, mysteriously second-hand language, at our disposal?

'Well,' I said, after too long a pause, 'a lot of us don't like what we did either.' Miri Rangi stiffened, as if she had heard of this point of view among the Pakeha and didn't believe it, but, on the other hand, had never actually heard the words spoken to *her* before. It was not much of a remark, not a very handsome apology, but I think that she believed me.

It was, as I said, only a slight electrical storm. After that, we became friends.

3

A captive in the lens

The news of the little trophy, one captured child, did not make a great impact on the public mind. One newspaper turned him into a girl; another increased his age to ten. And the military intelligence in the possession of the six-year-old was not of high value. He was, however, able to tell his interrogators that two or three white men had of late been fighting on Titoko-waru's side, and that one of them had recently been murdered.

Both these pieces of information were gratifying to the authorities. It was still difficult for some people to believe the Maori could ever defeat Englishmen on their own. There must be an evil genius, a turncoat, a renegade Irishman or American among them, who could account for the phenomenon. And if such a renegade was then to be slaughtered by his Maori friends, so very much the better.

Omahuru also told his interrogators that on the morning before the battle, which was known to be impending, Titoko-waru had asked the women of the *pa* to dance a *haka* for him – 'an entertainment of which he is fond,' said *The Taranaki Herald* darkly, although only fifty years after Waterloo the paper couldn't quite work out why dancing on the eve of battle should be the object of censure.

After that, the boy slipped from sight. He is not mentioned again, among the requests flying from Patea to Wanganui and to the capital for slippers for the wounded, port and brandy, crutches and walking sticks. Nor does he makes an appearance in the final, formal report on the disaster written by the Minister of Native Affairs, a man named Richmond, to the Governor. Richmond was one of the new men who had led the colony into war in the early 1860s.

The stalemates and the savagery of the war, then the catastrophe at The Beak of the Bird all gave Richmond an opportunity of doubting his own wisdom but he did not consider taking such a drastic step as that. He could not, however, now diminish the gravity of the situation as he wrote to the Governor.

'A disastrous defeat the like of which has never before befallen our arms in New Zealand,' he called the battle. 'After the loss of several of the officers there appears to have been an utter absence of order or command in the rear-guard – many of the men threw away their arms and accoutrements and had it not been for the help of the friendly Native contingent, our loss must have been even more severe than it was. There is too much reason to fear that some barbarous cruelties were afterwards perpetrated by the Maoris upon the wounded, including one officer, who fell alive into their hands . . . The enemy's loss is not accurately known.'

Richmond did not in the end mention the murder of the child or children found in the clearing. But he considered it: in a first draft of his report, which is still in the National Archives, he wrote: 'All that is accurately known is that three men and two children were killed.'

Then he removed the words: 'and two children'.

There are many other deletions in the first draft, and they are just simple black strokes of the pen. But over the words *and two children*, Richmond paused. His pen hovered; he pondered, he wondered. Then finally he expunged the words with a long series of interlinked 'o's, like a child's scribble of train smoke, or the voices of small ghosts in a comic strip.

That hovering erasure – *0000000000* – grows heavier and darker as it goes along, so that over the third word it has become a dense mass of black rings. It is the sole notice from any government source that the children ever existed.

While this letter was being written to the Governor, the third child, the little captive, was safely in the hands of Mr and Mrs Herewini, at the military base at Patea. He was then taken to the town of Wanganui when the Native Contingent retreated westward, along with other forces and many settlers.

At that point he vanishes from sight into a Maori world, and there he might well have remained, like a moth against its native bark. Many years later he himself said that he knew of several children who had been captured during the wars and carried away in roughly the same circumstances as himself; they disappeared against their new background, and were never heard of again.

This could easily have happened to Omahuru. But one day, soon after he arrived in Wanganui, the wide-set, slightly staring eyes of the Residential Magistrate, Mr Walter Buller, fell on him.

Buller was a strange man, a kind of baggy Victorian monster, but, although he was a monster, he was a human rather than inhuman one. He was greedy and generous, the worldly and ambitious son of a Wesleyan missionary, a great naturalist whose slaughters helped to drive the country's rarest and most noble bird, the legendary *huia*, into extinction.

The first colonial–born member of the Royal Society, he was a correspondent of Darwin and Lady Hyacinth Hooker of Kew, Lord Kelvin, Sir John Lubbock, Lord Walsingham and Dr Sclater: at the same time, he was an impenitent fraud who once concocted a 'new' species of laughing owl out of duster-feathers and tried to sell it to one of the English Rothschilds, who indignantly rejected the object.

He was disliked and distrusted by many settlers in Wanganui

51

as a 'philo-Maori', a phrase which had the same drift as 'nigger-lover' in America, though perhaps less force. Buller is credited with a famous remark: 'The Maori are dying out and nothing can save them. Our plain duty as good, compassionate colonists is to smooth down their dying pillow.'

One biographer, contemplating his career, said: 'He did not so much smooth down the dying pillow of the Maori as snatch it away from under them.'

In 1868, when young Ngatau Omahuru came to his notice, Buller was only thirty-one, married with children, hard up, eager to rise in the world. He rose and rose – on the back of rare birds and more or less exploited Maori – and he became a millionaire, a magnate and friend of royalty. One morning, at Windsor Castle, he sat down to breakfast with a little old lady who wore black mittens, poured the tea, told a little joke, *tittered*, and then later that day made him a KCMG. It was the last knighthood that Victoria personally conferred. Buller died some years later in the shadows, in some degree of disgrace.

The first glimpse we have of him, a few years before he met Omahuru, was at a great land sale on the banks of the Rangitikei river, fifty miles east of Wanganui. This meeting was described by a British MP, Sir Charles Dilke, who in the mid-1860s toured the empire and wrote a book, *Greater Britain*. His description of the land sale is worth quoting at length, for what took place that day, and the personalities involved, were all to be of importance in this story. It is also a wonderful evocation of the ideal and official vision of the colony, the two races gathered under the Union Jack.

The place where the sale was actually completed was named Parewanui. Today it is flat, rather drab farmland near the country's main air-force base, Ohakea. Jets boom and flash across the sky. The Englishmen who arrived there that day in 1866, in their black suits and with their ledgers under their arms, felt as if they had wandered into a gathering on the plain before Troy.

The scene opens with a Maori song sung by the women to greet the Superintendent of the Province, Dr Featherstone (*Petatone*, in Maori which lacks an 'f' or any other sibilants), when he finally arrived with the money for the completion of the sale.

Here is Petatone
This is the 10th of December;
The sun shines and the birds sing;
Clear is the water in rivers and streams;
Bright is the sky and the sun is high in the air.
This is the 10th of December
But where is the money?
Three years has this matter in many debates been discussed,
And here at last is Petatone;
But where is the money?

A band of Maori women chanting in a high strained key stood at the gate and with this song met a few Englishmen who were driving rapidly on to their land.

Our track lay through a swamp of the New Zealand flax. Huge sword-like leaves all but hid from view the Maori stockades. To the left was a village of low houses, fenced around with a double row of lofty posts carved with rude images of gods and men. On the right were groves of karakas, children of Tane Mahuta, the New Zealand sacred trees. In startling contrast to the dense masses of the oily leaves, there stretched a great extent of light-green sward where there were other camps and a tall flagstaff from which floated a white flag and the Union Jack, emblems of British sovereignty and peace.

A thousand kilted Maoris dotted the green landscape with patches of brilliant tartans and scarlet cloth. From all corners of

53

the glade the Maori cry of welcome came floating to us. We found ourselves in the midst of a thronging crowd of square built men, brown in colour and for the most part not much darker than the Spaniards but with here and there a woolly negro in their ranks.

Glancing at them as we were hurried past, we saw that the men were robust, well limbed and tall. They greeted us pleasantly with many a cheerful open smile, but the faces of the older people were horribly tattooed in spiral curves. The chiefs carried battle clubs of jade and bone; the women wore strange ornaments.

The purchase of an enormous block of land – that of the Manawatu – had long been an object worked for by the Provincial government. The completion of the sale had brought the Superintendent, Dr Featherstone, and humbler *pakehas* to Parewanui.

It was not only that the land was wanted for the flood of settlers, but purchase by the Government was the only means whereby war between the various native claimants could be prevented.

The pakeha and Maori had agreed upon a price; the question that remained was how the money should be shared. One tribe had owned the land from the earliest time; another had conquered some miles of it; a third had had one of its chiefs cooked and eaten upon the ground . . .

The Ngati Apa were well armed; the Ngati Raukawa had their rifles; the Wanganuis had sent for theirs. The greatest tact on the part of Dr Featherstone was needed to prevent a fight such as would rouse half New Zealand.

On a signal from the Superintendent, the heralds went round the camps and *pas* to call the tribes to council.

The summons was a long-drawn, minor-descending scale: a plaintive cadence which at a distance blends into a bell-like chord. The words mean:

'Come hither! Come hither! Come! Come! Maories!

54

Come —!' and men, women, and children soon came thronging in from every side, the men bearing sceptres of ceremony,
the women wearing round their necks the symbol of nobility,
the *Hei-tiki* or greenstone god.

We, with Mr Buller, the resident magistrate of Wanganui,
seated ourselves beneath the flagstaff. A chief, meeting the
people as they came up, stayed them with the gesture that
Homer ascribes to Hector, and bade them sit in the huge
circle round the spar.

No sooner than we were seated on our mat than there ran
slowly into the centre of the ring a plumed and kilted chief,
with sparkling eyes, the perfection of a savage. It was Hunia te
Hakeke, the young chief of the Ngati Apa.

Throwing off his plaid, he commenced to speak, springing
hither and thither with leopard-like freedom of gait and
sometimes leaping high in the air to emphasize a word. Fierce
as were the gestures, his speech was conciliatory and the Maori
flowed from his lips — a soft Tuscan tongue. There ran around
the ring a hum and buzz of applause.

Karanama, a small Ngati Raukawa chief with a white
moustache who looked like an old French concierge, followed . . . and, with much use of his sceptre, related a dream
foretelling the happy issue of the negotiators. The Maoris
believe that in their dreams the seers hear great bands of spirits
singing chants: these when they wake they reveal to all the
people; but it is remarked the vision is generally to the
advantage of the seer's tribe.

Mr Buller — a Maori scholar of eminence and the attached
friend of some of the chiefs — interpreted for Dr Featherstone
and we were allowed to lean over him in such a way as to hear
every word that passed.

Dilke describes the violent invective exchanged, the applause,
the poetry. He mentions the existence of a fourth party who are

not present, who are against the sale altogether, who are said to be armed and in the neighbourhood, urged on by some mysterious 'white men who are not friendly to the sale'. The next day, a war seems to be looming. The Union Jack is pulled down. The English officials walk out. Tempers then cool, the sale goes on, and Dr Featherstone – Petatone – returns.

The next day, Dr Featherstone drove into the camp sur-rounded by a brilliant cavalcade of Maori cavalry, amid much yelling and firing of pieces upwards. The assembly was soon dismissed and the chiefs withdrew to prepare for the grandest war dance that had been seen for years. The allies were led by Hunia in all the bravery of his war-costume. In his hair he wore a heron plume, and another was fastened near the muzzle of his carbine; his limbs were bare but about his shoulders he had a pure white scarf of satin. His kilt was gauze-silk, of three colours – pink, emerald and cherry – arranged in such a way as to show as much of the green as the other two colours. The contrast, which upon a white skin would have been glaring in its ugliness, was perfect when backed by the nut-brown of Hunia's chest and legs. As he ran before his tribe, he was the perfect savage.

The instant that the heralds had returned, a charge took place, the forces passing through each other's ranks as they do on the stage, but with frightful yells. After this, they formed two deep, in three companies, and danced the 'musket-exercise war-dance' in wonderful time, the women leading, thrusting out their tongues and shaking their long pendent breasts.

It was not hard to understand the conduct of Lord Dur-ham's settlers, who landed here in 1837. The friendly natives received the party with such a dance, which had upon them such an effect that they immediately took ship for Australia, where they remained.

The next day, when we called on Hunia to bid him farewell, he made two speeches to us worth recording as specimens of Maori oratory. Speaking through Mr Buller, he said – 'Hail, guests! You have just now seen the settlement of a great dispute – the greatest of modern time.

'This was a weighty trouble, a grave difficulty. Many Pakehas have tried to settle it – in vain. For Petatone was it reserved to end it. If Petatone has need of me in the future I shall be there. If he climbs a lofty tree, I will climb it with him. If he scales high cliffs, I will scale them too. Where he leads, there will I follow. Such are the words of Hunia.'

To this speech, one of us replied, explaining our position as guests from Britain.

Hunia then began again to speak:

'O my guests, when you return to our great Queen, tell her that we will fight for her again as we have fought before. She is our Queen as well as your Queen – Queen of the Maori and Queen of the Pakeha.

'When we wrote to Petatone, we asked him to bring Pakehas from England and from Australia – Pakehas from all parts of the Queen's broad lands. Pakehas who would return and tell the Queen that the Ngati Apa are her liege-men.

'May your heart rest here among us, but off you go once more to your English home, tell the people that we are Petatone's faithful subjects, and the Queen's. Enough.'

Hunia kept his word. He became one of the great *kupapa* chiefs. The word originally meant 'those who crouch' – i.e., to duck the blows of a quarrel between strangers. But the *kupapa* tribes were usually those who found their fortune magnified by an active alliance with the whites. Hunia was leader of the Ngati Apa, a formerly powerful tribe which had come down in the world. They were, according to the Native Secretary in 1850, a

57

'rude and uncivilised race', numbering only a few hundred, but through alliance with the whites they were now rich and powerfully armed again. Hunia was one of the chiefs at the battle of The Beak of the Bird which took place two years after this scene, and it was two men under his command, Herewini and Pirimona, who kidnapped the boy. And it was through Hunia that his 'attached friend', Walter Buller, Resident Magistrate, heard of the child when he arrived in Wanganui.

At the sight of the little captive, Buller's eyes must have widened, like a cat's seeing a bird. Scientist, linguist, government agent – he was above all an entrepreneur, and he had a journalist's nose for a story. Here, for a small outlay, was an opportunity to make some money.

For some years he had been involved in a trade in Maori artefacts, tattooed heads, venerable pieces of jade, greenstone clubs and *hei-tiki* – fantastical pendants or amulets, representing in embryo the figure of the first man created by Tane, some of them hundreds of years old and with a long genealogy of former owners attached by memory to each of them. This trade was profitable but it also brought the ambitious young magistrate into contact with great museum directors and aristocratic collectors abroad. When he got to England in the early 1870s, he was in their doors in no time. He dined with the Duke of Newcastle, His Grace was 'very kind'. He supped with Lord Kinnaid, who took him back to his country seat and showed him a 'well-tattooed head kept in the Entrance Hall . . . very highly valued'.

'I have not forgotten your request about a Hei-tiki,' he wrote from Wanganui. 'I have "made love" to every old lady wearing one since I came here.'

But he also knew there was a profit to be made from other areas of the Maori world, especially in the booming market for the *carte-de-visite*, the stiff little ancestor of the postcard, which first appeared in the early 1860s. In New Zealand the most popular *carte-de-visite* ever made was a picture of von Tempsky; after that came images of the Maori.

The white attitude to Maori in the 1860s was quite incoherent. On one hand, they were 'fiends in human form' and 'swinelike niggers' and so on. But at the same time they were 'a superior race of men, the very counterpart of Englishmen', 'the finest race in the world – not excepting the British' (according to the historian Froude) or simply the 'Noble Race'.

'I cannot name them, but chose them for their great beauty of countenance etc.,' wrote one settler packing off a set of *cartes* to his friends in England. 'Among the men there are some noble heads worthy of better deeds than have befallen them to their lot [sic]. However they are a fair sample of the Noble Race.'

It was clever of Buller to have recognised in the forlorn little Ngatau Omahuru an opportunity to get into business. Wanganui was awash with displaced people, settlers in rags, their farms burning in the distance, Maori coming in to town to escape the troubles, militiamen trying to lose their uniforms. But Buller reached into his pocket and bought the child a good suit, a new white shirt, excellent English boots; possibly it was even he who combed the boy's hair and showed him how to put one hand in a trouser pocket when he stood before the camera.

Buller saw that the Noble-Race *genre* could be altered to suit the times. On the back of the sole surviving *carte* are written these words:

The nephew of Ti Kuwaru, a rebel who said he had tasted the flesh of the white man and it was good. This boy's parents were both shot and he was found in a hut all alone. He was brought to town, sent to school and named William Fox.

The boy was not Titokowaru's nephew; his parents were not shot. He was not an orphan. He had not even been found in a hut all alone. And Titokowaru himself probably never ate human flesh. But by emphasising the Maori darkness from which he had emerged, and showing him in a semi-classical, civilised world and a good pair of boots, a clever image-maker could combine all three components – savagery, potential Maori nobility and the goodness of the colonial enterprise – together in one frame.

A photographer charged fifteen shillings for a dozen *cartes*. Buller, who was always short of cash, could have them sold for half a crown each, a hundred per cent profit.

Perhaps, as well, at this early juncture he was unconsciously rehearsing the pinnacle of his career nearly twenty years later. We are now in London in 1886, at the Colonial and Indian Exhibition. Buller, retired at forty-nine and vastly wealthy from dealing in Maori land, is in charge of the New Zealand pavilion, for which he has had commissioned twenty paintings of 'Maoris in characteristic costume' by an artist named Lindauer.

Here is an account of what happened next, which appeared in the *New Zealand Free Lance* some years after his death:

Sir Somers Vine, a friend of Buller's, succeeded in inducing the Prince of Wales to inspect the New Zealand court at the Exhibition. The Prince glanced politely but wearily at the kauri gum, wool and flax and was apparently about to go when he caught sight of a picture on the wall, a Lindauer painting of a pretty Hawke's Bay Maori girl with a wreath of clematis thrown carelessly over her head.

The Prince asked for a chair and sat there looking at the picture for several minutes.

At last as he rose to go he said to Sir Somers Vine and Dr Buller:

'Do you know, that is one of the most beautiful pictures I have ever seen!'

Immediately the Prince left, Sir Somers Vine rushed back and said:

'Now, Buller, there's your chance! Pack that picture up at

once and send it round to the Prince of Wales and ask him to accept it as a memento of his visit.'

This was done *instanter*. The bread cast upon waters returned *the very next day*.

The announcement was made in a list of additional Birthday Honours that Dr Walter Buller had been made a KCMG.

Within a few days Buller and his wife were in the breakfast room at Windsor Castle. The Queen poured the tea. She told the Bullers a funny story: 'A grandson when at college wrote and asked for the loan of a pound. I replied that as he had overspent himself, he must wait until his pocket money was again due. His reply was to this effect. "Never mind, Grandmother. I sold your letter to a chap for £3, so now am in funds."'

The Queen giggled.

'Tell me, Dr Buller,' she said, 'are the Maori ladies *very* pretty?'

'Pretty enough, Ma'am – for the men.'

'Oh, Sir Walter!' said the Queen, and the tittered again. Her fingers, even behind the panes of her fingernails, were quite white.

When they rose to leave she kissed Lady Buller on both cheeks.

'I was overcome by her motherly sweetness and felt like giving the old lady a good hug,' wrote Lady Buller later.

This wasn't bad going even by Buller standards – being kissed on both cheeks by the Queen of a fifth of the world, and all on the basis of a wisp of clematis in a Maori girl's black hair.

And it is a very Bulleresque moment: strictly speaking, the painting was stolen property. Buller, under the terms of his commission, had no right to give away state property to the first royal who strayed into view, and merely for his own aggrandisement ('Now, Buller, there's your chance!'). But he seems to have covered his tracks quite well. The rest of the Lindauer portraits were returned to New Zealand and most are now on display in the Wanganui Museum. In 1999 I asked the curator about the twentieth painting, the Maori girl with clematis in her hair. She had never heard of her. But the Surveyor of the Queen's Pictures confirmed the newspaper story. The picture is still in the royal collection, where it is described as:

Terewai Horomona. Half-length portrait of young maori girl, facing the front, her hands raised in her dance; from her left hand hangs a long poi: long dark hair surmounted by a wreath of white clematis; white blouse and dark pleated skirt; landscape beyond BP 2323 406702.

Terewai Horomona, of course, knew no more about a KCMG and breakfast at Windsor than, twenty years before, young Ngatau Omahuru knew about the hundred per cent profit that could be made in the *carte-de-visite* business. And probably she wouldn't have cared less, one way or the other. Her portrait was to affect other lives, Buller's especially, not her own. She departs from the story, the picture vanishes into the Royal Collection. But for five-year-old Omahuru, the case was different. His photograph was to change his life. It was to bring him to the notice of a number of interested parties, both Maori and Pakeha, in and around the river town of Wanganui, to which the war was coming closer.

So finally there he is, the boy from the forest darkness, in front of the camera, peering anxiously at the photographer. As well as woe, there is perhaps a hint of anger darkening his brows. This is something you often see in Maori children, who seem to have a keener appreciation of their rights than most infants. He is afraid, but he also does not approve of the proceedings. He does not like the man who has dived so importantly under a black veil, removing his own head.

When I first saw the picture reproduced in one or two books, the captions indicated that it was taken after he had been adopted by Sir William Fox. By then he would have adjusted a little to the ways of the Pakeha gentry in their big wooden houses along The Terrace or behind Parliament in Wellington.

In fact it shows him on his first day, perhaps his first hour, outside the Maori world. It is possible that he was in the Wanganui studio on the same morning as the 'Te Ngutu heroes' – the survivors and wounded men transported to Wanganui after the battle of The Beak of the Bird. The spiral-stand table on which he rests his hand appears in their portraits as well, nearly hidden by trouser-legs, crutches and walking sticks. The veterans tilt their beards defiantly camera-wards.

The boy is lost. He is entirely surrounded by the Pakeha, the strangers of whom he has heard all his life, and he has then been placed in front of the machine with its attendant and black impenetrable eye. In front of the Pakeha machine, whose purpose he could only have vaguely grasped, Omahuru appears stern and angry but also quite lost, like a child fallen down a well — not only alone now, but perhaps alone for ever.

4

Fingerprints on the trophy

But in the end, of course, things weren't as bad as all that. When the photo session was over, Buller, who had vanished off somewhere, came back and reclaimed Omahuru. They walked through the town hand in hand, Buller talking to him in Maori, a proper language without any of the hissing sounds that the boy heard from all sides. They came to Buller's house. It was warm and pretty inside, though it smelled strange as if food and sunlight formed different compounds among this tribe. Omahuru had never before stood upon a carpet.

Mrs Buller hugged him, then took him into another room where there was a fire burning in an iron cupboard and she gave him a drink of a liquid that fizzed and popped, for it was trying to speak to him. Buller and Mrs Buller both watched him as he listened to the speaking liquid, and something made them smile at him.

Then Buller took him out the back of the house and showed him some cages with birds in them – a sleepy owl, several wild tui, one piratical weka (a native woodhen) prowling the perimeter of its gaol.

In an empty stall in the stables, hiding in the straw, were three or four kiwi, curled up and lying on top of one another like little pigs. Buller fetched a stick and poked at them. They made a kind of growling chuckle and struggled away from the stick, trying, each of them, to find the darkest place in their prison.

In another cage, separate from the rest, was a *mokai*, an old, wise, tame tui, which had learned to talk. Whenever Buller spoke, the bird interrupted, intoning the same word: '*Tito . . . tito*' – 'Liar . . . liar.'

This made Buller roar with laughter, and suddenly Omahuru too burst out laughing; it was the first time he had laughed for several weeks.

Then Herewini arrived at the house, and took Omahuru back to the camp near the river sand where some of the *kupapa* were living. Mrs Herewini clapped one hand to her cheek when she saw the splendour of his new attire. She made him take off his new clothes and laid them carefully inside a flat box. Dressed in his ordinary garb, a grubby calico shirt and loose pants and with his feet bare, he went out to play in the mud with some other *kupapa* children he had become friends with. And there, a moth against the bark, he became invisible to the outside world again.

This was in October. Quite why and how, by the following January, Ngatau Omahuru was transformed into Master William Fox, godson and namesake of the most powerful man in the country, is not simply answered. The circumstances, as a historian would say in these circumstances, are obscure. One problem for a researcher in this area of Maori–white relations is the extraordinary number of fires which swept the country. Colonial New Zealand, built of wood, seems to have been in a semi-permanent state of conflagration. For our purposes the most disastrous fire was not until 1907 when Parliament and much of the national archive, including most of the records of the Native Department which would have thrown light on lives such as that of Ngatau Omahuru went up in flames. That great blaze constantly rises between us and our quarry, young Omahuru/Fox – sometimes he is silhouetted against it, then he disappears

66

again among the flames like a small *ignis fatuus* itself which one is chasing.

Among the few Native Department documents that did survive were the Letter Books, in which a copy of all outward correspondence was made. A Letter Book, like so many things in an archive, is a sorry and disappointing object. Your hopes rise at the sight of its battered leather bindings. Then you open the pages: the handwriting is illegible; the paper is extremely thin and absorbent; every pen-stroke has become furred; wherever a nib long ago paused to make a full stop or to punctuate the dullness of an office afternoon, the pause has over the years spread out into a dense blot. Hundreds of such sepia blots, each visible through several days of correspondence, are scattered across the transparent pages like dwarf brown stars on a spectograph. Furthermore, a record that consists only of *outward* correspondence is necessarily enigmatic. You only get half the picture. Mysterious subjects are taken up, dealt with curtly, and dropped without conclusion.

And yet one afternoon, in the midst of that wormy and riddling universe, you turn a page and there, beautiful as a blue and white planet, is a document that is perfectly legible, relevant to your search and even self-explanatory.

Here for instance is a copy of a letter from the secretary of the Minister of Native Affairs, Mr Richmond, to the Leader of the Opposition, Mr Fox. The two men disliked each other and from time to time replaced each other in ministries. Their correspondence is therefore extremely polite and this letter carefully repeats Mr Fox's earlier communication back to him.

Dec 29, 1868

Sir,

I acknowledge receipt of your letter to Mr Richmond of the 22nd instant upon the subject of a young lad captured by two of the Ngati

Upokoiri tribe, and whom the Ngati Raukawa Hauhaus had expressed their intention of retaking by force if necessary and stating that to prevent a probable conflict you had proposed that the child should be given up to the Government which proposal had been agreed to by both parties, with a reservation on the part of the captors that he should, on the completion of his education, be handed over to them.

The Government will be glad to provide for the maintenance and education of the boy in Wellington but an engagement to restore him to his captors would probably be impossible of fulfilment as it will rest with himself to decide where he will reside when his education is completed.

The better plan would probably be to get him sent here as soon as may be, without, if possible, giving any undertaking as to his future destiny leaving it for <u>time</u> to remove present difficulties on that point.

Would you have the kindness to have the boy sent to town by Cobb's Coach to be handed over to the Custodian of the Maori Hostelry, who will be instructed to take charge of him.

And three weeks later, in the *Wanganui Evening Herald*, this report appeared:

It will be remembered that a little boy was captured at the commencement of the attack upon Te Ruaruru [the clearing outside the Beak of the Bird] in a *whare* [house] which constituted the advance post of the enemy. The Rev. B. Taylor considered that it was necessary for him to undergo the ceremony of baptism (of course all staunch churchmen think the same) before he could be brought up in the Christian faith like other natives of Putiki, and accordingly, preparations were made with all becoming haste, and in keeping with the importance of the event by such an extraordinary course of circumstances, to perform the sacrament.

Tuesday was the day fixed and at the appointed hour, Wm.

Fox Esq. MHR [Member of the House of Representatives], Aperahama Puke and Wikitoria Tumua were in attendance. The boy was baptised and received and named William Fox after one of his fathers.

There is a very great legal question arising out of this matter. The little Foxite was sprinkled at the time of his capture by Father Roland [sic], lest, as this worthy clergyman himself informed us, he should be killed and die a Hau-Hau. By such an act he was admitted to the body of the Church of Rome and will, canonically, remain in it until, by his own consent, he leaves it.

Considering the danger that heroic man braved, he should surely be allowed to retain within his own Church the little convert he made.

So it was all quite simple. War at that moment was raging to the west of Wanganui and any little spark, it was feared, could carry the conflict away to the east as well, to the settled districts of Rangitikei and Manawatu. In this district lived a tribe named the Ngati Raukawa, whom we met during the land sale described earlier. A section of these Raukawa were Hau Hau and they had been alerted to the boy's existence – possibly by his photograph – and had decided to retake him on behalf of their co-religionists. The boy was the spark which could ignite a war fifty miles away to the east.

By agreeing to give him up to the government, both Maori parties could save face and avoid the conflict. To seal the bargain, and to make it irreversible, William Fox had the boy christened and renamed after him. Then the child was to disappear off to the capital, far from the troubles.

It is all very neat and makes perfect sense. But there is one difficulty: the story is not to be believed. For William Fox, MA (Oxon), Barrister (Inner Temple), five times colonial Premier, gentleman-farmer, artist and total abstainer, was also a liar. He

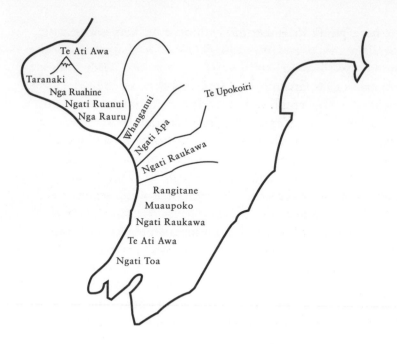

Tribal Areas, Central and Lower North Island

Note: All names above are of tribes, none are place names

lied throughout his career. In this case, he merely lied to Richmond and to Herewini and arranged the insertion of a few falsehoods on the boy's baptismal certificate.

Two days after the christening ceremony, Fox, back at Westoe, his country house forty miles east of Wanganui, in the Rangitikei district, wrote this note:

My Dear Buller,

On my return home I heard that Herewini had been down here with a gun on his shoulder to recapture our captive. Nobody could understand what he said beyond asking for a *pukapuka* [letter] to you to give him up. This hint may mean that he is going to Wanganui to look after him, so I pass it on . . .

One thing is clear from this – Herewini had not agreed to give the boy up. The child was now, in Fox's own words, 'our captive'. The figure of Herewini, prowling up to Westoe with a gun on his shoulder, shows up the untruthful Mr Fox like a silhouette against a newly-risen moon.

The exact circumstances of the boy's second abduction may never be known, but to understand the background better and at least see the scale of Fox's deceit in this instance it is necessary to go back to October and November in 1868, to the grim months of early summer when war came closer and closer to the outskirts of Wanganui. After the battle at The Beak of the Bird, things went from bad to worse for the colonists. For a hundred miles west of Wanganui, the forces of Titokowaru were in the ascendant. Houses and farms were burning in all directions. Nearly all the settlers had fled. A third of the Maori in the district joined the insurrection, others headed for the bush or came to town. Only the old, the stubborn or the most fanciful optimists stayed at home.

In early November there was a second major battle between colonial forces and the insurgents, which resulted in another Maori victory. Worse still, a squabble over the chain of command meant that most of the Maori *kupapa* allies had refused to join the fighting.

Titokowaru came nearer and nearer, crossed the Kai Iwi river and burned houses within five miles of Wanganui.

One night, on patrol on the edge of town, Captain Dawson of the Wanganui Cavalry heard: 'a terrific yell, gradually dyeing [sic] away into the distance. There was scarcely a breath of wind. The air was extremely rare . . . it was a Hauhau cry of the most fiendish description.'

71

He raised the alarm and men, women and children ran through the streets of Wanganui in their nightgowns seeking safety in the army stockades. However, the enemy did not appear and in the morning there was no sign of their whereabouts.

One day, Father Jean-Baptiste Rolland set off across the vast no man's land to visit his parishioners on the other side of the war zone. He was alone, and carried only his breviary and one prized possession, Von Tempsky's whip. He rode for mile after mile and saw not a single living soul. At one place, near the Waingongoro River, he thought he heard 'a cry resembling that of a Maori woman', but then decided that it was only the scream of an inland-whirling gull.

When the enemy is at the gates but doesn't actually come through them, life has a way of carrying on as usual. Buller was busy in his Magistrate's Court. There was a suit for damages on account of a shipment of flour which 'tasted strongly of kerosine'. Kate Hickey, 'well known to the bench', was charged by Mr Trimble with stealing a handkerchief. James Nixon, servant, was fined five shillings for 'most revolting language'; William Alfrey came before the court as a lunatic. J. Griffith and someone known only as Pompey were fined ten shillings for being drunk and fighting, charges being brought by Constable Coakley.

'This is a nice little place but the people are . . . detestable,' wrote a new arrival, a Colonel Lyon. He had one arm, and his wife was far away and hard of heart. 'I am half distracted, one letter in 5 weeks,' he wrote. 'Do you call that kind? I am tormented with awful thoughts. I have made a wee drawing very like your legs. Am I not naughty to think of drawing them but I think so often of you day and night that I am surely mad . . . Did you know there are *two* chapters in the Bible exactly the same, one in Kings, the other in Isaiah?'

The Wanganui Races were held on schedule, but the attend-

72

ance was small. In the Welter Stake (one and a half miles) the favourite, Titokowaru, owned and ridden by Mr J. Day, won easily.

The local papers did not neglect the great world. The Earl of Dudley's funeral address in London for a certain Baron of the Exchequer was quoted: 'He was a good man, an excellent man. He had the best melted butter I ever tasted in my life.'

A wistful letter appeared in the press deploring the horrific nature of modern weapons. 'Soon,' the author suggested, 'there shall be no one left to kill. Shall we be forced into loving one another?'

Two sleeping settlers were caught by a war party a few miles out of town and were about to be slaughtered, when a young Maori girl from their district burst into tears. The executioners turned on her.

'What's the matter with *you*?'

'Oh,' she said, making more noise than ever, 'you are going to take our Pakehas away to Okotuku, and kill them!'

'At which,' reported the *Wanganui Evening Herald*, 'the Hauhaus relented.'

Back in town, meanwhile, something ugly was brewing. There was a growing animosity between the whites and their Maori allies, the *kupapa*. The blame for this rests most clearly with one man, a certain John Ballance, the editor of the *Evening Herald*. Ballance, an Ulsterman in his late twenties, makes his first appearance in this story at the great land sale at Parewanui, described earlier, when Dr Featherstone drove into the camp with £25,000 in gold in a wooden chest on the floor of the carriage.

In his wake, like a flock of gulls following a trash barge, came a number of Wanganui tradesmen eager to part the newly enriched Maori from their money. Ballance at the time was in the jewellery business and he came along with his pockets full of gold watches and other trinkets. The Maori chiefs whom he approached gazed doubtfully upon him. There was something about the little man with his wispy moustache and truculent lower lip they did not quite trust. They applied to Buller for advice. Were these gold watches and chains of good quality?

Buller – himself of course a fraud, but a subtle one, and conscious of his magisterial rank – declined to offer any opinion of the merchandise. The chiefs therefore sent Ballance on his way. He rode off through the golden afternoon full of rage. He never forgave Buller, and his thoughts on the *kupapa* chiefs who had waved him elegantly away were unprintable.

Except that one day Ballance, who had the indignant gaze of a bullfrog and eventually owned his own evening paper, did print them.

Vehement and ignorant, Ballance was one of the colonists who had acquainted himself with the full title of Darwin's work: *On the Origin of Species by means of Natural Selection, or the Preservation of Favoured Races in the Struggle for Life.* He rose to his feet at a public meeting called in Wanganui to discuss the war. 'The Maori must be taught they have a Superior Race to contend with!' he shouted, according to one report.

But at this stage, most of his venom was directed not at Titokowaru marauding to the west but at the *kupapa* allies within the town. Ballance could not bear the fact that the white people of Wanganui, Britons, should be dependent on an Inferior Race for their safety.

'McAuley's dream, about the Maori sitting on a broken arch of London Bridge and picturing the ruins of St Paul's, is likely enough to be realised,' the *Evening Herald* prophesied. 'This is not a *kupapa* organ. We are read by our own countrymen.' On the other hand, when some of the Maori allies refused to fight in the recent battle at Moturoa, the *Herald* said they were 'cowards

74

or traitors' whose performance was 'disgraceful'. When a Maori cavalry unit was set up, the *Herald*, whose editor himself rode in a town cavalry corps, was beside itself: 'A motley band of Maoris in regulation forage caps . . . some in boots, some in shoes and others in their more natural costume of nudity. A ridiculous exhibition . . . simply preposterous.'

Ballance and the *Evening Herald* denounced allied chiefs, at one point seemed to be calling for a lynch party to attack certain Maori visitors to town, and wanted mass reprisals against the whole race for the actions of those in insurrection. For a while, to put the natives in their place, the *Herald* reduced the capital M of Maori to the lower case.

The atmosphere grew ugly. There were jeers in the street and shoving and pushing in hotel bars. A few years earlier, the Reverend Taylor had complained in his diary about drunken white and Maori soldiers staggering through the streets at night, singing, with their arms around each other's shoulders. Now the *kupapa* stated that they believed that the cavalrymen were on the point of attacking them.

But at the same time, out of sight, something more deadly than public dissension between allies was taking place. A flower of evil – to use a phrase coined in that decade – had quietly opened. There were only hints and winks and veiled phrases in the *Herald* to signal what had taken place:

War is not made with rose-water.
The enemy now has a wholesome dread of cavalry and this will be increased . . .
The Kai Iwi Cavalry are a perfect pack of devils and most un-controllable. If they smell the natives, they follow Bryce like a pack of hounds and cut, slay and destroy the poor natives before you have time to look around you . . .
The Cavalry have always professed they would kill every male they

came across on the other side of the Kai Iwi, unless there was some
proof he was a kupapa.

The full facts behind these sinister words, wreathed in smirks, did not emerge for twenty years in a great libel case in London. Briefly, this is what happened. Following the formation of the Wanganui Cavalry, which was useful in keeping open lines of communication and patrolling the borderlands, a second troop was set up. This was the Kai Iwi Cavalry, which consisted for the most part of young white farmers, many of whom had lost their land and been chased into town by the Maori insurrection. The two corps saw themselves as the elite troops of this little war – dashing, sporting, often drunk, a cut above regular forces, well-horsed (they supplied their own mounts) and commanded by officers they elected themselves.

Late in November the Kai Iwi Cavalry under Lt. John Bryce, a black-bearded young farmer from Kai Iwi, set out on their first foray into enemy territory. Two days later they were back in town covered in glory. They had sighted the foe, swooped upon them, sabred and shot and killed. It was only a small party of ten or a dozen Maori, admittedly, but the rout was complete. Two certainly were slain, four or five badly injured; the rest fled in terror.

At the conclusion of the affray, the horsemen gathered around one of the fallen enemy. Blood was pumping from a bullet wound, and he had a great sabre cut across his head. They did not dismount while they watched him dying.

In the official and unofficial reports, no one mentioned that he was a child of eight.

Under cross-examination two decades later, a witness gave this account of that incident:

Q. Was he a small boy or a large boy?
A. He was about four feet six inches in height.

Q. Was he nude?

A. He had only a shirt on.

Q. Could you see his private parts?

A. His penis was sticking out and not skinned as a boy of 14 or 15 would be.

Q. Could you judge from what you saw of his private parts as to his age?

A. Yes.

Q. Did you notice whether there was any hair on his private parts?

A. I noticed there was no hair there.

The enemy force which had been attacked consisted of a dozen children, aged from six to ten, chasing a flock of geese and a pig near the woolshed of an abandoned farm.

The chase and the slaughter among the squawking geese took about ten minutes. The men, in other words, knew what they were doing. They were not bad people – young red-faced farmers and surveyors and seed-merchants named George or Arthur or Ginger. There were several sets of brothers among them, they played cricket, they danced, they got 'jolly well drunk'. The old question which arises here – why is it that young men can always be found to carry out a massacre of the innocents? – is easy to answer. On their own George and Arthur and Ginger were sociable, cheerful, anxious to please. Even in a group they would not have taken it into their heads to kill children. But the presence of some vague authority – an implied consent, the imagined approval of a newspaper – was all that was needed to turn the Georges and Arthurs, for fifteen minutes or so, into a 'pack of devils'.

Years later, there was a suggestion from his obituarists that Ballance was present at this scene, but whether or not he was there in the flesh, he was there in spirit. If this 'dashing affair', as the *Herald* called it, were to be painted in the baroque style, with prancing horses, a distant forest, and a dozen children chasing the geese, there would also be a deity among the clouds, with an outstretched finger. Its pinions would be inky, its cuffs dingy, its name would be something like *Power of the Press*.

When the troopers got back to town the story was both a sensation and instantly hushed up. Some of the troopers were heard boasting in the pub, describing how difficult it was for a horseman to sabre a child that is hiding in a hedge. The authorities got wind of the facts. In Wellington, the Superintendent of the Province, Dr Featherstone, went to see Archdeacon Octavius Hadfield, the leading moral figure of the colony, and said: 'This war has become *barbarous*,' and he wrung his hands. The two other Wanganui newspapers were at first elated about the affray but then, on learning the facts, fell silent and published no further details.

The facts also soon reached the Maori community in Wanganui town and just across the river in Putiki, the headquarters of the *kupapa* and home of the greatest chiefs, Mete Kingi and Kepa Te Rangihiwinui. There was disbelief and disgust.

Me i mohio au ka penei to mahi e kore ahau e haere mai. 'If I had known what you were capable of, I would never have come to your side,' Kepa said in a rage to Lieutenant John Bryce.

Although the Wanganui *kupapa* would continue to defend the town – which was in their tribal territory – against Titokowaru, their appetite for making war on him dwindled away for a while. It was at this juncture that Mr and Mrs Herewini seem to have decided to pack up and leave Wanganui and go back to Hawke's Bay. As they prepared to depart for Ahuriri, Herewini's old home on the estuary near Napier, the question arose of what should happen to the child, their stolen goods, Ngatau Omahuru. His presence in Wanganui was already known as a result of the *carte-de-visite*. After the massacre of the children at Handley's Woolshed, he must have become the focus of uneasy considerations among the Maori. It should be remembered here that tribes in the same area, even those which were at war with one another, almost always had strong links of intermarriage and sympathy, links which, to the annoyance of the whites, could suddenly surface at inconvenient moments.

Could it have been that at this point a feeling sprang up among some of the *kupapa* that the boy should be given back to his own people? Too many children had been killed and, as a salve to their conscience and to the feelings of the bereaved, the stolen child should be sent home. Enough, in other words, was enough.

It is also possible that an odd coincidence came into play here. The name of the smallest boy killed, precisely the one whom the cavalrymen surrounded as he lay dying, happened to be Herewini. A child Herewini had died. An adult Herewini had stolen one of his cousins and made off with him. There was something wrong here, an asymmetry, ill-omened and unlucky, which should not be allowed to persist. Herewini himself may have felt this most of all.

To give the boy back, however, would have been easier said than done. What had become of his parents? Where were Titokowaru's patrols? Who could safely play the role of nursemaid and guide in that angrily humming no man's land to the west?

There was another solution to be found in the east. Fifty miles away, among the mixed tribes of the Rangitikei and Manawatu, were a number of Hau Hau adherents, 'very peaceable and good neighbours' according to some of the white settlers. They were connected by old ties to both the boy's tribe and to Herewini's people. This group, a section of the Ngati Raukawa, could take care of the boy and in due course deliver him safely home.

But here another obstacle appears. Fox and Buller at that time were involved in a bitter legal battle and a personal feud with these same people, the Ngati Raukawa Hau Hau. The idea that they should be allowed to play the discreet and honourable role of trustees and go-betweens would have been anathema to the two lawyers. To understand their animosity we have to go back once again to the land sale held at Parewanui a few years before, to that beautiful golden after-noon, as described by Sir Charles Dilke, in which *floated a white flag and the Union Jack, emblems of British sovereignty and peace. A thousand kilted Maoris dotted the green landscape with patches of brilliant tartans and scarlet cloth. From all corners of the glade the Maori cry of welcome came floating to us.*

It was all extremely picturesque, but, as is often the case with the picturesque, it disguises the full story. Dilke outlined the transaction and described the Maori disputes over sharing the sale-price. Later, he heard the women lament the loss of their ancestral lands but understood this was mostly acting, as they had never actually occupied the land they had just sold.

Thus we have met the sellers and we have met the buyers. But throughout the report there was only the briefest mention of another party – those among the many Maori owners of the land who were against the sale. Dilke, the distinguished transient from the House of Commons, was probably told very little about them: they were, in fact, a great embarrassment, for they had the best title to the land of all. Where the other tribes and sub-tribes had only glancing claims, based on old battles and distant marriages, the Non-Sellers, as they were called, were the people who actually lived on the block of land in question. The sale, that picturesque and beautiful occasion, was in fact a conspiracy by both Maori and whites against the one group to whom the block of land really mattered – those born and bred there and in actual possession of it.

But they were a small minority, only about two hundred strong. Buller, in the years before the sale, had travelled far and wide gathering signatures agreeing to sell from people with the remotest connections to the land imaginable. No one listened to the complaints of the occupants. Featherstone blocked his ears. Fox was eager to see hundreds of white farmers in the region. The Maori sellers vanished over the horizon with their share of the loot. Suddenly the Non-Sellers found themselves impoverished and homeless, beggars under their native sky. And in that state they might have remained, like a few other defrauded tribes too small to matter, drifting here and there, moored to nothing.

But in their case something else happened. They acquired a champion. He was just a local settler, and the word *just* is both right and wrong for him. He was a whirlwind, a Daniel come to judgement. Justice was precisely what Alex McDonald, forty-year-old government sheep inspector, and father of twelve children, discovered he had a passion for.

The Non-Sellers managed after two years of agitation to have an appeal heard in the Native Land Court, but as soon as the session began they knew they were in trouble. They had no money for a lawyer and without one were no match for the clever Mr Fox who appeared for the Crown. McDonald, who had wandered into the courtroom that day by chance, saw that the Non-Sellers – 'as honest and straightforward a people as God's sun shone on', he called them – were hopelessly out of their depth. A woman named Poi-Te-Ara asked him for help, and suddenly he found himself on his feet.

Fox, who had expected to breeze through the case without opposition, was outraged.

'This is disgraceful,' he shouted. 'This man is a servant of the province and he is stirring up and encouraging the Maoris to resist the government!'

McDonald revered Fox, who had 'once done me and mine a very great service', and he felt that he was under a 'deep moral obligation to him'. But now he fired back: 'She is as honest as you, and in distress, and I will help her if I can.'

The hearing was adjourned. McDonald went home and buried himself in law books. He was dismissed from his government job, but when the hearing resumed he was back in court. In November 1868 he won an important tactical battle against Fox. He wrote to the Native Minister and complained that Crown counsel was relying on technical arguments to delay the judgement. Fox was reprimanded and he conceived a violent hatred for the younger man, his neighbour and former protégé, who until recently had never opened a law book in his life.

Fox also stepped up his smear campaign against the Non-Sellers, and spread alarming reports through the district that the Ngati Raukawa Hau Hau were about to rise and attack the whites. 'There is not a shadow of truth in it,' the *Wanganui Chronicle* said. 'They have no idea and no wish to disturb the peace.' The Ngati Raukawa themselves protested their peaceful intentions. They had put a *tapu* on the whole coast, against war, they said. But the panic spread, stockades were built, Ngati Raukawa sheep-shearers were ordered off farms, and Fox continued to fan the flames and stoke up his anger against those parties, McDonald and the Non-Sellers who had defied him.

McDonald was a charming, volatile character, well known in every hotel bar up and down the coast, in precisely the rooms, that is, where the teetotal Mr Fox could never set foot. He had arrived in New Zealand in 1840 aged eleven. On the voyage out he fell in love. His sweetheart was nine. He courted her for a decade and then they married and set off for the outer wilderness of the Rangitikei. The languages spoken in that wild district were then, in order, Maori, Gaelic and English. McDonald, looking back to the early Rangitikei from his old age, was as loyal in friendship as in love.

'We were as happy as Larry . . .' he wrote. 'It was no uncommon thing to get up a dance to the music of a hair comb covered by a piece of paper, and accompanied by the beating of a tin milk dish by way of a tambourine . . . Oh! Bob Knox – Bob Knox, friend and mate of my young days. You are now dead but well do I remember your beating of that tin dish till knuckles bled!'

Alex's father was deputy-Lieutenant of Argyllshire, thus making him in his own eyes quite the social equal of Sir William Fox, whose father was deputy-Lieutenant of County Durham. But he set more store on the fact that he was a Glencoe McDonald. A great, great uncle, Aeneas McDonald, was with Bonnie Prince Charlie when he landed in 1745 – among a mixed bag of Scotsmen, Irish rogues, marquises tottering with age – 'as allagrugous fellows as ever I saw', one eyewitness said. 'Allagrugous' is not a word to be found in the dictionary, not even in the twelve volumes of the Complete Oxford, which if anything adds to the force of its presumed meaning. Allagru-gousness must have run in the blood: Alex had a myriad of friends, English, Gaelic, Maori – even the *Evening Herald* which abhorred his politics couldn't help admitting that it liked him and from time to time had a drink with him when he came to town.

His friendship with the dispossessed Maori of the district was a personal affront to Featherstone, Fox and Buller who had run native affairs there for years. But it was more than that – it was dangerous to them as well. 'I am a Tory to my bones,' McDonald wrote. 'The Tory is always found to be sitting on the rock of Principle . . . the Whig on the crest of the ocean wave, driven hither and thither as the wind blows.'

He sat on the rock of Principle! He was a Jacobite reborn and he remembered the wickedness of state power as exerted against his own ancestors at Glencoe. Now he kept reminding the Maori of their wrongs, and of the Treaty of Waitangi, the founding document of the colony, by which Maori rights were expressly guaranteed. Fox, especially, had been at pains for years to jeer at the treaty. It was a device to amuse savages, it meant nothing, it had been disproved by positivism and by Dr Arnold of Rugby. The Maori themselves had never understood it and only remembered it now, he told the court, because of the 'mysterious shower of red blankets' which had descended upon the signatories.

For Fox to have to sit in court and hear McDonald preach on the Treaty before a judge was bad enough. The thought of him roaming about the Manawatu, drinking whisky with the Maori and telling them of their rights sent a red mist in front of his eyes. 'He really is a far greater savage than the Maories are or ever were,' Fox wrote of his neighbour, 'and far more dangerous to the community than a 100 Hau Haus foaming at the mouth.'

It was at this point, towards the end of the year, that Fox became involved in the question of the captured boy, and wrote to Richmond, the Native Minister, about him. It seems that there was more than one lie in the letter. His claim of a 'probable conflict' over the boy is impossible to believe. Even if they wanted to fight, the Ngati Raukawa Hau Hau were in no position to take on the numerous and better armed *kupapa* tribes with their new carbines and cavalry corps. The Non-Sellers numbered fewer than a hundred fighting men. They had never resorted to violence against the other tribes over loss of the land they lived on: it is incredible to suppose they would attack the same people over a boy they had never seen and who was only remotely connected to them.

So now, having disposed of Fox's letter, we are left with the problem of guessing what really happened. Why did he lie about Herewini and about the Non-Sellers? Why did he get involved in the story at all? Could it have been that he could not bear the idea that the boy, who by now had acquired some celebrity, should go to the Non-Sellers and their champion McDonald? Fox, as we shall see, was not personally interested in the child, but he was a strange man, a great hater – 'the essence of undying vindictiveness', McDonald later called him, he was 'crabbed, spiteful and envious' in the words of one of his own allies, the *kupapa* chief Hunia. Could he have stepped in simply to spite his high-minded and popular neighbour?

Exactly how the next part of the plan was carried out is not clear. Somehow Buller managed to spirit Omahuru away from his Maori guardians and get him down to the Reverend Taylor's church where a small party was assembled. There was Fox. There were two new Maori godparents from the *kupapa* community. It was a hot summer afternoon. The church was dark, timbered, with shafts of sunlight slanting at the door and through tall pointed windows.

The ceremony began. For at least the second and probably the third time in his life (his father had been a Wesleyan lay-preacher), the boy was doused with water like a small persistent fire and prayed over. For a few moments, one imagines, the sunlight outside the door and the shouts and echoes from the river dwindled into the distance. When the boy emerged from the church, he was in possession of a new name. Ngatau Omahuru had become Master William Fox.

At this point, William Fox senior had no intention of adopting the child. We can only guess at his reasons for imposing his own name on him. Vanity may have played a part. The Queen herself had been godparent to at least one Maori girl who was naturally named Wikitoria. The last Governor, Sir George Grey, had done the same and there was at least one Maori George Grey running around the colony. A small Maori William Fox would put stout, white-bearded William Fox into a select category. Vanity, therefore, but also spite . . . By turning Omahuru into a Fox, by putting his own fingerprints all over the trophy, the leader of the opposition was demonstrating that no one else would get their hands on the boy.

Whatever the motives were, they must have been compelling,

for the renaming process was not simple. It involved telling several lies, in that least likely of places, a hushed and nearly-empty church. The lies had to be written down in the baptismal register, where they may still be consulted. This is what the register says:

Child's Christian name: *William Fox, age 7.*
Parents: *Hane and Ani.*
Surname: *Ngaruahine tribe.*
Quality, Trade or Profession: *Little Hau Hau Captive.*
By whom ceremony performed: *Basil K. Taylor.*

To rename a child without the consent of his living parents raises some difficult problems. Omahuru's parents, therefore, had to be killed off or at least rubbed out of the official record. 'Hane' was the name of one of the three enemy Maori known definitely to have died in the battle of The Beak of the Bird and the only one who was not a chief. 'Ani' is so commonplace a name it defies identification. In the place of the surname (which could have been supplied – the boy must have known his own family name), only the tribe is stated.

His real parents, Te Karere and Hinewai Omahuru, alive and perhaps only fifty miles off, were thus excised from the child's life.

The category 'Quality, Trade or Profession' applies, of course, to the parent not the infant. Other answers in the register to this question are, for example, *Farmer*, or *Infantry*, or *Road Contractor*. Here, the boy's new masters avoided the question by turning it on to the boy himself. What was his Quality? What was his Profession? Why, he was nothing but a little . . . captive. They revealed more than they intended: the answer is very like the expression used by Fox two days later. 'Herewini [has] been down here with a gun on his shoulder to *recapture our captive.*'

By accident or for good measure, a year was added to the child's age.

After the ceremony, Buller led him away and hid him somewhere for a few days before he could be packed off to Wellington by coach. His godfather and new namesake set off to visit his constituents and apparently forgot about him. Herewini soon realised something strange was afoot. He had been swindled. It took him two days to walk to Fox's house, where he appeared 'with a gun on his shoulder' demanding a letter which would order Buller to give the boy up. He went away empty-handed.

Fox was cautious, however. He did not like the idea of a dark Maori grudge aimed at him from afar. He arranged with the Native Department in Wellington to have a government 'present' of £15 sent to Mr and Mrs Herewini for looking after the boy, and finally the cash caught up with them, on the edge of the Ahuriri estuary near Napier, where they had gone to live and from where never another word was heard from them.

As to McDonald, Fox kept up his grudge against him to the edge of the grave. The land case was resumed and the Non-Sellers, with McDonald as their agent, had the impudence to win it. They were awarded thousands of acres of land and Fox, Featherstone and Buller were made to look unstatesmanlike and foolish.

Fox then had his revenge. He came to power, he was Premier once more and he stepped in to deal with the case personally. Infinite delays emerged in granting the claimants legal title to their new land. They could not lease it; the rent revenues held from their former ownership before the land was sold were frozen. A new high road from Palmerston to the booming little town of Bulls was run without permission across their land.

The present inhabitants of Bulls are under the impression that their town is named after the animal, and on the approaches to town they have erected a great silhouette of a bull rather like the hoardings advertising Osborne Sherry which make the approach to Madrid on a dark winter's day so portentous. In fact the settlement was named after its leading citizen, an English carpenter named James Bull who first carved the panelling for the waiting room of the railway station in Worcester, then the interior of the House of Lords, and then came out to Rangitikei to turn its forests into weatherboard. The mill was working furiously, workers flocked in, coaches and pedestrians went up and down the new road, and a new mail service was soon promised. Once again all ears were deaf to the Non-Sellers' complaints.

Then once again, the Tory rose from his rock of Principle, the Jacobite McDonald re-emerged. On the first morning that the Royal Mail coach appeared on the road crossing the Maori land, Alexander McDonald stepped forward with a gun and called on the coachman to stop. He refused, at which point McDonald shot the leading horse, which fell down, apparently dead.

Fox was delighted. 'He really has gone too far this time!' he exulted in a letter to a political colleague. McDonald was arrested and tried and sent to goal for three years. The *Wanganui Evening Herald* condemned such a sentence for a 'man of sensitive mind'.

'Our view of the justice of the sentence includes a feeling of sympathy for a man whose honesty of purpose has always been recognised.' The *Herald* did not, however, believe the shooting was a political demonstration but merely 'caused by drink . . . a common failing which has prompted him to commit unwarrantable acts'.

In fact the protest worked perfectly. The Governor himself rushed north to see what the problem was. Fox was circumvented. The Non-Sellers were given title to their original grant of land and to thousands more acres of land to boot.

The horse, a grey, recovered and years later was seen running the coach to Otaki down the coast. It had a scar above its eye and had been wittily renamed 'Mac'.

McDonald, however, was not pardoned. One night soon after he had departed to his prison, his wife, alone in the house with her children, looked out and saw shadowy Maori figures in the yard. Several of the Ngati Raukawa then walked into the house.

'You have looked after us, and now we shall look after you,' they said, and they poured out 999 guineas into a pool of lamplight on the kitchen table. They also laid down on the table the title to 850 acres of their land as a gift for the family. The golden guineas were enough to stock the land and to keep Mrs McDonald and her brood – twelve living children – for two or three years. 'Who shall say that Maoris have no sense of gratitude?' McDonald demanded rhetorically.

In later years, some of the McDonald children married into the Ngati Raukawa who had lost, regained and finally given away the land around the McDonald house. Today there are Maori McDonalds to be met with on *marae* all across the windy, green plains of the northern Manawatu.

For two or three months, when I first began to follow the story of the kidnapped boy, I could see no connection with the story of Alexander McDonald. I could see in the distance that great tangled law case, and I went to some pains to avoid it. This became increasingly difficult – everywhere I looked, in newspapers, government files, Fox's letters and so on there they were – McDonald and his Ngati Raukawa friends and the Manawatu land. McDonald began to annoy me in fact; he seemed to be trying to force his way into this story and I couldn't see the point of him. Finally and with reluctance – for archives are full of red herrings and bridges that end in mid-air – I gave in and turned to him, not to put him into the story but to assure myself that he could be kept out of it. Thus I found his unpublished reminiscences and other material and so pieced together the story I have just outlined.

I also discovered something else important, important to me at least, although it was on a completely different plane from the story I was tracking. Alex, it seems, may have been a distant relation of mine. My own great grandfather was also a Glencoe McDonald who came out to New Zealand, though some decades after Alex. His name was Archibald, and only one clear image of him has been handed down through the family – Archibald walking up and down the platform of Timaru Station in the 1890s with the Prime Minister, 'King' Dick Seddon, discussing the issues of the day. Archibald's social position seems imprecise. His occupation is given as 'carter', yet he was a friend and confidant of one of the greatest of the colonial premiers. His people in Scotland were 'gentlefolk' – my great aunts were very firm on that – and he was related to the Bowes-Lyons family, although that was always mentioned in an undertone as if it was something to be ashamed of. Perhaps the aunts feared derision for claiming a link with the nobility, or perhaps they assumed that, as that particular branch of the family had gone up in the world, their manners must have gone down.

Archibald had the finest team of greys in Timaru and these horses were his downfall. People were always borrowing them for funerals, the dying, on occasion, booking them for the trip to the cemetery in advance. He began to spend too much time farewelling the dead and the funeral whisky finally got to him. His wife and children left him and he succumbed to an early and soon-forgotten grave. I myself, for example, heard little about him and never thought about him, until that is I read about Alex and the Non-Sellers, the horse with a scar over its eye, the 999 guineas. Could the two men have been related? Glencoe was a small place, and perhaps in the waves of emigration it was a younger cousin or even a younger brother who followed an elder out to remote New Zealand.

There was some wishful thinking here: I would have liked to claim some connection with Alex, the only settler, as far as I know, who ever went to jail for acting in defence of Maori rights.

And, in any case, the symmetry interested me. I liked the possibility that Alexander McDonald not only may have caused the life of young William Fox to take the shape it did, but also, by perhaps remotely bringing about my presence in New Zealand a century later, he helped a book about that same life come into existence.

5

'The house moves fast'

Naturally the boy knew nothing about these storms raging high above his head at adult altitudes. All he did know was that, early one morning, he was taken by Buller across the river on the wire-ferry and along to the Red Lion Hotel at Putiki and there put aboard the Cobb & Co. coach for Wellington. This was probably on 25 January 1869. Young William Fox was still with Buller on 24 January, but he was in Wellington by the end of the month. On 1 February a curt note was sent from the Native Hostelry to the Department of Native Affairs and thence referred to the Colonial Secretary:

'The boy Wm. Fox cannot be kept for less than 10 shillings and 6 pence per week.'

This was from a certain E. Clark, Custodian of the Native Hostelry, a man of whom we shall hear more. It is remarkable how only fourteen words from E. Clark conjure up a new world – a cold parlour, the soup ladle, carbolic soap, bureaucrats at their ledgers. In short, your heart sinks for the 'boy Wm. Fox', sent out of his green forest and into the custody of E. Clark, of the Native Hostelry, on the corner of Molesworth Street and Tinakore Road.

But we are getting ahead of ourselves. We are still at the Red Lion. The perfume of stale beer and old night issues from its front door into the shining morning. There are shouts and yells and last-minute packages arrive on long legs. Buller lifts young William Fox up and installs him in the coach. An acquaintance of Buller's, an old man with mutton-chop whiskers, is travelling to the capital and promises to keep an eye on the boy. And then they are off.

'It is a very good house, it moves very fast.' That is the first recorded Maori response to the sight of a coach, made by a visitor to London early on in the century, and young Fox must have felt something of the same. There he is inside a small wooden cabin filled with Pakeha and suddenly, to the crack of a whip and the shouts of urchins, the room begins to jolt and rock and then it moves smoothly out of the Red Lion yard and down the dirt road leading south, out of town.

The Wanganui–Wellington coach departs from the Red Lion every Monday and Thursday at 7 a.m., calling at:

Turakina,
Tutaenui,
Upper Rangitikei,
Bulls,
Lower Rangitikei,
Scotts,
Manawatu,
Otaki,
Waikanae,
Paekakariki,
Porirua,
Johnsonville,
and Kaiwharawhara, before terminating at:
Wellington.

The coach is a six-seater. Occasionally, a seventh passenger is allowed inside as well, but only if he or she is dead. The coffin goes on the floor and the living then must travel with their knees up and the soles of their shoes resting on the wooden roof of the departed.

The journey can take up to three days, depending on the state of the road. The road is always bad, but is better in summer than winter. At one point down the coast it runs through marshy ground and is sometimes quite impassable, in which case the coach turns right and for twenty miles or so runs along the ancient Maori highway – the hard-sand beach between Manawatu (soon to be renamed Foxton, after Sir William Fox) and Otaki. A few years before, that route had been considered dangerous: a huge black bull had taken up residence in the sandhills and rushed bellowing upon travellers, especially those on foot, forcing them to run into the surf up to their necks and stay there, bobbing up and down, until the beast lost interest and wandered off. But by 1869 the animal had been despatched by some local Theseus or had retired peacefully inland and was heard of no more.

We know few details of the boy's trip, but anyone who has read Dickens will have an idea of the nineteenth-century coach journey seen through the eyes of a waif or orphan. The long-nosed waiter with dirty apron . . . the stout lady with a friendly, quaking bosom, the clergyman with his nose in a book. A cold mutton chop for dinner, a tattered moon, a shouting ostler, the coachman's capacious pockets and marked aura of rum. It is possible, of course, that none of these items – apart from the mutton chop, which is a dead cert – applied in the 1869 journey of young William Fox from Wanganui to Wellington, but the point is not lost – how strange the wide world looks to a child being hurried through it by strangers.

Reading that list of little towns which the boy passed through in 1869, I learned something unexpected about biography. I had been surprised to find that, through Alex McDonald, I had a possible link with the subject of this book and thought that there would be no more. But now I saw that biography is, at its simplest, only an attempt to reconstruct the memories of another person, and during this process one's own memories come into view. Between any two lives, in other words, a shared pattern can be found; they will look similar or run on parallel tracks for a few minutes at least or maybe even a year. Here was another example. That list of wayside stops, or to be precise the latter part of it, from Otaki to Wellington, were the same places that I passed through one afternoon on the day that I left home for ever.

I hasten to state the differences. I was eighteen, on a train, and it was a hundred years later. But there were also some similarities. As we got nearer Wellington I began to feel a nervous apprehension, the dread of arrival. The train seemed positively to gather speed and howl along, just as I would have preferred it to go slower and slower. The names flashed past at station platforms or to the jangle of bells at railway crossings: Otaki . . . Waikanae . . . Paekakariki . . . At Porirua, a semi–industrial sprawl across a harbour, it was late afternoon; red lights were already winking from transmitter masts on distant hills, and, from a radio someone had turned on further down the carriage, Simon and Garfunkel were going:

I wish I was homeward bound
I wish I was ho-omeward bound

At that moment I wished *I* was homeward bound. I realised with a shock that I would now never go home again, to the home I knew in Napier, or rather that I would not be homeward bound if I did. By leaving it, home had ceased to be home.

An hour or two later, of course, once I had arrived, I forgot all about this, and although the same sensation, the dread of arrival, was to occur again in the next few years – flying into mid-summer New York, a set of spindles on a brown horizon, approaching an under-lit Madrid one Christmas Eve, driving through a fluent snowstorm into Cincinnati – it was never with the same intensity. But when I read that roll-call of place names in the Cobb & Co. coach service advertisement, my *homeward-bound* moment passing through Porirua came back to me distinct but transparent, like a lens through which I might see as far back as 1869. And it seemed a reasonable supposition that two memories – the memories, that is, of two people – though inherently different, should occasionally form an almost natural alignment like a telescope and a star or a microscope and a cell.

All the same, the differences were great. I was on my way to begin university in the city where I had been born. On the rack above me were my suitcases, a tennis racket and a new fawn duffel coat with a tartan lining. I had a bursary, a room in a student hostel, and one of the great aunts mentioned earlier lived on the hill below the university. Young William Fox, on the other hand, did not know where he was going. He spoke no word of the heavily-sibilanted language being spoken all around him. He understood, however, that he had lost his old name and now had a new one which he could not himself pronounce. His father and mother and his elder brother, Ake Ake, whom he hero-worshipped, had dropped below several horizons. And he had no more say in these matters than a brown-paper parcel tied up with string. *Have the kindness to have the boy sent to town by Cobb's* . . .

At this point, another memory, from a much lower level of my past, from a prehistoric epoch you might say, came back to me. I was in a high-ceilinged room. There was a smoky fire in the fireplace and some other children were present. For supper we were given jam sandwiches and cocoa.

I was not quite three years old. My father, who was a scientist working at the time on radar installation, had to go away, and my mother had fallen ill, so I had been brought here to this strange place for a week or two to be looked after by the nuns. I did not understand this; to this day, a smoky fire and a jam sandwich seem to me to be preternaturally dismal objects.

97

Some giant beings – boys aged seven or eight – put me on a rocking horse that was in the middle of the room. It had a black mane and a mouth made of a piece of black leather. A rocking horse is about the same size to a three-year-old as a real horse of uncertain temper to a grown man. The big kids began to push the horse from behind and I was swung higher and higher. I was afraid, but I did not cry, since I was among complete strangers. In other words, at that moment I felt that I was nobody and, for that matter, was nowhere. *Have the kindness to send this boy towards the ceiling* . . .

6

In the capital

Like most towns in the world of 1869 – a world wider, more airy and more narrow-minded than ours, where black-faced cherubs blowing along sailing ships could still be remembered inhabiting the corners of maps – the Wellington into which the child arrived, capital of a colony of a quarter of a million people, has now entirely disappeared under the harrows of the twentieth century, the harrows of peace and prosperity – steel, concrete and glass – being much heavier than those of mere war or natural disaster. The Native Hostelry, to take one instance, where William Fox was sent, has not merely disappeared – the actual solid ground on which it stood no longer exists. It took me some time to work out where the building had been. Then I found out that, after parking my car on Mt. Tinakore (in English, Mt. Nothing-for-Dinner) and walking down to one of the libraries near Parliament, I had, every day for a month, been strolling right through the middle of its former site, through its vanished hallways and bedrooms, as I walked over a bridge fifty feet above a motorway that the engineers had sent through the oldest part of town in the 1970s, ridding the place, in the process, of thickets of workers' cottages, colonial mansions, an avenue memorial to Katherine Mansfield, and a steep, pine-clad cemetery where the early citizens of the town lay in graves raked like the tiers in a theatre.

In 1869, the hostelry, a long, two-storeyed, verandaed building with dormer windows in the roof, stood on the corner of Tinakore Road. It had been set up by the Department of Native Affairs as a 'respectable lodging' for Maori chiefs visiting the capital, but the thing had been done in a miserly, cheeseparing spirit. For example, the place was built at the wrong end of Molesworth street, a mile from Government House and Parliament. Tinakore Road had not yet become a street of rich bankers' houses and Mansfield's *The Garden Party*. In the 1870s that end of the Thorndon district was 'renowned for overcrowding, disturbances and brothels'.

In winter the sun sets early behind the hill and Tinakore Road stands in shade from three o'clock onwards. Brawls, bawdy houses and the army barracks, all in cold, windy shadow, were what visiting Maori chiefs admired from their veranda.

Being a state-run institution, the hostelry was closely monitored and badly run. To judge from the records in the Native Department's General Register and Index, not a single expenditure or domestic decision could be made without office approval. The Register and the Index, which summarise departmental correspondence (the letters themselves were burnt in 1907), are great, battered, leather-bound tomes two feet wide and a yard long. You need two hands to lift them, but the entries are no more than a few words each.

Requesting that Blankets in use at Hostelry may be washed, it reads.
Authority to procure lanthorn, tin boiler calico for Tablecloths &c for Native Hostelry.
Requisition for boots for Native Boy, W. Fox.
Calls attention to stagnant pool on land belonging to Native Hostelry.
Two spare blankets from Hostelry to be given to a lame man and old woman released from the Hulk.

But there was another aspect to the place, worse than these little whiffs from the scullery suggest. The Hostelry was not only mildly squalid – it was an unhappy, bad-tempered, and even at times uproarious place. The blame for this rests largely with the custodian E. Clark (or E. Clarke – even the clerks at the Native Department treat him with disdain in their notes, sometimes carelessly giving him a final 'e' and sometimes carelessly taking it away again).

He was originally hired by the Department of Internal Affairs as an office messenger and then promoted to the custodian's job. But he was quite unequal to the task of arranging hospitality for the Maori chiefs from the interior, some of whom were great magnates in their own world, able to put a thousand or more men in the field, filled with fantastic ideas of honour and valour, incapable of telling a lie, and determined to get as drunk as possible, if they so desired, while in town.

It is impossible, however, to imagine a house-rule of E. Clark prevailing against even a whim of Kepa Te Rangihi-winui, the 'Maori Achilles', a great general who, however, 'cannot be kept sober'. Or against Wi Tako, who had sold the site of Wellington to the settlers and who stalked through the Government House ballroom and around the streets like a landlord keeping an eye on unsatisfactory tenants. Or against Hunia, haughty and vain as a peacock. Or Mokena Kohere from the East Cape, who once, at the snap of his fingers, had a thousand of his men baptised as Anglicans – probably the fiercest Anglicans in history – the vehemence and thunderous precision of their hymn singing once so alarming a visiting cleric that he fainted on the spot.

Men like these would never have encountered a species like E. Clark, a kind of back-office, backstairs beetle of a man soon to be demoted for 'irregularities' and sent back to his old job as office messenger. In due course he was to be sacked from that, for absenteeism. Although the chiefs themselves would not have

101

deigned to notice him, it is pretty clear that they let their retainers torment the poor man. And so the departmental Register is scattered through with bitter little complaints, fired from both sides at the Hostelry:

Report from E. Clark: *That Taia Rupuha was drunk last night and insulted him.*
From Mr Rangitakawaho: *States that Mr Clarke is always angry when he comes into the room.*
From Custodian Native Hostelry: *Had not provided sufficient food for Wi Waka and others on acct. of their arriving just at dinner hour. States that Wi Waka and most of the other natives were intoxicated.*

It was through the front door of this deplorable household that the boy William Fox was blown – probably, if the roads were in good condition, one dark Saturday night, with the wind banging the doors shut and making the tree-shadows jump and skitter all the way around the garden:

One Native boy, Wm. Fox, for delivery to E. Clark.

And yet . . . in a way, you have to conclude that the boy was lucky. He had at least been delivered into an environment that was partly Maori and, apart from the unprepossessing E. Clark, one that was kindly as well. We know this from a tiny detail that survives from his years in the Hostelry. There he acquired a nickname. He was called 'Awhi'.

Awhi as a verb means: *to embrace; to foster; to cherish; to sit on eggs, as a hen.* As a name it means, roughly, 'the cherished one, the embraced one', or, in short, 'darling'. In other words, young William Fox became the pet of the establishment. He was, so far as the records can be relied on, the only child to live there, and he was there for about three years. During that time he was taken

102

under a wing, under several wings in fact, and powerful and protective wings at that.

The great chiefs visiting the capital were not merely bloody war captains coming to claim their reward. They included several of the formidable personalities of the era. There was Renata Kawepo, for instance, an extraordinary man, splendidly ugly with his empty eye socket, a famous orator, witty and grave. He was the leader of the Ngati Te Upokoiri, a small tribe but 'virile and bellicose', two of whose members, Pirimona and Herewini, we have already met in the battle at the Beak of the Bird. Kawepo himself had been up to his neck in strife since childhood. When he was sixteen, he and his people were caught in a seige by a raiding army from the far north. After some time passed, he offered himself as a hostage to save everyone else from starvation. The offer was accepted and the sixteen-year-old went out to meet his fate (slavery or torture and death were the usual options) with these words: *Kia kawe au ki te po* – 'Now I deliver myself to the night.'

That is how he got his name. *Kawe-po*: Deliver-to-the-night.

He was carried off into slavery for many years. As a young man he learned to read and write and when he was freed, with the coming of Christianity, he wrote an account of his journey home, hundreds of miles on foot, in the company of Bishop Selwyn. It is the first extended piece of Maori prose. It reads like some of the first sentences ever written. Here he finally arrives at a village of his own people:

Then when I reached the shore I untied the knot in my garments and looked at the tinderbox. It was not at all wet, and I got a fire going.
I said to my friends 'We will be hungry.'
My friends said to me 'So what can be done?'
I said 'You must buy something for a shilling.'
I gave them a shilling and they bought only three potatoes . . .

We slept.

Next morning, only then did they [his relatives] come to fetch me.

Then together we wept.

When the weeping was over a man stood up. He said . . . 'Now you have come here, you must stay.'

I answered them 'I will not stay. That is that.'

Now, decades later, he was fighting a war on two fronts: against the Hau Hau movement and against the settlers' greed for Maori land. The latter was the more dangerous campaign and often brought him to the capital. Although his lands were being whittled away, he was still immensely rich and held receptions on his estate in Hawke's Bay where, Richmond noted with a mixture of approval and envy, 'he served champagne to all, Maori and pakeha, who would have it.'

Kawepo had a way of piercing the English conscience with a pithy remark. 'It is strange,' he said. 'When you first arrived here, we heard much about the sons of Japhet [the Maori] welcoming the sons of Shem [the English] into their tents. And so we did. We said: "Come in, Shem." But what we do not like is this: now that Shem is inside the tents, he says "Get out, Japhet!"'

Then Kawepo pointed to a pile driver working by the river. 'You English are very like that monkey engine,' he said. 'You drive our heads down to the earth.'* And again: 'No doubt it is quite true you English are a noble race, and we Maori are a wretched set. It is quite true. God made you to be a good and fair-skinned people, and made us to be "bad and black", as you say. But had we not better leave that consideration to the God that made us?'

It is hard to imagine that Kawepo, with his single gleaming clever eye (the other had been plucked out in a battle − by a woman he later married), would not have looked with interest on young William Fox, the 'little Hau Hau captive' who in the first place had been captured by two of Kawepo's own tribe, and who was now delivered up into the hands of Pakeha custodians.

Mokena Kohere, another important visitor to the Hostelry, was also walking on a tightrope between the Hau Hau, whom he saw as wild men going back into the dark, and greedy settlers. But he was a subtle strategist, adroitly unreliable as an ally, now embracing the whites to his bosom, now ordering them from his territory. 'If not for Mokena, what then?' are the words in a *haka* still performed in his home district, the East Cape. What indeed? The sky would have fallen in, as it did for so many other tribes at that time. But Mokena and his people emerged with most of their land, and at the same time he was loaded with honours and appointments. In 1872 he became a member of the Upper House, the Legislative Council, one of the first Maori to sit in Parliament and he was often in the capital on business.

* *Our Maoris*, Lady Martin, London, 1884.

Mokena Kohere's surname means 'protector of the people'. He too must have sometimes looked down thoughtfully at 'Awhi', the little fellow wandering somewhat sadly in the gap between Maori and European worlds. Men like Mokena and Kawepo were in a sense manoeuvring in the same space. They wanted the benefits and stories of European civilisation, but they also intended to remain themselves, to keep something safe at home – a Maori room, as it were, at the centre of their lives.

Some of them succeeded. The first time that I myself ever set foot inside a Maori household, I was shown a weapon hanging in a long, dark hallway. It was a sword of honour that had been sent to a great chief by the Queen of England. The chief was Mokena Kohere. I was twenty years old and visiting his great, great grandson, Taunoa Kohere, a friend from university.

I have no clear recollection of the sword itself. The room was dark, lit only by sunlight shining through a door at the far end of the hall. In any case, something else then happened which impressed me more than the sword. I went down the hall, a door was opened, I walked in two paces – and found myself in another world. It was a sitting room – fireplace, sofa and chairs, scattered books – but from floor to ceiling its walls were covered with wooden ancestral figures, with glaring eyes and small images of more recent generations carved between their thighs. Until then, the house with its bay window and verandas had seemed like any other old rural homestead surrounded by sheep. I could not have been more surprised at that moment if I had walked into a sea cave filled with echoes or the chamber of a Sybil – but then I came from precisely the world, domineering, assured, and in a sense one-dimensional, that men like Mokena had foreseen long ago and had tried to keep at bay.

The Koheres were a gifted and aristocratic family. For two hundred years each generation has produced at least one outstanding individual. Taunoa Kohere, my friend, himself died young, in an accident – within a few months of the day I saw the

106

sword in that remote farmhouse at the East Cape. He was described by his English professor as one of the most brilliant students he had ever taught and one who would have been a great writer had he lived.

When he died six of us carried his coffin down to his grave a hundred yards from the beach. When we buried him and lost sight of that calm, surprised and thoughtful gaze, we felt we had also lost the key to a door, a door difficult to find but easily opened, and which led to a room where two cultures could interact simply with nothing of their best being lost.

For me, at least, it is pleasing to imagine that Taunoa's great grandfather, Mokena, might have sat with the child, while the southerlies rattled around the Hostelry and told him tales every Maori child should know − of the dazzling Tawhaki, who arranged a Flood, cured blindness with his spittle, and one day was seen climbing to the summit of a hill where he 'laid aside his mean raiment and stood arrayed in lightning'. Or of the Pakepakeha, a legendary race who were never seen but only heard singing as they floated downstream on the driftwood of swollen rivers. And even of the children of Whanau Moana, from the tribal district of young Fox's own mother − a unique race of winged human beings who lived side by side with ordinary people and flew about openly in the day, sometimes to the tops of mountains, sometimes far out to sea. The Rev. Taylor of Wanganui reported in the 1850s that their descendants were still living, but that the last man with wings had lost the use of them, his wife having most unfortunately rolled over in her sleep and damaged them beyond repair . . .

And the Hostelry itself, despite the brothels and barracks nearby, was not in a completely unfamiliar environment to a Maori child. Tinakore Road, like the mountain behind it, took its name from the night when the road contractor failed to provide his gang of Maori workmen with their food. *Tina? Kore:* Dinner? Nothing at all.

This, for some reason, piqued their amusement even more than their indignation. *O, Tina-kore!* they said. The name refused to leave the locality. Perhaps the Maori were just pleased to learn that the Pakeha with their chronometers and noon-guns and scolding lectures against 'beastly' tribal communism could also make things *pakaru* – that is, could mess everything up.

In those days the mountain looming above the Hostelry roof still had some of its native bush (it was all soon to go; now the hill is covered with pines) on its upper slopes and lower gullies. From his room, young Fox would have heard at least one sound familiar to him all his life, the call of the morepork owl, *ruru,* which still haunts the hills of Wellington. Perhaps he even heard the occasional screech of the nocturnal kiwi. As late as September 1926 a kiwi was found wandering about in Molesworth street one night – the last occasion on which New Zealand's national symbol is thought to have paid a visit to its capital.

To a boy who had seen only the Taranaki forest and the town of Wanganui on a bend of a brown river, the capital through whose streets young William Fox set out for school each morning must have been an eye-widening place. Photographs of the time show the harbour busy with ships, some docked at the wharves, others slowly on the move, their sails blurred in the time exposure. There are pubs with figures at their dark doorways, and a certain smudge of sticks and shadows marks the little Maori *pa* at Te Aro, shortly to be removed from sight. In photographs taken from certain angles there appears a recession of belfries and steeples, crockets and buttresses. Wellington, like other colonial capitals, was a wooden simulacrum of the imperial ideal of Westminster.

The little town which straggled over hills and beaches was probably only three times the population of Wanganui, but by comparison it was the great world. There were royal visits and parliamentary feuds, and then there was the fact and presence of government itself, which gives to any capital, no matter how small, an air of preoccupation with a view further than its own rooftops, a view at least further than that seen from other towns.

There was also a good deal of fighting and drunkenness, especially at the wrong end of Molesworth Street, although there was little serious crime. Let's see: John Thomas is sentenced to two months with hard labour for stealing a feather pillow. William Morris appears on a charge of being disorderly and drunk; the bench sighs and observes that he is *always* disorderly and drunk. Wi Patene is charged with stealing eight chickens; the public galleries are packed with Maori eager to observe British law in operation. He gets two weeks' hard labour.

The papers complain of dust clouds in the unpaved streets, and of an epidemic of 'furious riding'. The upper classes drive out in carriages in the afternoon and leave cards at one another's houses. There is a discussion in the press on the merits of the different varieties of artificial eyes available for horses, the choice being glass, porcelain or gutta–percha. Glass is thought to be too brittle but gutta–percha is too soft. How many horses passed through the streets looking out with a cold porcelain eye we will probably never know.

The nebulae in Argo and four nebulae in Scorpio have been photographed for the first time. In weather reports, the wind speed is given not in miles per hour but in miles per day. On average the wind in Wellington blows at 262 miles a day. But during a gale, the atoms that blow your hat off at dusk on the corner of Willis Street had begun the day six hundred miles away out to sea.

They were 'a queer and cantankerous lot,' one visitor said, of the citizens of Wellington. Mostly they were Londoners whose main interests were commerce, politics and the law. They did not exercise themselves greatly over education or religion. Unlike other cities in the colony, Wellington in 1869 had no secondary school or college; the children of the wealthy had to be sent away to the South Island to continue learning anything.

There were a handful of establishments for junior students. Mr Grundy kept a school on Clyde Quay, Mr Flux one in Rintoul Street. There was the Terrace School run by a 'big Highland Scot who on occasions donned the kilt, flourished his dirk and "danced and hocked" till the rafters rang, to the delight of the boys except for one timid youth who was so alarmed by the Celtic mood that he was deterred from further attendance'.

Further down the hill stood Mr Grace's schoolhouse, into which, from time to time, 'dusky faces might peep to see what the Pakeha youths were doing while the wiser Maori was stretching in the sun'.

William Fox was sent to a school in Thorndon run by a man named Mowbray. Mowbray's was the obvious choice. It was near the Hostelry and there were at least three other Maori pupils on the roll, two of them the children of the great chief Wi Tako, who had sent them there to board on the advice of Sir William Fox. The school was a rather gloomy-looking wooden building in the gothic style with ogival windows and a steep roof. It long ago went up in smoke, like most of 1870s Wellington. Of William Mowbray himself there is not much to say. He was tall, he was young, he had sandy hair and also a sandy moustache. He liked opera. After two or three years of marriage, his wife presented him with a son, and then, a year or two later, lo and behold, she presented him with a daughter. At the start of term, one newspaper noted approvingly that, unlike the other schoolmasters of the town, Mr Mowbray made an address to the whole school and he counselled diligence and hard work.

One year, his pupils 'presented him with an opera glass as a mark of respect'.

He taught for four decades and retired without a blemish on his record except, possibly, that of leaving the newspapers with not much they could think of to say about him.

There was in his long career only one possible imputation against him, and that did not appear in the press. It is marked by a small flurry across the pages of the Native Department Register and Index of 1871:

21 January: *Complaints by chiefs about your treatment of the Maori boys under your care.*
21 January: *Ihaia Porutu and Wi Tako complain that Mr Mowbray makes the Maori boys who are at his school peel potatoes &c.*
11 March : *Mr Mowbray replies to certain charges brought against him by Wi Tako. To whom referred? Hon Premier.*
2 September: *Mr Mowbray. That Pene Te Hiko one of the boys at his school has run away.*

Once more here is the usual difficulty: the letters themselves do not exist. The flames of 1907 blaze up again. Whether for instance *only* the Maori pupils were put to work peeling potatoes, or whether the chiefs thought that this work may be acceptable for the children of the Pakeha but was quite improper for the sons of great nobles, or *rangatira*, like themselves, we cannot tell. One gets the impression, it is true, that being schooled by sandy Mr Mowbray was not pleasant for a Maori child, but that is just an impression and in any case it is not really the point.

The most interesting fact about the fuss over supper at Thorndon School is revealed in the 11 March note. The reply to the charge is referred to no less than the Premier, Mr Fox, himself. The affair has become a matter of state.

It is not just that Wi Tako was an important man, a friend of the Governor and an acquaintance of royalty. Nor is it that he is dangerous. He has on several occasions declared his disgust with the Pakeha, threatened to turn against them and gone off to brood in his seventeen-room mansion over the hills. But the time when he could pose a real threat to white power in the Wellington district is now over.

What was at play here was something more subtle than that, more insubstantial, yet sombre and powerful, like a memory of forked lightning. It is the fact that this windy capital with its turrets and picket fences had once been the setting for an extraordinary British experiment in political and racial relations.

It was called a 'humanitarian' plan, although that word rather limits its revolutionary scope. When British sovereignty over New Zealand was proclaimed in 1840, the Maori, unlike any other colonised people, were immediately given full citizenship and equal rights in law. Miscegenation was frowned on in other parts of the Empire but here it was seen as most desirable. 'Through love and intermarriage the two races shall become lost the one in the other,' Governor Grey told the chiefs in 1847.

The idea was, in the words of *Blackwoods Magazine*, 'to make New Zealand a kind of moral centre for the diffusion of high principles and enlightened civilization'. The proposals can also be seen as a further step on from the American and French revolutions which, promoting liberty for their citizens, had failed dismally where people of other races were concerned – Jefferson's slave-pens and the treatment of Haiti's leader Toussaint are all that need to be said on that score.

Now, by 1869, the great experiment in New Zealand had failed – but not officially and not entirely. The Treaty which enshrined the plan had never been repudiated. It was mocked by men like Fox, but not too often and not too loudly.

Furthermore, many of the men who had first arrived in the colony to carry out the plan were still alive, still watching closely and were still powerful. They were well connected in England, and they remained closely connected to one another. A surprising number of them came not just from Cambridge but from St John's College, Cambridge, where for about thirty years there

112

seems to have been a common-room/playing-field myth that New Zealand was 'theirs'. Perhaps the young gentlemen at St John's were inspired by the activities of the first missionary to the colony (a St John's man), or even just by this description of his first night among the feared Maori, with its faint echoes of Blake's *Tyger! Tyger!* and 'When the stars threw down their spears':

> We prepared for repose and feared not to close our eyes in the very centre of these cannibals (who had massacred and devoured our countrymen). An immense number of men, women and children, some half naked, and others loaded with fantastic finery, were all stretched about me in every direction; the warriors, their spears stuck in the ground, and their other weapons lying beside them, were peeping out from under their [capes] or shaking from off their dripping heads the heavy dew.

Graduating from St John's a few years later were William Martin, the colony's first Chief Justice, and George Selwyn, friend of Gladstone and New Zealand's first bishop, who walked thousands of miles around the new land 'planting a church'. There was the bold and brilliant J. E. Fitzgerald (Christ's College, Cambridge), who warned the settlers against the 'great crime' of confiscation, not only on behalf of the Maori, 'but on behalf of your own sons and daughters . . . in virtue of that mysterious law of our being by which great deeds once done become incorporated with the life and soul of a people.'

Even Samuel Butler (St John's), who kept aloof from politics while he was in New Zealand, turned the final pages of *Erewhon* into a sly attack on racial prejudice among the settlers in the South Pacific.

Selwyn left the colony in 1868, in despair at a war which he thought had ruined his life's work and sent so many Maori out of the church. He went back to England, but there he was as dangerous as he had been in New Zealand. He was in close touch with Martin and knew everything that was going on in the colony. In England he was a great figure; he preached at Windsor, was Bishop of Lichfield, and had access to powerful figures in Whitehall and the universities (Keble was founded in his memory). For the rest of his life, New Zealand remained his preoccupation. On the afternoon he died, his mind wandered back to the fields of his early days, to his thousand-mile walk with Renata Kawepo and his church building with Mokena Kohere in the hot, dry valleys of the East Coast. Over and over again he muttered to himself, and to his old friend Martin, who was at his deathbed: 'They will come back.'

His last words were Maori: *Ko te maarama* – 'It is the light.'

Even today, down the dark, secretively curved nave of Lichfield Cathedral, there lies Selwyn in alabaster effigy with a Maori warrior standing guard above him, depicted in shiny Victorian tiles.

Against the establishment power and residual authority of such figures, men like Fox and Richmond had to tread cautiously. They wanted Maori land, as much of it as possible, they wanted not equality but domination and they went after both land and domination by fair means and foul – but for that very reason it was important to keep up appearances. Trouble between the races should not be allowed to fester for its own sake. Even the most trivial issue – who peels the potatoes at a school where the government sent children on Native Scholarships – had symbolic importance. If some teacher had begun to mistreat his Maori pupils, he should be stopped in his tracks.

And in any case, certain aspects of the relationship – Maori citizenship and parliamentary representation, and interracial marriage – which were unthinkable in most parts of the world caused them no disquiet.

So that was the Wellington into which young William Fox had been delivered – a queer, cantankerous town of currents and cross-currents as contradictory as its winds, a great experiment and half a fraud, with Maori chiefs in the ballroom at Government House and others – for example young Fox's own relations would soon arrive there – in the prison hulk on the harbour. When men like Kohere rose to speak in Parliament, young white women in the Ladies Gallery begin giggling. 'When the Maoris happen to be speaking . . . at present their rising is the signal for ill-suppressed laughter and conversation' (letter to the *Daily Advertiser*, 18 September 1871).

The same newspaper printed, without comment, this letter from a German named Von Hagen, writing from Melbourne and offering:

> To raise an auxiliary force of say 1,500 to 2,000 men to go to New Zealand and mercifully secure an everlasting peace to your splendid country. I have visited my countrymen and for £200,000 we can contract to exterminate every native in two years . . . provided . . . no interference from your imbecile Colonial Councils. Of course I expect your Government to supply the Prussian needle rifle and ammunition.

At the same time five thousand citizens, almost all white, followed the coffin of a local chief, Te Puni, the pallbearers being several government ministers.

Another newspaper, the *Wellington Independent*, with which William Fox Snr. had close connections, discussed his godson's tribe in the following terms:

> There are a certain number of natives on the West Coast . . . who must be shown no mercy. They should be treated as wild beasts – hunted down and slain. Modern History teaches us that irreclaimable savages, who rendered colonisation impossible, and the lives of peaceful settlers insecure, have been, in the interests of society, exterminated . . .

there are certain *hapus* of tribes on the West Coast whose deeds of rapine and murder have made them the curse of the colony, *and we would exterminate them*. It does not matter what means are employed, so long as the work is done effectually. Head-money, blood-money, killing by contract – any or either of these means shall be adopted and we shall be content . . .

But at the same time the Governor himself was addressing a Maori meeting near Wanganui:

The Queen desires that the Maori and pakeha should grow up together as one people, and that they should flourish as the everlasting green of your native forests. The Queen has sent her son, the Duke of Edinburgh, to visit this land and assure both races of her love for her subjects and her earnest desire for their mutual welfare and happiness . . .

Meanwhile, the country's first noted English poet, another St John's man, named Domett, was dreaming away in the General Assembly Library, writing a long, yearning and at times quite sexy poem about a love affair between a Maori girl and an Englishman, 14,000 lines of it – named *Ranolf and Amohia*, which Tennyson found 'remarkable, full of thought' and Long-fellow 'splendid'.

In private, Domett regards the Maori with a kind of cold loathing: 'Your nigger philanthropy rather sickens me,' he writes to a colleague. 'You talk of *swindling* the natives . . . They must be ruled with a rod of iron. After all it is unthinkable that savages should have equal rights with civilized men. Nevertheless they are not cattle and if they can be educated up to a firm belief in the white man's domination, it should be possible to treat them with some degree of kindness.'

It was Domett who during a short period in office as Premier in the 1860s had proposed the single most iniquitous act of government in the country's history, the confiscation of Maori land. Perhaps one day some psychologist-historian will unravel the story of this strange man with his swooning verses and vengeful politics, both directed towards the Maori. It is tempting to think that his was a case of Eros turning nasty, that Domett had once been rejected by some pretty Amohia. Dozens of young Englishmen had affairs with Maori women. The lordly young Francis Dillon Bell, for instance, wrote to a friend in the pidgin-Maori then fashionable among the upper-crust: 'I am to be *marenatia* [married] as you know, soon to a *pakeha* and my *puremu* [fornicating] days alas are numbered.'

But Dillon Bell was tall and dashing and looked at the world through supercilious, heavily-lidded eyes. Domett was stout and balding and 'sweated – awfully'. Could it be that behind the policy of confiscation, which kept the war going for another six years, uprooted thousands of lives and poisoned the relations between the races for a century, was some girl's light and mocking laughter?

Domett did not return to England until 1872. Every day he sat in the parliamentary library in Molesworth Street and dreamed over his poem. Stars winked, cataracts sounded, raven tresses half-hid incomparable breasts. Ranolf – square-jawed and golden-headed – worries himself to distraction about taking Amohia, 'a savage wife', back to Kensington, where, of course, savage wives have never been sighted . . .

Meanwhile, outside the library, young Fox, the small owner of one of the lives uprooted by confiscation and war, was on his way to Mr Mowbray's school. It is unlikely that Domett, ex-Premier and personal friend of Browning and Tennyson, noticed such an insignificant being. Yet the two would in time come to meet. For there was trouble brewing at the Native Hostelry which would soon have its effect on both the William Foxes.

As usual the records are cursory and puzzling. The police have been called to the Hostelry, but do not seem to have got in the door; orders are given that they are to be given admission 'at any time'. At one point E. Clark is actually dismissed:

to E. Clark: *I am directed by The Hon. Mr Bell, to inform you that the Govt. having caused enquiry into the charge brought against you, it has been decided yr. services are no longer required.*

Yet three months later he is still at the Hostelry, reporting that:

Mr Porter up with his hand and give Maria Morris a severe slap on the side of her head.

And a year later, in 1871 – nearly three years after the boy arrived there – there are still police reports on their visits to the Hostelry and complaints about 'irregularities'. What exactly was going on, who Mr Porter and Maria were, why the police had the door slammed in their faces – we can make no headway here. But the general impression of uproar will suffice.

To understand why this became important to the story, we need to know one crucial thing about Sir William Fox.

In many ways Fox was a peculiar man, inconstant as smoke, capable of cruelty and kindness, treachery and decency – never knowing his own mind, a poor Prime Minister, a wonderful leader of the opposition. He was against the war, he was violently for the war. He was a philo-Maori, he despised 'these contemptible savages'.

There was only one question, throughout his public life, on which he was as solid as a rock. He hated alcohol.

He would do anything to get land from the Maori – except stupefy them with rum. For a year or two he gave up politics altogether and spent three months in New Hampshire witnessing an early abolition experiment and then toured Great Britain for a year lecturing on Temperance. The only party he ever threw (though he was notoriously stingy anyway) was a 'picnic for 500 Total Abstainers' on the lawn of his country house in the Rangitikei. During the war against Titokowaru, he rushed to Wanganui to give a lecture not on war or peace or taxation but on the evils of Strong Drink. He bounded on stage and began:

In no part of the Continent, Great Britain or America is there such a consumption of rivers, lakes, seas, and oceans of strong drink as in this Colony . . . One in twenty of all the houses in the land are engaged in the sale of drink . . . I cannot conceive how a publican could lie down and sleep at night after taking his till out and counting the money . . .

Drunken doctors are the worst of all, and should be tied up by the heels (laughter) . . . I have known three magistrates in one province who were eternally drunk, and I have known two clergymen drunkards – one of the church of England, and one of them, I am sorry to say, of the church of Scotland (laughter) . . .

Woman is the greatest sufferer from strong drink. She is the cause of the introduction of it into the world and now she is suffering the penalty . . . Every petition for a new licensed premises should be signed by three-fourths of the adult women in the district, and then if the women were not fools – they *are* fools – (laughter) there would be very few licenses . . .

If I were a pretty young girl, and any young fellow came fossicking after me, I would say: 'Young man, I don't believe you are perfectly sincere! – just you walk across the street, and put your name down, and if you keep the pledge for twelve months I will marry you; but if you don't, then don't keep funoodling after me.' (loud laughter)

On and on the words roll – rivers, lakes, seas, oceans of words. The audience seems suspiciously hilarious (Wanganui's drunkenness was notorious) – but Fox takes no notice. On this topic – he admitted it himself – he would talk the hump (or humps; there is a dispute in the press about the anatomy of the phrase) off a camel. This is his passion, his life work.

At some point during the next three years, when reports of the upheavals at the Native Hostelry reached his ears, Fox's conscience must have pricked him. He had after all plucked a child from his Maori world only to deposit him there, in the stews. And although the Hostelry staff might be disciplined or dismissed, the problems were more complex than that. There was no way that the chiefs and their entourages who lodged there could be prevented from drinking when they came to town.

And so finally – probably towards the end of 1871 – he stepped in and took the child himself. In the end it was fumes of alcohol that shot the boy, like a stopper from a bottle, out of the Hostelry and down to the other end of Molesworth Street, into the calm, sober and silent household of the Hon. Premier and his wife, Sarah Fox.

7

Family life

Wiilliam Fox (the elder) was born at Westoe, County Durham, in 1812, took his BA at Wadham College, Oxford, in 1828, entered the Inner Temple to read law in 1838, married Sarah Halcomb, daughter of a Wiltshire landowner, in 1842, three days after he had qualified as a barrister, and arrived in Wellington, New Zealand, on 7 November 1842 on the *George Fyfe*. They arrived in the harbour well after sunset.

All that was visible on shore was a long line of fires. This was the two-year-old settlement, in its entirety, going up in flames after a fire had started in a wooden chimney.

Towards the end of his life Sir William climbed Mt. Taranaki or Egmont as it was then called. He was the oldest man – and the slowest – ever to make an ascent of that most beautiful of the world's solitary mountains. He looked down from the summit but the view was obscured by an immense pall of smoke. The settlers were burning the forests and marking out their fencelines. That was a result of Fox's policies. The smoke was his monument.

Between these fires of 1842 and 1896, he led an extraordinary, vexatious, contentious and vituperative existence, lecturing, hectoring, advising, complaining, denouncing. In short, he never shut up. Here is a contemporary sketch of the centre of this whirlwind: 'A small man with a long head vanishing upwards into a tall, rusty, black hat. Lank hair fell from hat to sandy mutton-chop whiskers linked tenuously across the upper lip by an untidy moustache. With his sharp aquiline nose and tight mouth he looked mean in appearance and thin in person.'

On exploring expeditions he always rushed ahead of everyone else; he liked to swim in the coldest glacier-fed rivers. He poked his nose into everyone's affairs, especially those that least in fact concerned him. He owned a string of horses (Chestnut, Tormentor, Shandygaff, Havelock) and fancied himself a horseman. At seventy he wrote: 'Some elderly gentlemen affect a steady cob but I find the longer I go the more I enjoy a pulling, tearing, lively beast.'

As soon as he landed in the colony, he was at daggers drawn with the Chief Justice, William Martin, who required that a new barrister submit to an examination and swear an oath that he had never done anything that would make him unfit to be a lawyer. Fox refused to make such a declaration 'humiliating to an English gentleman'; for some years he was unable to practise law, and never forgave Martin.

He then extended his feud to the whole government and missionary establishment – to the very vision of men like Selwyn, Martin and Fitzgerald – following an event which became known as the Wairau Massacre. In this incident, an armed party of settlers led by some young gentlemen from Nelson marched on to a block of land, which they claimed to have bought, at the north of the South Island and attempted to arrest a number of Maori, including two of the most formidable warriors in the country.

The chiefs yawned politely and declined to consider themselves under arrest. The English began shooting and one chief's favourite wife was killed. The settlers, who then began to get the worst of it, waved a white flag, but when the Maori laid down their guns they started firing again.

Infuriated, the Maori rushed in, captured, and then killed almost all of them. Fox and other settlers were outraged and all for war. But the government refused to launch a punitive expedition, pointing out that the whites had started it, and had been foolish enough to kill the wife of one Te Rangihaeta – perhaps one of the most excitable warriors in the entire country. In any case the young men had had no right to go on to Maori land waving arrest warrants in the first place. The words 'whippersnappers' and 'pipsqueaks' hover not far above the page on which the official response is printed.

The Wairau Incident, as it is now called, took place between a deep narrow river and a flat-topped hill at the edge of a grassy plain which the Maori had decided not to sell. That day was the beginning of two downward spirals – in relations between Maori and white, and also between men like Selwyn and Martin, with their dream of interracial justice, and those like Fox, who preferred simple domination.

(Domett was another outraged by the events at Wairau. His friends in England were dismayed at his letters. 'If black is the colour about you,' wrote Robert Browning, 'and may not be softened, away, take ship in heaven's name! and be here in the cursed six months!' Browning in any case seemed mesmerised by – almost half in love with – Domett:

My love is here. Where are you dear old friend?
How rolls the Wairoa at your world's far end?

And he wrote:

I must say how unutterably thankful I and all your friends are that you are out of the horrible story of the 'massacre'. But what melancholy work for you – most of the poor fellows must have been your friends.

The poor fellows were indeed Domett's friends. He himself was not involved in the fight only because he was at the time lying on a sofa at home with a broken leg. But he turned violently against his old college friends, Martin and Selwyn, and perhaps his anti–Maori rage began here. But that does not account for the moony fantasies of *Ranolf and Amohia*.)

Unable to practise law, Fox was, in turn or in different conjunctions together, journalist, explorer, militiaman, farmer, political agent, land–dealer, pamphleteer, Total Abstainer and politician. He was also a painter. Two or three of his early watercolours of great empty South Island landscapes, steeped in silence and surmise like the peak in Darien, are extremely beautiful. The first time I saw a reproduction of Fox's *In the Aglionby [Matakitaki] Valley, 1846*, it was hanging on the wall of the council flat of a Maori friend of mine, a lateral descendant of the hot–blooded Te Rangihaeta. He did not seem troubled by the irony. The painting was too beautiful to care about that.

As time went on, and the country became uglier in strict accordance with Fox's policies of burning and clearing, his paintings became uglier as well – not because he was accurately reflecting the new reality but because of the obscure law which forbids artistic talent and political power to co-exist in the same person at the same time. Fox's brush-strokes grow coarse, the skies garish, the landforms fatuous; his later *Mt. Egmonts* gape at the sky like gun muzzles pointed at heaven. Some of his later paintings are simply either childish or hideous.

He was never at ease with the human figure although on the voyage out from England he drew some strong caricatures of various sailors and male passengers. He could hardly manage women at all, except at a distance, much veiled and cloaked.

The house into which the boy William Fox arrived one day in 1871 was childless. It was also notorious, even in high official circles, for its silence, order, and a kind of spotless dreariness. Not to mention parsimony. 'An oasis of piety and temperance –

clever ones took their own liquor,' an early biographical note states. One visitor – a waggish judge – wrote:

With Fox I lately chanced to dine
The servants spared the food and wine
But carefully the plate displayed,
The eye was pleased, the guts dismayed.

'I am staying at the Foxs',' one of the Richmonds reported to his sister. 'I am leaving today. I can't say I feel much at home here – the house is very clean and orderly but desperately dull.'

C. W. Richmond belonged to a crowd of brothers and sisters of two intermarried families who were on fire with ideas, talk, letters, love; they, 'the Mob', were like a scattered commune and saw themselves as forming the country's first political dynasty. 'Without our set,' wrote one, 'where would Taranaki be now, for everything written, said or done of any importance . . . on behalf of this province, has emanated from an Atkinson's or a Richmond's pen or tongue or sword – rifle I should say perhaps.' They fired one another up with great debates over vegetarianism, divorce, the Resurrection and the flax industry. One Richmond brother spent years writing an immense paper proving 'That Matter Is Force'. It came back from the Royal Society with the terse judgement attached: 'Not enough mathematics.'

Sir William, by contrast – 'a perfect disciple of Adam Smith, reducing everything to £sd and Manchester opinion' – would rather have his head boiled than bother it over whether Matter was Force or Force Matter.

(Fox was not given his knighthood until 1879, but since we have two William Foxes in the same house, and sometimes in the same sentence, no one will mind if, for clarity's sake, we knight him early.)

'Fine plate – and a miserable spare-rib of pork for supper.' 'The guts dismayed . . .' 'Mean in appearance and thin in person.' 'Too bitter, too sarcastic, too violent, too fond of personal denunciation.' The complaints and sidelong glances drift in thick and fast around the Fox household and Fox himself. Yet nothing about Sir William can be settled easily. One astute observer also has him as eloquent, humorous and good-natured, although he adds that Fox 'rushed from one view to the other so whole-heartedly, it became extreme'. And there is another contradictory set of evidence: his photographs. What do we find, but a beaming stout Santa Claus with twinkling eyes and long white whiskers.

Here, for example, he is sitting in a canoe about to be paddled up the Wanganui River, in 1869. He is, admittedly, wearing a very odd hat, a kind of bowler with a black crown and a white band that looks like the single eye of a bull glaring heavenwards, but he himself contrives to look benign enough underneath it.

He is on his way to visit some neutral tribes with a view to securing their alliance. Secretly he despises them: 'I did any amount of hongi-ing [pressing noses] and tena-koe-ing [good-health-to-you-ing],' he grumbled to a friend, but he also wrote:

I was [enchanted?] with the Wanganui River which after the first twenty miles surpasses the Rhine and the Hudson.

Of course it has no castled crags [but] it is one continuous succession of fresh beauties that I saw and many more beyond that which I hope I shall see. I have arrived at the conclusion that Maories have no more eye for the picturesque, the sublime or the beautiful than the beasts that perish and I doubt that any man whose eye is not educated has. Our own labouring people seldom admire a fine view. A primrose by the brook a primrose is to them – a mountain is a mountain and a valley a valley.

I suspect there are many money grubbers and other two-legged creatures who can see nothing more admirable in nature's beauties than Maories and clodhoppers.

Very few people study clouds or skies by day or by night, yet they are often more beautiful than anything to be seen on the surface of the Earth. One of the chief advantages of dabbling in the fine arts is that it opens the mind to other things and as David has it 'Spreads a table in the Wilderness'.

Fox's canoe was paddled up the Wanganui by Maori oarsmen. For hundreds of years the children on the river had played a game, lying down at the edge of the cliffs, looking up, their heads between two abysses, and naming the different shapes and beings they saw moving past in the clouds.

For adults, these games evolved into chants used by the paddlers, addressing their own reflections among the reflections of clouds seen on the surface of the water. Here is a typical Wanganui chant:

I am a bird, I fly in the sky.
I am a spirit! I have escaped
I have escaped to heaven
O bird of the clouds.

Fox, in forty-two years dealing with interracial affairs, did not learn to speak Maori. On this trip upriver, musing on David, a table spread in the Wilderness and the advantages of an educated eye, he never enquired what the men poling and paddling around him were singing as he and they all went upstream together.

Fat or thin, stingy or jolly, bitter or good-humoured, Manchester man or aesthete, Fox is difficult to sum up except for one certainty. He was unalterably self-centred. His wife, Sarah Fox, you will not be surprised to hear, was the opposite. Of her no certain photographs exist, although as we shall see there is a small group of people who have eagerly sought one over the years. Small, thin, shy, dull, lonely – she was often left on her own for weeks at a time while Sir William rushed about the country – she has attracted little notice, none of it very favourable.

At one point, in the late 1850s, she seems to have had a nervous breakdown, which in the fashion of the time went unregarded.

'She is *quite* deranged,' reported young Dillon Bell coldly. 'While her sister was dying she did all sorts of most astounding things, such for instance as going all day about the house seizing a large mop and having the windows cleaned incessantly and floors scrabbled.' Of course the supercilious Dillon Bell, with his wilful Ngati Raukawa girlfriends and sheep-station heiresses flocking around him, would have found little Sarah Fox, whose highlight of the week was the Sunday School she ran in a cottage at the gate, well below his speed.

The Richmonds tended to agree. She was, declared Richmond, 'very niminy-piminy, but kind in a frigid way. Married to anyone but Fox she would have been a little narrow-minded, church-going missionary-box of a woman.' She wore black gowns quivering all over with black bugles and white caps quivering with white bugles. In short, said Richmond, she was a 'perfect aspen of a woman'.

The Foxes' house stood in a bare garden on a slight eminence behind Parliament, set well back from the corner of Molesworth and Hill Streets. One day Sir William took his easel into the garden and painted the place. The painting is oddly stiff and lifeless . . . a row of tall windows, a conservatory, a desponding shrub or two, a determined gravel drive. Nobody appears to be home. 'Home', in fact, is the last word that comes to mind when you look at the picture.

The house is now gone. But the site retains something of the mood of Sir William's painting. Wellington is a narrow, noisy town with steep streets and traffic jams; the wind blows, roofs creak, gulls scream, the cable-car twangs up Kelburn hill. An earthquake will rock you awake in the middle of the night. Yet on the rise of Hill Street even today there is an odd sense of silence, of someone holding their breath. There is a little Greek temple, rather flaking and empty, which serves as the Catholic basilica. There is the Gothic-revival parliamentary library which a lunatic or a committee has had painted pink. There is still a grey picket fence, a great tree or two, some deserted stairs, and a statue of Ballance looking stoat-like under a pohutukawa tree.

You are in the open air, yet it all seems very quiet. Everything has been swept and dusted. The floors have been scrubbed, the mops have been put away, and a young Maori boy aged about eight is coming, very quietly, down the hall of a big, gleaming, silent house . . .

This of course was the irreversible step, the point of no return. In a way it is the moment we have been waiting for. There is to be no more 'Awhi', the pet of the Hostelry, no more great chiefs coming and going with their retinues and grievances and tales. Even the call of *ruru*, the native owl, becomes faint and infrequent. Hidden away on the slopes and gullies of Mt. Tinakore, he is not heard often in this part of town.

For young Fox, this is the moment of transmutation.

There is a long tradition behind it. There are perhaps half a dozen New Zealand stories of lost English cabin boys, ship-wrecked or spared in massacres, and found decades later tattooed to the eyeballs, living among the coastal tribes. In 1874 a little blonde girl called Caroline Perrett vanished from a bush-dark farm near Leppertown in north Taranaki. She didn't turn up for fifty years: by then she was Maori to her bootstraps, even her cheekbones had acquired a kind of blunt Polynesian shape and she remembered nothing of her former existence. In a wistful, oddly unsuccessful short story published in 1908, Katherine Mansfield, who as a child lived along Tinakore Road, dreamed up a white girl named Pearl Button, swinging on her gate, who is lured away into a Maori background where the sea is bluer and the colours warmer. And behind Pearl Button surely there is a memory of Jemmy Button, the most famous of the nineteenth-century changelings, a young Indian from Tierra del Fuego who was taken to London in 1820 and turned into a young gent. His return to his native land a few years later was one of the main tasks of the voyage of the *Beagle*.

A young Cambridge graduate who was aboard, Charles Darwin, watched as Jemmy was put ashore along with the essential items of civilisation – a mahogany sideboard, tea trays, and several chamber pots.

A year later the *Beagle* came back. Jemmy came across the bay in a canoe and climbed aboard. He was stark naked, his hair hanging over his shoulders.

'I never saw so grievous and complete a change,' said Darwin, who was a great genius in the natural sciences and a very bad anthropologist.

Walking quietly down the hall, under the grandfather clock with its potent white face and swinging pendulum, young William Fox was travelling in the opposite direction from Jemmy Button. He has crossed the threshold into an entirely

European world. And after that, as we shall see, he could never really get back.

He could, of course, have done whatever he wanted in later life, but something strange was to happen to him which marked him for ever. It was not really strange so much as simply unexpected in that silent, sad, spotless house. And here, for the first time in this story, we hear young William Fox's own voice:

'She *loved* me.'

To find out more we have to go back to see Amiria Rangi, Aunty Miri, in the house set about with gnomes at Mawhiti-whiti. I made several trips from Wellington to see Miri in Taranaki, driving north past the sea at Paekakariki and on through a string of small towns, Foxton, Levin, Bulls, each time, as it happened, under brilliant cloud-flecked skies.

Over the months I learned more about Miri from Miri herself. She had worked for many years as a waitress at the Egmont Hotel in Hawera, rising to head waitress, and for forty years has been teaching classical Maori music. She has a married son who was christened, rather against her will – there was a *coup* carried out at the baptismal font by, I think, a domineering uncle – William Fox Rangi. He is known in the family as Foxy Will. Miri herself was brought up speaking and writing in Maori. She deprecates her command of English. Occasionally she writes to me to give me more information about the young William Fox, her uncle who died before she was born. She writes in a rather grand eighteenth-century style, with infinitely branching details of long-dead family members, and she takes a lofty attitude towards the apostrophe.

On the way north I pick up something to take as a gift – a cake, a dozen peaches from a roadside stall. Miri greets me at the back door. 'Oh!' she says angrily. 'You shouldn't give me these peaches! That cake, that's too good for me. You take it back.'

'No, Miri. You have to eat it.'

She pauses.

'*Oh* well,' she says, 'maybe I'll give some cake to Nga Rauru. They're coming here tomorrow for the smoking.'

Nga Rauru is the neighbouring tribe to the south. Anti-smoking campaigns are big in Maoridom at the moment.

At times I felt rather uneasy going to see Miri and asking for more information. There is a theory among some Maori that whites have no right to tell stories which relate in any way to their own race. It is seen as a kind of theft, not unlike the land thefts of a hundred years ago. An angry Maori poetess, to whom I outlined this tale while I was beginning to research it, glowered upon me. 'That's one of *ours*,' she said. 'He's just another Pakeha stealing our stories,' she said after my back.

I thought about this for a while. Then I thought about the clever and curious long-lost gaze of Taunoa Kohere and I knew that the poetess was wrong. It seemed to me that I was dealing with the one thing in the world that can *not* be stolen. A story is like the moon: it is either hidden, or it is out. And when it is out, it can be seen anywhere or everywhere at once, across rooftops, down freeways, on a puddle in the woods; not even a poetess may restrict its reflections.

Now Miri and I are sitting in her dark lounge with the summer day outside and she is telling me about Sarah Fox and young William Fox.

'She *loved* me.'

She is speaking in the voice of young William Fox, although she never in fact met him.

'I was the only child she ever had,' said William Fox. 'She was a mother to me. And — I loved her.'

Miri is keen to know if I have ever seen a photograph of Sarah Fox. Sarah has always been held in high regard in this small corner of South Taranaki. Shy, childless, dull Sarah, in fact, turns out to be one of the heroes of the story — a timid little hero, admittedly, but all the same, determined. And she was to be punished for it.

'Yes,' Miri went on. 'She loved him. She always had something in her pocket for him' – here Miri put her hand towards her skirt as if she herself at that moment was wearing a black gown quivering all over with black bugles. There was something secretive about the action, a fact that I nearly missed. I was more interested in the gesture itself; it reminded me of a quick touch on an old polished stone that has been handled and passed among different people for many years.

Then Miri went on.

'She loved him. When Sir William Fox was out, she used to sit and read stories to him. But when they heard his footsteps in the hall, they'd – *sit up*—'

Then Aunty Miri, once more being the boy for a moment, trembled.

So – here is the unpleasant fact. A child, who has been wandering up and down motherless for three years or so, is found by a lonely woman who has always been childless. They form a bond. But when Sir William's footstep is heard on the step, the murmur stops, a book is dropped, the two jump apart – and the boy begins to tremble.

That gesture I had seen, of putting hand to pocket, *was* furtive. The gift in question – whatever was in Sarah's pocket for the boy – was forbidden. It had to be slipped to him on the quiet. Sir William's wife was not permitted to love the child. The child had no business leaning against her listening to a story.

And why did he tremble? There is no suggestion made to me of actual bodily harm, although it crossed my mind Miri might have been sparing me something here out of interracial politeness. In any case, one stare from the bitter and sarcastic Sir William, the terror of the parliamentary chamber, would be enough to make an eight-year-old quail. Whatever the answer, you know that there was something wrong in the atmosphere of Sir William's house.

The three of them lived together for four years. Then Sir William meted out his penalties.

In the meantime, school continued at Mr Mowbray's. In the summers, the Foxes went to Westoe, their house in the Rangitikei. Westoe is still there, a few miles off State Highway 1, looking remarkably as it does in Sir William's paintings. The grounds are open to the public. Through a dark gate of Californian redwoods and Lawson cypresses planted by Sir William, one descends a gravel drive that loops past his Oregon pines, his umbrella pines, his great cedar of Lebanon. The house is painted grey. It has oddly narrow windows – clearly sunlight was no more welcome inside this house than jolly judges tucking in their napkins – and a tower designed to give wide views of the surrounding countryside. Sir William, however, disliked going up the stairs and the room was never entered.

I walked around the garden for a few minutes among the shrubberies. The Foxes left Westoe in 1885 and the newcomers, a family named Howard, have lived there ever since. It was a hot summer's day. From the house, which is not open to the public, came the sound of talk and laughter. For some reason – perhaps the contrast between that cheerful sound and my own train of thought, which seemed flimsy and dark – I was suddenly depressed and I got in my car and drove away and kept driving for an hour or two until the tower of Westoe from which no one ever looked out was well below the horizon.

In 1874, William Fox left primary school and was enrolled among the first students at the new Wellington College, the secondary school which the town had taken thirty years to get round to building. It was yet another Gothic castle, but this one was a mile from the harbour in a waste of tall grass and marshes.

134

Beside the school rose the new lunatic asylum, also Gothic. There was no road beyond these buildings, just a footpath through the high grass leading to the black and rocky south coast, from which can be seen, sixty miles away across the strait, one high mountain on the South Island, Tapuae-Uenuku, the 'Footsteps of the Rainbow God'.

The college, according to the newspaper, had a 'noble entrance', was panelled with native red pine 'not inferior to the finest wood in the world', it had a 'noble staircase' leading to 'a magnificent lecture hall with five Gothic windows and a fine Gothic ceiling, much loftier than any other room'.

There was also a tower, which, however, like the tower at Sir William's country house no one ever entered.

On the summit of the bare hills beside the school were remnants of several very ancient *pa*, first built by Tara, whose people colonised the district in, probably, the fourteenth century. 'We must build these forts as a shelter, lest we be rent by man as the sun is shining,' declared Tara – which suggests that earlier tribes, of whom little is known, were already present in the country.

After the school opened, its grounds were dug and drained by the Hard Labour Gang, which was made up of a mixture of whites and Maori prisoners, some of the latter being from young William Fox's own tribal area.

The headmaster and senior staff were mostly Cambridge men. Mr Wilson, MA (St John's), 'could reprimand with great severity a boy detected in an ungentlemanly act,' and at the midday meal, 'it was a brave sight to see him attack a large sirloin of beef,' a pupil wrote. Sometimes Mr Tuckey BA (St John's) used at times to assist him in the carving.

'During the meal, Mr Wilson used to discourse on general matters of interest, thus we got mental fare as we listened to his comments upon the wreck of the *Avalanche*, the suspension of the Glasgow Bank, the death of the Prince Imperial and the Rimutaka railway catastrophe.'

Mr McKay, MA, who had recently got married, had the disconcerting habit of addressing boys in his lessons as 'my dear'.

The French master, Monsieur Adam, began his class each morning by asking 'Are we all complete?' Since he himself was extremely short, this made his pupils laugh. Then towards the end of 1874 he suddenly fell ill and died, which made the boys – since schoolboys are ghouls – still laugh, although not in front of adults, when they thought of the question.

The boys played cricket and football and there were sometimes excursions to the wild south coast, to Island Bay, where there stands an island named Tapu Te Ranga. The name is obscure, and very old, probably dating from the first Polynesian explorers. The sea swells and rises and falls around it with a lazy amplitude, rather like the slow roll of water one sees on the reef of the atolls in the outer Pacific.

By the 1870s, the island had become infested with rats, and was named Rat Island by the settlers.

Further around the coast, in both directions, various pinnacles of black rock stand among the bull-kelp. To the Maori, these spray-beaten figures, twenty, thirty, forty feet high, are none other than the petrified children of Kupe (the earliest Polynesian explorer), left there as coastal guardians 'whose food is only the wind'.

In the National Library archive I found a photograph, probably taken on Inauguration Day in 1874, of the college staff and students. The teachers have great black beards, prodigious beards, streaming beards that owls could nest in. The boys, forty or so of them, display the usual crazy range of expressions of adolescents – sleepy, snarling, vacant, blithe. Young William Fox, aged about thirteen, is there. He is a big husky kid wearing a dark suit and a dashing white hat with a wide brim.

Miri Rangi had never seen this picture and was delighted with it.

'Oh, but he looks *sad!*' said someone else who saw it.

I looked at it. He looked sad. Then I looked at it again. He didn't look sad. A magnifying glass did not resolve the issue. It turned him into three or four grains of grey, which spelt no emotion at all.

But if he was sad, or even if he wasn't, by the year 1874 there were real reasons why he should have been.

8

A silent land

One morning in the summer of 1869, at 7.15 a.m., about the time that William Fox was waking up on his second or third morning at the Native Hostelry in Wellington, a great silence fell across a hilltop twenty miles west of Wanganui as three men, watched by hundreds of others, climbed out of a ditch, walked across a space of open ground and stood before a tall palisade behind which, for the last few hours, no sounds or voices had been heard. No one realised it at the time – or even for several months – but their short walk in the morning sunlight marked a critical moment in the history of the wars, and in the history of the country. It was the moment that European military ascendancy had finally arrived.

The men were Ben Biddle, an ex-sailor aged twenty-one, and Solomon Black, a Scot aged thirty-four, and a third whose identity is now unknown. They were part of a great army assembled to challenge Titokowaru – the 'largest solely colonial force ever raised', according to James Belich, a historian who in 1989 published a masterly account of Titokowaru's war.* More than two thousand men – several hundred veteran volunteers, about four hundred *kupapa* troops from the local tribes, the Kai Iwi and Wanganui Cavalry units, five hundred seasoned soldiers

---

* *I Shall Not Die. Titokowaru's War, New Zealand 1868–1869*, Wellington, 1989.

from the Armed Constabulary, and five hundred new recruits from around the colony and Australia – had been marshalled in Wanganui. The Australian press jeered at the New Zealanders who could not defend themselves, but more than a hundred and sixty Australians, Americans and Britons joined up in the streets of Melbourne and crossed the Tasman Sea to fight the Maori.

The place where the two forces met was called Tauranga Ika, within a mile or two of Handley's Farm, where the children had been attacked by the volunteer cavalry two months before.

Tauranga Ika, according to Belich, was the most formidable position ever built by a Maori general. With numerous bunkers and underground tunnels, it could withstand far heavier bombardment than the attackers might offer, and with three types of firing positions – trenches, loop-holed palisades and *taumaihi* or bastions built at each of the four salients – a withering fire could be delivered to any takers. Even in simplified two-dimensional plan, says Belich, the fort had a 'certain fatal beauty'.

TAURANGA IKA

It was 'a fearful place to rush', the colonists said later, 'beautifully built', a fortress which 'no troops in the world' could have taken by storm.

By five in the afternoon of 2 February, the advance party of the attacking army, moving slowly and entrenching as they went, had come within a hundred yards of the *pa*, and the artillery opened up. The defenders remained in their underground bunkers and were virtually unharmed. Maori rifle fire during the day had been desultory, Belich says – most of the details given here of this battle are taken from his book – but as night fell the two armies, now close enough to shout to each other, exchanged more volleys. The firing increased in the darkness, as did shouting and singing, the exchanges reaching a crescendo at 3 a.m.

To keep up their spirits, the white forces sang military songs, including 'Marching through Georgia' from the recently ended American Civil War.

'Go on, Pakeha, go on,' the Maori replied, 'give us some more.'

Less politely, one warrior shouted, 'Come on, Pakeha, and be food for the Maori; send all the fat ones to the front.'

The exchanges died away in the last hours of the night. As dawn came and men in the colonial army began to stir, some noticed an 'ominous silence' from the *pa*, but that in itself was not an unusual Maori tactic – to present an appearance of an abandoned position which, when approached, erupts in a storm of fire.

The minutes ticked by.

Then finally Biddle and Black and the third man got up and began to walk towards the *pa*. 'The colonial army,' says Belich, 'held its collective breath'. They reached the palisade unharmed. Then they climbed the wooden barrier and let themselves down into the *pa*.

Tauranga Ika was deserted.

Even today arguments about what happened during the night inside Tauranga Ika continue. Some, including Belich, believe that the chief was caught committing adultery – or even incest – fatal to his *mana* as a warrior-priest. This is bitterly repudiated by Maori today, which does not necessarily mean it is not true. Reports to the same effect appeared in Wanganui papers almost immediately afterwards: 'Tito's men are deserting him in large numbers. He appears to have been misbehaving himself in reference to the women in the camp.'

Whatever the reason for the flight of the Maori forces, it is certain there was a spiritual or superstitious element at work. The Maori, whether pagan or Christian, were generally a more religious-minded race than the British. (On Christmas Day in Wanganui, it was said, the Maori flocked to the churches while the English flocked to the races.) Titokowaru himself, according to modern Maori sources, became convinced that his god, Uenuku, had been cursed by the 'angel of McDonnell'. The evidence for this was perfectly clear to him: during the night the north-east sea breeze, the symbol of Uenuku, had sprung up . . .

The colonists of course knew nothing about all this. The empty, impregnable *pa* they found the next morning seemed to them altogether sinister, a sign not of weakness but of strength and confidence. The gloom in the colony increased. In Wanganui, house prices had already collapsed and a sizeable fraction of the citizens sailed away to Auckland or Australia, never to return. The streets were full of destitute people flocking in for food and shelter. The women of Wanganui sent a petition to Queen Victoria begging her to 'avert their extinction'. Advertisements in the paper read: 'Mourning. A nice assortment of coburgs, baratheas, crapes &c.'

A merchant ship, the *Wild Duck*, arrived from London filled with farming implements and a complement of thrushes, blackbirds and starlings, but no one had kept up their subscription to the Acclimatisation Society. What was the point of a landscape filled with English songbirds if the English themselves all had to fly away? The *Wild Duck* sailed off with its living cargo, to a shore more suitable for transfiguration into England.

Then, ten days after Tauranga Ika, worse news arrived. On the coast north of New Plymouth, a settlement of military farms in a hitherto peaceful area was attacked. Not only was the commanding officer, one Bamber Gascoigne, killed, but his wife and children were murdered. The children – even five-month-old Louisa and three-year-old Cecil – had been tomahawked. Not content with that, the raiders despatched the family pets, a cat and a dog, in the same way.

After these killings, the Maori looked out and saw another white man riding into view. He was the last person they wanted to meet. It was the Rev. John Whitely, a Methodist missionary who had years before baptised the leader of the raiding party.

'Go back, Whitely, you have no place here,' they are said to have shouted to him.

'My place is here and here I remain, for my children are doing evil.'

Five bullets ripped into him from a distance of thirty yards.

The murder of Gascoigne's wife and children may have been a deliberate riposte to the events at Handley's Woolshed two months earlier. 'You say A B C, we say A B C,' ran the standard Maori answer to criticism of atrocities on their part.

The colonists' horror was not merely at the thought of murdered civilians. The raid was a challenge from a powerful group of tribes, some of whom had suffered from confiscations even more severe than those in Taranaki, but who had kept out of the latest fighting. There was now an insurrection in the east, an uncertain war with Titokowaru in the west and a grave threat from the north. General conflict across the whole island loomed, and this time around there would not be thousands of Imperial troops coming to the settlers' aid. 'East and west, the war cloud shows no signs of breaking' lamented a Wanganui paper. 'The Maori has shown he has the brutal thirst of the tiger for blood.'

But the *Wanganui Chronicle* was wrong. The powerful north-ern tribes waited for a response to their challenge but no response came; so they did nothing. In the east, the insurrection sputtered out quietly. Meanwhile Titokowaru fled further and further west, shedding supporters as he went. This is not the place to give a full account of Titokowaru's retreat under fire. It was a long, complicated chase with no clear conclusion. More of the pursuers died than the pursued. There was a disaster in a peach grove where a party of men, including two young Australians not long off the streets of Melbourne, were caught in an ambush among the late-summer fruit. Once, Titokowaru and his followers – down in numbers to about a hundred – had to flee, some of them stark naked, into a ravine during a pre-dawn assault launched in a fog. He later led the colonial forces splashing and cursing into the heart of an immense swamp twenty miles across and managed to escape them by a whisker. In the end he reached safety on the other side of the Wain-gongoro River. He was back where he started near the Beak of the Bird. And there the government, tired of war and nervous about the northern tribes still waiting in the wings, decided to leave him in peace.

It is what happened in the territory that he left behind, that sixty-mile stretch of coast through which Father Rolland a few months before had journeyed and heard only the cry of a Maori woman, which, in the ensuing silence, he amended to the cry of a seagull, that this story is concerned with. Most of the inhab-itants of this area – all the whites and about two-thirds of the Maori population – had fled during the war. When the hostilities with Titokowaru ceased, or rather moved rapidly away into the distance, many of the Maori prepared to go home to their villages and gardens and resume their lives.

This, however, was not to happen.

Instead a new policy was adopted. All Maori, friendly, neutral or former rebels, were swept from the area.

Some responsibility certainly rests with the head of the military, Colonel Whitmore, although Whitmore too had other things on his mind. While he led the pursuit of Titokowaru, he garrisoned the territory behind him with several hundred volunteers who, as far as can be made out, were allowed to operate as they pleased. One is left with the conclusion that this extraordinary new policy simply grew up in the dark, in secrecy, behind closed doors, under the hands of men like Ballance, a certain Major Noake and Captain John Bryce (formerly Lieutenant Bryce – he was promoted after the 'battle' of Handley's Farm), nonentities who by chance had the terrible fate of being allowed, for a short time, to do what they liked.

It was the newspapers, unable to resist boasting to their readers, which opened up a tiny chink in the wall of secrecy.

30 March 1869: 'Col. Whitmore has expressly handed over the Waitotara natives to the tender mercies of the local cavalry forces and Capts Hawes, Kells and Bryce,' Ballance wrote in the *Wanganui Evening Herald*. The reports in the *Herald* and the *Wanganui Chronicle* of the operations to the west of Wanganui were all written in similar code:

'We know that . . . there is nothing to fear from the Waitotara natives. The villages have been captured and burnt and Major Noake and his officers have shown the darkies we are determined and able to beat them by river and by land.'

'The Waitotaras are skulking back near town. They may as well consult their own safety in keeping from these districts.'

'Noake is on their trail. A long rope and a short shrift is their own desert.'

'If the rebels ever return they shall be cared for in a way that need not be mentioned.'

The forces which Whitmore left in the rear consisted of several infantry volunteer units, and the Kai Iwi Cavalry, captained by

John Bryce. The Kai Iwi corps was no longer that 'perfect pack of devils in all manner of habilements' praised in the *Herald* after their attack on the children at Handley's Woolshed the previous December. They were now well kitted out with blue peaked forage caps, brown leather equipment, blue jackets, fawn Bedford cord breeches and black boots. The officers, who were elected by the men, had the same uniform but their caps were picked out with silver lace, and their jackets trimmed with black lace.

The 'scouring', as it was called, began in earnest towards the end of March with Bryce and the Kai Iwi corps harking back and forth like bloodhounds around the area of their old triumph, Handley's Farm. On 1 April, Major Noake, having sent a letter to the Minister of Defence stating that 'any Native found in the Waitotara was liable to be treated as a rebel', led a nine-day expedition up the Waitotara river. The force left nothing behind them, according to Belich, but 'devastated fields and smoking ruins'. In mid-April, the volunteer forces reached Whenuakura and searched upriver while Bryce and the Kai Iwi corps scoured the countryside immediately to the south.

On May Day, a party of Maori 'returning to their haunts on the Patea river were surprised and a few were killed'. A week later, three young men, an old man and an old woman found in the same area were 'all killed except for one man who escaped'. A further expedition was sent back up the Waitotara in mid-May. 'The meaning of the movement', said the *Chronicle*, 'was to destroy the enemy's property and shoot down as many of the rebels as could be met with.'

By the end of May, the Waitotara district, extending thirty or so miles from Wanganui to Patea, the ancient tract of the Ngarauru tribe, was deserted. Not a single one of its Maori inhabitants remained. All, according to the papers, even including those friendly parties who during the war had saved settlers, had 'fled'.

The implication is clear: they fled because those who did not

146

flee, even women and children, were killed if they were found. There is one other piece of evidence that leads to the same conclusion. It is an extraordinary Maori name which was given to Captain John Bryce.

Bryce, a farmer and local politician, had arrived in the colony at the age of seven with his brother, sister and father, a Glasgow cabinet-maker. He left school at fourteen and worked as a cowhand, at which point he appears to have acquired a reputation for sadism towards animals. He then spent some time in the Australian goldfields, returned during the wars and volunteered to join the military, where he was described by his commanding officer as 'the dirtiest and most negligent trooper we ever had'. He was unanimously elected commanding officer (lieutenant) of Kai Iwi and Goat Valley Cavalry in October 1868. Europeans, as we have seen, were generally referred to by transliteration of their names into Maori form. Thus Sir William Fox became Wiremu Pokiha, Governor Grey became Kawana Kerei, Featherstone was Petatone, Selwyn was Herewini, and so on. Very few people earned the distinction of a name deriving from their special characteristics. Von Tempsky was one of the elect, being known as Manu Rau – 'Hundred Birds' – since during a campaign he seemed to be everywhere at once.

John Bryce was another. He was known as Bryce-kohuru, which means Bryce-of-the-murders. Alternatively, he was referred to as Kohuruhuru, an intensified form of the word, which means simply Wickedness, or Black Murder.

Many years later, when Bryce had risen to great heights and become Native Minister, he disputed the charge that such a name had ever been attached to him. But the authority behind the claim was unimpeachable, the Bishop of Wellington, Octavius Hadfield.

In 1883, Hadfield sent a private letter to an Australian historian named Rusden who was writing a three-volume history of New Zealand:

147

Early in 1871 it became my duty to visit the people north of Whanganui. I found it impossible to do more than speak a few words on the subject of religion to the Natives before they turned the conversation to the recent war and spoke of the savage conduct of the white people, especially in the case of the children . . . When he [Bryce] became Native Minister, Natives near Whanganui asked whether it was Bryce-kohuru. Natives on the West Coast were greatly astonished and alarmed when he became Native Minister.

On Hadfield's visit, he was given the names of at least five women who had been killed by Bryce or his men, and in 1886, when the matter was aired in a libel case in London, a witness named Whakarua-te-Kariki deposed that Bryce was 'known as the murderer [kohuru] of women and children'.

All of this, as Hadfield himself recognised, was hearsay, after the facts, and unverifiable, and in any case the government itself would have no interest in investigating the claims. Though nothing could be proven and nothing would be done, Hadfield was convinced that a great crime or series of crimes had been committed between 1869 and 1871 in the district of Wanganui and southern Taranaki. Hadfield was one of the old school of idealists who, by 1869, had seen their influence wane away before men like Fox and Richmond. He was, unusually for the colony, an Oxford man – he had lived in the rooms at Pembroke once occupied by Samuel Johnson – but had never taken his degree. Ill health forced him to leave college and he emigrated to New Zealand, where he remained a semi-invalid all his life. Naturally he lived to an immense age, infuriating Fox who daily scanned the papers in the hope of reading that his Lord Bishop had departed this life. Occasionally Fox, the Premier, and Hadfield, the future Primate, met in the street. They looked hard at each other, but passed by without speaking. Hadfield is probably the 'gentleman of a liberal profession educated at an English University' who is mentioned in a pamphlet by Rusden:

> The scene of Titokowaru's success and reverses became a desolation in 1869. A gentleman, who afterwards went to that part of the country to make enquiries, assured me that he was horrified at learning from the lips of one who had lived in the neighbourhood at one time every Maori creature old or young, 'omnis sexus, omnis aetas,' [both sexes, all ages] was ruthlessly slain. 'I had no idea' (he said) 'that we had been so wicked.'*

What took place west of Wanganui in the first few months after Titokowaru's retreat was horrible but not surprising. The volunteers were mostly youngish men, not properly supervised, angry and ignorant. They were urged on by a savage press, itself under the thrall of the new, racist 'science' of Neo-Darwinism against which the Hadfields and Selwyns could make no headway. Many of the troopers were farmers who had had their houses burned to the ground and their cattle and sheep dispersed. (For years after the war herds of cattle of the finest pedigree roamed wild in the bush.) Some of the volunteers had seen neighbours lying dead on their doorsteps. Their vengeance has an inevitable air, like looting or the starving of prisoners: cruel, short-lived, old-fashioned, hallowed by tradition.

It was what happened next that had a new appearance, sinister, and modern, or at least familiar to us who know what was to come in the twentieth century. For this distinction, the colony was indebted to Sir William Fox.

Fox had little to do with the first phase of the ravages. He was still in opposition and, in fact, watching events from the side-

* *Auretanga; Groans of the Maoris*, London, 1888.

149

lines, he concluded that the Maori of the Waitotara district were being allowed to settle down in peace.

'It surely can't be true that the Government is going to let the Waitotaras return,' he wrote to his brother-in-law in early April. 'They might as well have thrown all the money they have spent into the sea if they do. It will simply be an act of insanity and I *can't* believe it to be true.'

Twelve weeks later, he won a no-confidence motion in the House and became the leader of a new government. From now on, the fate of the Nga Rauru and the Ngati Ruanui tribes – the tribes, that is, of his namesake and godson, young William Fox – was decided by him.

Almost at once he put an end to the *ad hoc* and bloody rambles of the volunteer troops. First, the volunteer forces were demobilised. Fox, who could never resist a delightful phrase, no matter how many enemies it brought him, described them as a 'draggle-tailed bastard soldiery' and had them dismissed and struck off pay. Bryce, an angry man at the best of times – his studio photograph shows a glowering black gaze, a bearded head held oddly awry from the body – was furious. You can hear it in his speech to the men on their final parade.

'By constantly patrolling . . . by appearing at daylight in unexpected places . . . and by chasing headlong out of the district small parties which had ventured into it, you did I really believe, contribute to a considerable degree to the preservation of the district . . . It has pleased the Government in its wisdom to dismiss you now, after nine months service, without one word of praise or thanks, or acknowledgement . . .'

After the dismissal of the volunteer corps, military operations in the district were organised on a new basis. Major Noake set up headquarters in the town of Patea. His forces were comprised of some regular officers, an elite core of former volunteers and a new force of *kupapa* from the Ngati Porou tribe. They came not from the Wanganui area but far away on the East Coast, and thus had no ties with the local tribes that might temper their ferocity. 'The Ngati Porou have this high qualification: they allow nothing to live that they come across,' noted the *Evening Herald* drily.

Major Noake – a former riding master who had been present at the Charge of the Heavy Brigade at Balaclava – was a protégé of Fox, who was greatly impressed by his curt military manner, his handsome wife, his knowledge of horseflesh. When he arrived in New Zealand in the mid-1860s, Noake was unemployed; the first job he found was carrying out minor domestic commissions for Fox, such as riding a new mare, Gentle Annie, from Wanganui out to the farm at Westoe. It was Fox who found Noake some land in the same area, Fox who had him made a Justice of the Peace, Fox who fostered his career until he was 'quite a leading man in the district'.

Now, thanks to Fox, he was to become much more. He was given absolute authority in a territory stretching fifty miles along the coast, from Wanganui to the Waingongoro river, and about thirty miles inland. Fox withdrew the civilian authorities from the area. He expressly forbade the civil commissioner in Taranaki – the official intermediary between Maori and the Crown – from entering Noake's district. 'He cannot stop meddling . . . Why he wants to interfere I don't understand,' he wrote to his Minister of Native Affairs. 'There is not a single Native except our Ngati Porou south of the river.' The next obstacle was the Resident Magistrate, named Booth. 'I am anxious to get rid of him from the West Coast . . . Booth means well but is a great bungler and great meddler, and I am certain he will spoil Noake's work if he goes back to Patea.'

For nearly three years, Fox maintained this drastic policy – that no local Maori, ex-rebel or friendly, would be allowed to set foot in the district at the cost of their lives. The reason for Fox's policy was simple. Under the urging of the most extreme settlers, led by Bryce, he had decided that none of the original Maori

151

inhabitants, whether rebel, ex-rebel, neutral or friendly, would ever again live in the territory that had been ravaged by Titokowaru during the war.

On the day that the government wavered, then fell and Fox took power, there was an odd item in the *Wanganui Evening Herald*. A 'white horse of a dirty colour', it reported, had stood 'saddled and bridled all day in the market place'. The *Herald* itself did not seem to know why it ran the story. In a world full of horses, a saddled horse can hardly have been an unusual sight, or no more than a car left with its engine running outside the supermarket today. Later, for me at least, when I found out what happened during Fox's ministry, that saddled and bridled horse took on the appearance of a portent from Revelations. *Behold a pale horse and he that sat on him was Death*. For the next three years, across two thousand square miles west of Wanganui, death was in the saddle. The shape he assumed was that of Major Maillard Noake, the ex-riding-master with his freezing eye and upper-class accent.

From early in his career, his speciality had been crushing the powerless. At sixteen he had been on 'police duties' with his regiment in Ireland during the Famine. He had charged the Chartist demonstrations, he had been in India 'mopping up' after the Mutiny. There was something ridiculous and transparent about Noake, but Fox never saw through him. When I first came to his correspondence in the Wellington archives, I was baffled for a few minutes: Noake's letters to Fox look exactly like Fox's letters to Noake. Then I understood what was happening. When Noake wrote to his powerful patron, he adopted not only Fox's tone of voice and attitudes but even his narrow and clerkly handwriting.

Here, for instance, writing about the trouble he was having with his kupapa forces, he appeals to the teetotaller in Fox:

Patea is a nest of poisonous Pothouses. Ngati Porou avail themselves of every facility to drunkenness. In this state they render the place unspeakable for respectable females while their own women are corrupted in every way by the Europeans of the place . . .'

There was a drunken row of thirty mad Ngati Porou, but at my appearance a hush fell . . . at the appearance of Te Nuika. [The Noake]'

Therefore I want to send them away to Te Ngairi . . . Would you therefore put me in charge of two districts? I trust you will support me in this . . . for although I am not a *total* abstainer I have as great a horror of a drunkard as though I were.

Now, armed with the additional powers that Fox had got him, and with no civilian authorities to restrain him, Noake erected a wall of silence around his district and began his reign. Very few official admissions of wrongdoing are to be found, which is not surprising, but occasionally, in the early days, reports leaked out. In October 1869, three Maori, two old men and a woman, were found 'prowling six miles from Waihi'. The two men were shot immediately, the woman captured. They had been planting potatoes. The garden was destroyed. The following month, a party of Maori were found in the Waitotara district and were shot on sight: one man was severely wounded, and a woman was captured.

These reports caused difficulties for Fox. His new Native Minister, Donald McLean, had with some reluctance agreed to the policy of preventing the Maori of the district from returning home, at least temporarily, but he had not agreed to a policy of murder.

Fox resorted to bluster on the question of these shootings:

The natives were by no means the harmless unoffending persons they appear to have been reported to you, they were the most notorious ruffians in Titokowaru's cannibal band.

They were creeping back and getting cultivations ready with a view to future operations. They knew full well the risk they were taking.

What was done was in the spirit of my ministerial memo on Patea affairs, which every member of this Ministry approved.

It is true that they reversed the order by firing first, but you know how easily in the excitement of such circumstances such events escape the control of commanding officers.

The shooting affairs at [Waihi] and Waitotara have done us no harm, on the contrary, as I expected, they have caused the clearing out of Titoko's fellows who were creeping back to cultivate . . . It has operated exactly as desired . . . I don't think there is a Native inland nearer than Waitara.

McLean, although he was not above sharp practice regarding land deals, had some sympathy with the Maori, and they had some faith in him. He was a big, melancholy bullfrog of a man who had emigrated from the Hebridean island of Tiree, a perch of black rock, grey cattle and barley fields, inhabited by crofters, harassed by landlords and swept by horizontal rain. Among McLean's ministerial papers there are still to be found plaintive letters from his relations back at home: 'I think in a few years there will be very few people left on Tyree as they are so harassed with rent and taxes.' A man whose sympathies lay with the dwindling crofters of Tiree could not feel easy for long about the great silence that had fallen in the territories of Waitotara and Patea. 'Not a native inland nearer than Waitara,' boasted Fox. But where had they all gone? Human populations do not get up and depart *en masse* when asked to do so, or even under the threat of terror.

'Had the lame, the sick, the bed-ridden, suddenly died, or – what had become of them?' asked Rusden in the following decade. 'How many *unreported* slaughters were there? . . . Who can adequately pourtray [sic] the horrors of the time? Who can faintly imagine . . . how desperate had been the groans of the Maoris where in a once populous district, larger than some English counties, not one living soul remained?'

Ten years later, when he had become the elder statesman of the colony, Fox gave his views about the events of this period. He blandly excused himself from any responsibility. He had, he said, simply promised to keep *rebel* natives from the district. After that, the local settlers may have gone too far.

'Perhaps it was not unnatural that the exasperation to which they had been driven should have tempted many to distort the promise of the Prime Minister [Fox himself] from *rebel native* into *any native.*'

This was an astoundingly bold falsehood. His letters to McLean and his speeches to groups of settlers in Patea and Wanganui make it plain all Maori were to be swept from the region. The *New Zealand Herald* described one meeting with the settlers: 'There was a strong feeling of animosity against the whole [Maori] race, hostile and friendly; and they strongly urged on the Premier that no Natives be permitted to return to the district . . . Fox acceded to the wishes of the settlers and told them that no Natives would be allowed to light their fires between the Waitotara on the South and Waingongoro on the North.'

There are at least half a dozen similar reports. When McLean tried to soften the policy in 1870 and allow friendly Maori back to the Waitotara block, the settlers exploded: 'This is a breach of the most positive assurances of Mr Fox that the natives should *never* be allowed to return to the block in question,' the *Chronicle* said.

Fox's private letters confirm his policy: 'The essential condition to getting the settlers back on the land is that we should keep *all* natives outside of the block from Waihi to Wanganui,' he told McLean in September 1869. 'If we support Noake in the policy of perpetually scouring the Patea and Waitotara Plains, I believe we can keep the countryside free till the population can defend itself.' 'I am trying to keep the Kai Iwi and Waingongoro clear of Natives,' he wrote to McDonnell a few weeks later, 'and hope to be able to do it, as well as get the settlers back to their farms.' 'A district like the West Coast can be kept absolutely *clean* of the enemy in the open by a few active horsemen who know their ground,' he later wrote to McLean.

After three years Fox's experiment in racial clearance collapsed, for reasons which will be familiar to students of military occupations. First, corruption. Noake, commander and resident magistrate, turned into a thief and he was caught attempting to defraud the state. He applied for £1,000 for damage sustained to his property during the war. Then someone noticed that, during the war, he had not owned any property. In the meantime, while in Patea he had acquired a large farm a' few miles out of town and had put at least one of his own farm workers, a dairyman named Collins, on the military pay roll. At the same time the real soldiers, men in the ranks, were put to work cutting posts and rails for the new farm and carrying them out there by government dray.

This was all small beer, but it was enough for McLean who had conceived a loathing for the ex-riding master and his methods.

The second reason was the inherent absurdity of the programme. It was not just the muddle of its logic, though that was bad enough. If the Maori were allowed to return, Fox's reasoning ran, the settlers would attack them. Therefore the government should attack them first, and thus prevent a 'desultory war between the races'. His policy, he wrote in a memo to his ministers, was *for the sake of the Natives themselves.*

In the rest of the colony, under the soothing spells of McLean, peace and security had returned. Even across the

Waingongoro, Titokowaru had settled down and was growing grass and quietly making a fortune selling grass-seed to Pakeha farmers far and wide. Only in Noake's fiefdom was the atmosphere still charged with fear and uncertainty. Even Maori travelling through the territory on government business were attacked by Noake's men. Maori mailmen had their passes torn up and were sent packing. Maori road-workers, hired by the state and set up in government-issue tents, were surrounded and charged, their tents torn down, and they were sent back across the river at the point of the bayonet. Here things reached a point of lunacy, for it was Fox himself who was the leading proponent of the road-building project. This was not a case of the left hand not knowing what the right was doing; the left and the right were in violent conflict. Finally even the local press saw the absurdity of it all. The *Taranaki Herald* wrote:

> If Inspector Noake is allowed to send armed parties into the bush; if peaceful natives who are sent to make roads through the district are to be driven away on the point of the bayonet and threatened with instant death if speedy departure is not made . . . then we should blot out Taranaki from the map as a European settlement. We can hardly believe Inspector Noake receives authority to act in this way.
>
> Friendly natives . . . returning from voting in the election of a native member of the house of representatives – were actually driven from the district by armed men of the colonial forces. They had gone 30 miles to vote – an evidence of their privileges and rights as British subjects – [and were] immediately banished with a warning they would be shot as rebels if seen again.

The petty frauds of Noake, the dairyman on soldier's pay and so on came as a godsend to McLean. Noake had to go. Fox pleaded on behalf of his friend:

'I have known Noake for years as a settler and JP in Rangitikei. He was much respected there and quite a leading man and I have the fullest confidence in his ability.'

He appealed for mercy:

'Noake is virtually suspended and disgraced before the public, and his friends of whom he has many, and many most respectable, are very sore at the way he has been placed in the position he is.'

But the Native Minister, who had the final say in his own department, was unmoved. McLean cared nothing about the dairyman or the £1,000. It was Noake's cruelty and stupidity that offended him.

'The treatment of friendly natives that have come into the district has been harsh and inconsiderate . . . I do not consider he possesses judgement or other qualifications necessary to an officer entrusted with such a duty . . . It would be most impolitic to place restrictions on the right Her Majesty's subjects of both races have to travel without being subjected to threats or violence on the part of officers or men employed by the country for the maintenance of peace . . . Maj. Noake is continually guilty of acts of indiscretion which displays a great unfitness for his position.'

At this, Fox bowed to the inevitable. He could not afford to lose his Native Minister. McLean would now take over affairs on the West Coast. There was one final desperate play from Noake himself. He discovered that McLean was a freemason, and he wrote him this note:

Dear Sir

It being reported among the Craft that you hail from the High and Sublime Degree and as I also hail from the same place, I take the liberty to write privately to you. I seek only half an hour private conversation . . .

This was written in a round, upright script, quite unlike Noake's handwriting to Fox. There is no evidence as to whether McLean replied. Probably he did not, for the disgraced Noake departed from Patea and resumed his life as 'JP and leading man in Rangitikei'. Out of their hiding places and exiles and prisons, the Nga Rauru and Ngati Ruanui people emerged and came home, in some instances to find all their land, even their reserves, had been taken under a new and extra-legal further round of confiscation arranged by Fox. For several years the tribes had to perch wherever they could, but a decade later some land was given back to them in the district, and there they have remained.

★　★　★

Patea today is a small, depressed-looking town with bare, wide streets that seem somewhat cruelly exposed to sunny skies. The main highway westward swoops through and then, out among fields again, aims directly at the apparent mirage of Mt. Taranaki. Back in town on the main intersection, a big second-hand shop offers for sale some old bottles, a flat-iron, a bike pump; a hand-mower, a stack of *Reader's Digests*, all under the hopeful description of 'Collectables'. The main industry – a freezing works – has closed, and the wooden piles are rotting at the wharf where no coastal trader has docked for years. There is a museum, which an ancient, kindly farmer drove in from the country to open up for me. His grandfather was one of the leading settlers of the nineteenth century; we talked for a while but he became agitated and almost tearful when we disagreed on some question, and so I left him among the shadowy buggies and crinolines. Next door, in the Canoe Café, an angry woman was slamming down plates in front of the early lunch customers. Immediately across the road is the Canoe in question – a concrete hull forming the top of a memorial arch and containing eight or nine brown-painted concrete Maori paddlers. Their captain stands at the fore, shading his eyes towards the east.

Eastward, at the other end of the territory, near Wanganui, one can visit Bryce's grave; six panes of sun-blackened asphalt around an obelisk of shiny stone that looks as if it has no intention of ageing by a day. On it is the curt instruction:

Thy will be done.

Between these two points lie sixty miles of green paddocks, black pine belts, an occasional glimpse of the blue plain of the sea. There is no sign of public memory of the wars between Maori and Pakeha. One of the little towns you go through is called Maxwell; it was probably named after the young farmer – 'as brave a youth as ever went into the field of battle' – who killed two boys at Handley's Farm. But today, Maori and whites play golf together at Nukumaru, not far from the spot where the cavalry saw the children chasing the geese. Even at the small Maori settlements which you pass from time to time along the way, the particular events referred to in this chapter have become vague. On my last trip up that coast I stopped at Whenuakura, at the old Maori meeting-house where nearly thirty years ago I slept badly under an old green Chevy truck.

This time I was with a Maori named Matt, a friend I had made while living in London. We drove in the gate and parked and walked up to the house with some uncertainty. Maori *marae* are strange spaces for a white visitor to enter, neither public nor private, not sacred or secular; and you never quite know how you will be greeted. We were met by a nervous-seeming man who asked what we wanted. His name was Doug and he had suffered some injury to his hand, which he held like a claw.

It was dusk and the rain was just starting to fall. On the hillside opposite the meeting-house a farmer on the hill was still harvesting his wheat in the dim light. It seemed a sad, quiet little place. There was a child, about eleven, in a red jacket sitting hunched on a bench near the meeting-house. He did not look round at us when we approached.

'What was it you were after?' Doug asked again.

'Just to have a look at the old carved building,' I said.

He led us in and showed us around. It was just a little, old, dark village hall without a village. The walls were covered with photographs of Maori dignitaries from the 1880s, 1890s, 1920s. Some of them were dressed in fantastic finery. One was remembered as a prophetess but her fame had not spread wide. We looked at the prophetess and Maori Edwardians and men in straw boaters.

On the floor lay a great array of foam rubber mattresses, old and new, for the guests who slept the night here at funerals or other gatherings.

We went outside again. The rain had settled in. The boy or girl in the red shirt had disappeared.

What about earlier, I asked our guide. What happened here in the 1860s and 1870s?

'Ah, that's too far back for me,' he said. 'I've been living in Aussie.'

Doug locked the door behind us and we stood under the gable, looking at the rain and for something to say. Had something once happened here? Whenuakura was the absolute centre of Noake's operations. On Fox's orders, *all* land between the Whenuakura river and the Patea river was to be offered for sale to Europeans, for here especially it was intended that no Maori was ever to return. Could this have been the site of one of Rusden's 'unreported slaughters'?

When I began to follow the story of the abducted child, I did not expect to learn that, not long after his kidnapping and not far away, 'at one time every Maori creature . . . *omnis sexus, omnis aetas*, was ruthlessly slain', and that the victims were the child's own relations, and furthermore that the other main character in the story of his transformation, his foster-father, was responsible in part for some of their deaths.

Could those creatures, '*omnis sexus, omnis aetas*', be connected with the desolate dream which I once had here at the edge of the highway?

As we drove over the paddock and out the gate, I was assailed by doubt. Was I even sure that this was the place where I had slept under the truck? Surely the field I had seen then was wider than this and the hills were further away, and that second building beside the meeting-house – of that I had no recollection at all.

'Stop thinking about it,' commanded Matt. 'And you'd better stop coming back and *checking* things all the time. You'll get yourself in a tangle.' I accepted his advice. Matt himself was an expert at avoiding tangles – he was back from London to escape a tumultuous romance, tears, lawyers, a newborn baby and a midnight-blue Audi carelessly deposited in the middle of the Grand Union canal. We drove away south towards Wanganui debating the question of whether it had a Pizza Hut or not. I left the other questions, of Maori ghosts and voices crying out of the ground, where they belong, in the background, not quite visible and never to be resolved.

Waitotara in the dusk, Nukumaru, Maxwell, Kai Iwi . . . I had got to know this road quite well by now and I thought that, compared to the great dioramas of history, whatever had happened here was insignificant. At most, a few hundred people died over about five years of war. Since then relations have been peaceful and friendly.

There is one thing, however, which makes this landscape momentous, and that is the three-year silence which once reigned here. No one in the wider world noticed, but that was an early portent for the terrible century to come. The war along this coast was one of the first, perhaps the very first, fought in a haze of Neo-Darwinist ideology, the doctrine of struggle for struggle's sake and the biological necessity for conflict. Even the changes in Fox's language – from 'clearing' to 'scouring' to keeping a territory 'clean' of the enemy – prefigure the twentieth century when the enemy became bacteria, bacilli, dirt, whose removal, by one means or another, could be described as 'cleansing the terrain'.* It was only a straw in the wind, this little obscure war in the South Pacific, but the wind did not change direction or die away and it continued to grow until the 1940s.

Perhaps the point is best made by the Nobel Laureate Czeslaw Milosz, who watched history unfold from the dangerous but incomparable vantage point of Poland when the Nazis came streaming across the plains towards Warsaw. He argues that the events of 1939 were not an aberration of history, for far to the west and south there had already been a hundred years of burning native huts and moving 'inferior' populations. 'The coloured peoples did not suspect, when they were subjugated by the white man, that they were already avenged at the moment of their fall. The conquerors returned home with their greed and converted it into an idea of supremacy over inferior races – even white races . . .'† The ruins of Berlin, London and Warsaw were the logical conclusion.

There is one other aspect of these events to consider and that is their effect on the boy William Fox and his foster-parents. During the years of the Noake regime he probably had no inkling of what was happening in part of his tribal district. The policy was not fully in the public domain and not something that would have been discussed within the hearing of a seven- or eight-year-old at the Native Hostelry. But what can the atmosphere have been like when he was living in the Fox household – an eight-year-old boy whose mother was of the Nga Rauru

* The actual translation of the Serbo-Croat phrase usually rendered as 'ethnic cleansing'.
† Czeslaw Milosz, *Native Realm*, 1968.

163

tribe, and whose father was Nga Ruahine? Noake was a stupid man and Fox a clever one, but the same thought, perhaps at the same speed, must have occurred to them: under other circumstances, if for example this child, there in the room with them at Westoe, had happened to be sixty miles further west with his own people, he would *by their own orders* have been chased, hunted down and possibly killed.

Did the two men exchange glances? Did they avoid exchanging glances? Did they suddenly begin to talk in loud voices about the brown mare Gentle Annie, or Chestnut or Tormentor, or the new system for breaking in a colt which greatly impressed Sir William on a visit to South Australia? 'Horse breeders here have got what they call a crush pen – a very simple but efficacious invention for dealing with wild colts. It consists simply of a narrow adjunct to the common stockyard in which two gates are hung so that you get the colt between them and shut him up in a space 2ft 6in wide. You then halter or tie his legs or do what you like . . . They work to admiration.'

And what of Sarah Fox? She was an astute woman and must have known what had been happening in the country further west. Was the love she tendered her child an implied criticism of her husband? Was it that which enraged him when he saw the two heads, of wife and child, bent together over a book?

No word reaches us from the distance. But the subject must have hung over them all summer up there in the big house at Westoe, and even a child can sense the atmosphere created by an unspoken secret. There was a description current in the Maori language in the early nineteenth century for a landscape depopulated by war: it was 'a place where only the cicadas are heard'. The child William Fox was frightened of his foster-father. Was it because of a certain secret regarding a landscape, not far away, where, in accordance with Sir William's policy, nothing for three summers was heard but the sound of cicadas?

9

The years

S o that was how Titokowaru's revolt – Waru's march, as the Maori called it – ended. Titokowaru did not win, but he did not lose either. That angel-baffled general was back where he started, on the western bank of the Waingongoro, and there Fox's government left him, not caring to unleash more trouble. The country turned its mind away from war and towards sheep and railways. Young William Fox went every day to Mr Mowbray's school and in summer to Westoe. Sir William's government fell, then briefly rose again. Vast transfers of land from Maori to white ownership were now taking place legally, through the courts. Walter Buller gave up his magistracy, went into private practice dealing in Maori land, moved to Wellington, grew stout and began to grow very rich. In the evenings he presided at the Philosophical Society and gave lectures on Darwin and the fate of that extinct giant, the flightless moa. Occasionally he met the Foxes, and patted young William's head, chatted to him in Maori (a language which was growing vague to the boy) and, when Sir William was not looking, slipped him a sixpence.

'What else happened during those years?' I asked Miri Rangi.

'Ah, well . . .' she said. But she had no more information to give me. Perhaps nothing much happened at all. From nine to twelve, children often lead a mysteriously placid life. The dramas of infancy are behind them. Major storms – sex for instance – lie ahead. In the meantime, it is time to put on puppy fat, eat, sleep and read voraciously and without attracting undue attention, like the caterpillar under the leaf.

'Ah . . .' said Miri, 'perhaps you'd better ask Raukura Coffey.'

'Who's she?'

'She's my cousin. She's a lot older than me. She's got a *beautiful* memory. She's the one who knows all about the life of that William Fox.'

Several things happened in the course of this short speech: Miri became quite cheerful at the thought of someone else much older than herself. And she established that there are orders of memory other than merely good or bad, efficient or hazy. There is 'beautiful' for instance. And also she seemed, temporarily, to withdraw her own interest in her long-dead uncle. There was, I sometimes noticed, a certain ambivalence in her attitude towards the Maori William Fox. Once she went even further:

'We thought he was a *traitor*,' she said to me.

Raukura Coffey, although originally from Mawhitiwhiti under Mt. Taranaki, now lived in Hastings, my old home town, on the other side of the island. She had gone there to be with her daughter and to escape the cold, wet Taranaki winter. And so, to find out if there was more to find out, I went back to Hawke's Bay myself to see her. On the day I drove from Wellington the summer ended quite abruptly. Chilly, brilliant clouds were banked high over the hills. By the time I reached the string of rural towns – Dannevirke, Waipukurau, Waipawa – in central Hawke's Bay it was dusk. I stopped for gas at Waipawa, about thirty miles south of Hastings. A fog had crept up from the Tuki Tuki river and was smudging out details of the town. I re-membered Waipawa as a sunny, prosperous little place but now

168

it looked dismal, even slightly derelict. Across the road from a lonesome new shopping arcade, two gigantic yellow plastic ducklings stood forlorn on a stand on the river bank. They had been erected as municipal amenities.

Why? I wondered. Who thought them up? Who *wanted* them?

Probably everyone. Most small New Zealand towns have now appropriated some Disneyesque image for themselves. The ideal graven on the heart of every local councillor is to make their community look like a bit of America – not sleek, classy America, not Monterey or Aspen, but corny, fast-food, truck-stop America. This continental ugliness, done on the cheap, sits sadly in the gloaming of a large South Pacific island.

There was a man at the gas station and a woman frying chips in the chip shop, otherwise Waipawa was deserted. Smoke rose from one or two house chimneys. I drove out past the big yellow ducklings, the new and infantile guardians to the land of my childhood.

That night back in Hawke's Bay I stayed with an old friend, an Englishwoman called Rose who had married into the farming community, which sees itself as the local aristocracy in the province. The house she lives in, a big pink stucco mansion near the coast, about thirty miles south of Hastings, was damaged in the great 1931 earthquake and faint scars of repairs are still visible. We sat up late, looking out over a dark landscape that in daylight bears an odd resemblance to Tuscany, but a Tuscany with only one or two thin layers of history.

There is a Maori settlement a few miles from the farm. Rose told me about her burglaries. These are reasonably regular – one every four or five years – and she knows in each case exactly who the burglar is.

'I've been down to the *pa* and yelled my head off,' she said,

169

'and I've got my stuff back. Well, in a *way* I got my stuff back . . .'

Rose is one of those whites – a minority in Hawke's Bay – who, when the scandal of the Maori crime rate is discussed, tend to look for excuses. She sees a connection between the existence of a Maori underclass and a number of earlier crimes – the alienation of their land, not so much in Hawke's Bay by war or confiscation, but by judicial fraud and legalised theft.

But she is still rueful about her burglars.

'Gee, sorry, Rosie,' one of them told her. 'I was a wee bit drunk at the time. Anyway I only took your electricals, so's you could *upgrade*.'

'Oh, *fine*. Thanks a million. What about all my records?'

'I'll get them back.'

Her burglar turned up the next day.

'Here you are, Rose. A hundred CDs.'

'But . . . these aren't *my* CDs.'

'No. Yours have – ah – gone. These are *replacements*.'

'What happened to mine?'

'The Mungies had already sold them. But they sent you these instead.'

The Mungies, i.e. The Mongrel Mob, a Maori gang with criminal connections, have a strong presence in Hawke's Bay. When not fighting amongst themselves or against their great enemy, the Black Power gang, they are not above fencing stolen household goods.

Rose gazed around her expansive sitting room. Copies old and new of the *Guardian Weekly* and the *New York Review of Books* lay in drifts over the floor.

'What could I do? The real owner was never going to see his stuff again. So now I have an extensive collection of light-opera. If only you knew how much I hate Strauss.' She shuddered expressively.

'Still, they behave very well,' she mused, reverting to the burglars themselves. 'They never come when we're in, which would be embarrassing for all of us.'

The next morning I went into Hastings. It was a bright, sharply shadowed day, not quite convincing as representative of autumn. I drove in from the south and all the familiar landmarks seemed to be in place – the grandstand at the racecourse which I had never entered, the alien red-brick of the old rival school, Hastings Boys High, the big concrete clocktower at the centre of town on which every year a huge fibreglass Santa Claus was placed – an event recorded in the *Hawke's Bay Herald Tribune* one happy year – or happy for fifteen-year-old schoolboys – as 'the giant erection of Father Christmas'. Many of the old wooden villas in the inner city had gone; in their place a new ignominious architecture of low, windowless aluminium barns – discount warehouses, Kwik-Fix plumbers, office equipment rentals. The great cannery plant was still steaming and hooting down its series of side streets.

I met an old school friend, a lawyer, and we drove through town and out to a new suburb called Flaxmere. The city, in my absence, has grown both larger and smaller at the same time. That street corner we passed, where at dusk I used to meet my friends, was once on the outskirts of town and had seemed to be on the edge of the world: it is now disclosed to be about five blocks from the clocktower; beyond it new suburbs stretch far and wide. And what has happened to the two-lane highway, lined with orchards, that led gravely out into the riverine plains of Hawke's Bay? Isuzu, BP, Burger King, Mobil, KFC ('Hot 'N' Spicy is back!'). Giant letters and *words* in primary colours are littered everywhere, as after a revolution. I stopped to buy a cake at a commercial bakery, and my friend stopped at a garden centre to pick up some plants.

171

'No smoking. No blasphemy', said a sign on the wall. 'We Do Not Falsify Our Accounts.'

'Plymouth Brethren,' said my friend. We drove on: Daihatsu. Bitumix. Caltex. Mudgeways Wreckers. This was once Renata Kawepo territory. It was here that the great chief first dreamed of luring a European population to come and live among the Maori. He had his heart set on bread – a wheat crop, a flour-mill and a bakery. 'Japhet shall dwell in the tents of Shem and we, the sons of Shem, were very willing to receive him . . .' On hazy winter days, down the end of certain streets in Hastings, you can sometimes see the inland ranges covered after a rare snowfall, shining like tents. But Hastings has forgotten the man who enabled it to come into existence. In my years at school here I never heard of him. His name does live on, however: it has been given to one cul-de-sac in an area of low-cost housing.

Flaxmere has a bad name. The population is half white, a quarter Maori, a quarter Pacific Islander. The Mongrel Mob have a strong showing, with two fortified and mutually hostile chapter houses in the area. The crime rate is high. For a notorious crime-ridden estate, however, Flaxmere looks rather pretty. It was built on the site of a rich farming property and the polo fields and avenues were retained and incorporated into the town plan. The houses – or rather the 'homes' ('house' is now, as in most suburbs around the world, a word oddly avoided) – are neat and tidy; some are quite expensive-looking and the lawns well kept. There is a deep, green park dotted with low-skirted trees; 'It's dangerous to go too far in *there* alone,' said my guide briskly. He drove me around the worst side of Flaxmere – streets of run-down, state-owned housing with rusty letterboxes out front, each stuffed with untouched junk mail, an indication that no other kind is ever received. Here, the rates of child abuse, domestic violence, unemployment and so on are high. Here, as you approach, sullen faces look up from under the open hoods of parked cars and watch you go past.

He pointed out the rival Mongrel Mob fortresses – ordinary bungalows surrounded by great wooden palisades. Though they are both staunch Mongrel Mob, Mungies through and through, Mungies unto death, there is bad blood between them. One chapter are local boys, the others come from southern Hawke's Bay. Occasionally attacks are launched from one house upon the other. During these affrays, the police, working on the principle of divide-and-rule, generally turn a blind eye.

Inside one house which was eventually raided by the authorities, I was told, a room was found spattered with blood – blood of *several* types.

Further off, in better streets beyond a line of immense Australian blue gums, I found the house where Raukura Coffey lived.

Mrs Coffey is the granddaughter of Ake Ake Omahuru, the brother whom young William Fox had probably gone looking for in the forest on the day he was captured just before a battle. I rang the bell. And there she was coming down the hall, walking with two aluminium sticks, beaming.

Her daughter was standing behind her. There was, among the smiles of welcome, a faint air of puzzlement. I had rung a few days before to ask whether I could visit. Somehow I misrepresented myself: they were expecting a Maori from Taranaki named, I think, Joe Walker, come to discuss some family business. Instead, they got an unknown Pakeha, carrying a cake and wanting to talk about a boy who long ago had been lost and who had never really come home.

All the same, on we went. I was led into the front room. With her crutches laid aside, Mrs Coffey sat extremely upright on the sofa. She wore a black-and-white blouse and a silver brooch. She was the only person alive, or at least the only relation alive, who had actually met the boy who had gone missing during 'Waru's March'. She met him when she was a little girl of six living in Taranaki. He was an old man of fifty-five who lived far away – at least twenty miles away on the other side of the mountain. Once or twice he came to see her family at the *pa*. It was 1917. He was tall and slim. And he taught them how to make a cake.

'It was a Madeira cake,' she said. 'He read out a recipe for cake and then they made it. *I* ate some of that cake!' She beamed at me. 'And he told us how to make boiled pudding. We never knew about boiled pudding until that day. You see, he knew how to do those things, he learned them when he was a boy, living with the Pakeha.

'He put the pudding in a cloth and lit the copper. But no one at the *pa* would watch the fire under the copper, except for one old lady. She sat there watching the fire for hours. Then when the time was up, they took the pudding out and opened it up and – and it *sliced like cheese.*'

Mrs Coffey gazed at me, but she was really smiling at a fire under a copper boiler in 1917. I had an idea of what a 'beautiful' memory was, as opposed to a 'good' one.

'There was fruit scattered in it,' she said. 'It was a *plum* pudding. And it sliced like a cheese.'

Mrs Sturm, her daughter, laid out morning tea. There were Japanese biscuits and avocados, and the cake I had bought arrived, on a plate with a silver cake-slice. It was a bad cake, as I should have guessed, coming from that noisy, sign-littered highway – flimsy and textureless and over-sweet. The door opened and a small boy, dark and bullet-headed, rushed into the room. He shot me a glance, then saw the cake and advanced on it cautiously as if not wishing to distort a mirage.

'He's a bit of a Ngatau Omahuru himself,' said Mrs Sturm. 'Our little foster boy . . .'

'How old is he?' I asked.

'He's four – *don't* do that,' she cried as the boy picked up a knife and speared it down through the cake and into the plate. 'Would you like a piece of cake?' she asked gently.

'No!' he said, while cramming a slice into his mouth. The two women watched wearily as he clambered up in front of a computer on a desk in the corner.

'What did the name mean?' I asked. '*Ngatau* Omahuru?'

There had been a discussion between my brother-in-law and Miri Rangi about the various meanings of the name. Ngatau: A season. A song. A year. A sweetheart. The alighting of birds.

'The Years,' said Mrs Coffey with authority. 'Ngatau is a word that means a lot of things, but with him that's what his name meant. The Years.'

A breeze blew into the room, the curtain bellied tranquilly for a moment. I heard children yelling in the street.

'Why was he called that?'

'I don't know why he was called that name,' she said. Mrs Coffey beamed at me again. She was quite a star, I thought, sparkling for visitors, even if the visitor was the wrong one. She knew a lot of family history – the year that Ake Ake's house was burnt down; who married who at Mangamuka in 1936 – but not much more about William Fox Omahuru.

'I only saw him once or twice when he taught us to make a cake,' she said. 'You see, he never really resumed the family relationship.'

So young William Fox grew up. Eight, nine, ten, eleven. Years later, when he found his own people again, there was nothing much to report of this period of his life, or if there was the reports were forgotten. The Fox household sailed its difficult course under its own star. Sir William was still Premier, but, says the *National Dictionary of Biography*, 'he was not a policy maker and had few ideas about where to lead the country.' Increasingly he

175

left the important issues of government to the treasurer, a financial wizard named Vogel. While Vogel went to London and raised huge loans on the money market, Fox went on a leisurely tour of the hitherto little visited central North Island and Rotorua geysers and wrote a leisurely report on the lacustrine scenery and what he found it contained: 'sighing fountains, grunting fountains, fountains of mud, lucid fountains, fumaroles'.

'One peculiarity of this bath is, that in a very few minutes of immersion it covers the body with a most exquisite varnish or coating, quite invisible to the eye, but as smooth as velvet, which gives the bather the feeling of being the most "polished" person in the world.' Fox foresaw a great future for the district as an imperial and strategic resource. The hot springs were 'capable of accommodating whole regiments of soldiers at one time. [Rotorua] affords the finest conceivable opportunity of establishing a great sanatorium for Indian regiments.'

One way or another Fox was out of the house a good deal, although never away too long as far as one person was concerned. It was probably at this stage of his life, and during the absences of Sir William, that the boy learned to make his cakes. Perhaps we can imagine these as the happiest moments of his childhood. The rain of a Wellington winter is slinging itself against the kitchen window. Sir William is somewhere far away, safely beyond the gale. It is too early to light the lamps, but the fire in the range is starting to send shadows over the floor. And mother and son, the two sailors out of a storm, are making a Madeira cake, beating a pound of butter to a cream in one bowl, dredging in flour and sugar and lemon rind, and whisking nine eggs in another. They have the kitchen to themselves. They have the whole house to themselves. (Even the prime ministerial residence found it hard to keep servants, the shortage of women in the colony being so great. Some people took pains to import only the ugliest female staff, but that didn't help. Even a bearded lady cook, it is reported, was soon up and away, down the road in the arms of a passing drover.) And with Sir William absent and no servants to defend the scullery, why not, one afternoon, light a fire under the copper, send out for a quarter pint of brandy, and then:

Mrs Beeton's Book of Household Management, 1861.
Recipe No. 1834 – AN UNRIVALLED PLUM PUDDING

Ingredients. – One and a half lbs muscatel raisins, one and three quarter lbs currants, 1lb sultana raisins, 2 lbs finest moist sugar, 2 lbs bread crumbs, 16 eggs, 2 lbs finely chopped suet, 6 oz mixed candied peel, rind of 2 lemons, 1 oz ground nutmeg, 1 oz ground cinnamon, half oz pounded bitter almonds, a quarter pint of brandy.
Mode. – Mix all the dry ingredients well together, and moisten with the eggs, which should be well beaten and strained, to the pudding [sic]; stir in the brandy and, when all is thoroughly mixed, well butter and flour a stout new pudding cloth. Put in the pudding, tie it down very tightly and closely; boil from 6 to 8 hours, and serve with brandy sauce. This quantity may be divided and boiled in buttered moulds. For small families this is the most desirable way as the above will be found to make a pudding of rather large dimensions.
Time. – 6 to 8 hours. **Average Cost**. – 7s. 6d.
Sufficient for 12 or 14 persons.
Seasonable in winter.

Down to the scullery they go . . .

Only one truly momentous thing happened to young Fox in these years, and neither he nor the Foxes knew anything about it. His real family, his Maori family, that is, discovered he was alive. He was seen in Wellington by a man who knew him well.

This was Tauke Te Hapimana, the great priest-historian of the Nga Ruahine tribe, the 'beloved' Tauke, Belich calls him, whose stern bearded visage is to be seen among the crowds of photographs on Miri Rangi's sitting-room wall.

What the Nga Ruahine chief was doing in the capital, and under what circumstances he laid eyes on the Prime Minister's foster-son, is unclear. It was late in 1873 and Tauke may have been negotiating some delicate stage of rapprochement between his tribe and the government. Strictly speaking, they were still at war. McLean, however, had declared confiscation of their land suspended or impractical. Sir William raged at the thought of the tribe back at the Beak of the Bird – 'It would be justly offensive to Pakeha sentiment to have Titoko and his chums smoking their pipes on the spot where they committed their worst atrocities,' he told McLean – but for the meantime there was nothing that could be done to stop it. No one, or almost no one, on either side wanted war again. Tauke himself, whose attitude to Titokowaru's war had been ambivalent, was a perfect ambassador to discuss these delicate matters.

Somewhere he recognised his own relation, the boy who had gone missing and had been believed dead six years ago. He asked who he was. He heard the story. He said nothing.

But when he got back to Taranaki, across the Waingongoro, the 'snoring water' or the 'River of Snores', the boundary between two worlds that had been cut off from each other for so long, the news he brought came like a thunderclap. The family were astonished, in consternation, joyful, outraged. Hinewai was in tears. Her little boy was not dead! He was with the Pakeha! He had been with them all those years she had mourned him.

He was there *now*.

178

What did he look like? she asked Tauke. He was growing up. He was nearly a man. He was wearing a suit and a hat like an English gentleman.

This was terrible in a way — all those years of mourning her son and he had been alive all the time, growing up without her down in Wellington, where the Pakeha governor lived. At this moment he was there, possibly going out the door of a Pakeha house, putting on his hat. Hinewai felt almost outraged, as if she had not only suffered a loss, but a theft.

What was to be done?

This was a delicate question. The south Taranaki tribes and the government had no formal relations. Many of them were still seen by whites as rebels and monsters; and to them, the Pakeha were robbers, child-killers and aliens, *tauiwi*, who should go back to their 'own place in the midst of the sea'. And although they were safe in their fastness beyond the river, the tribes were now militarily weak and in no position to make demands.

And there was one further component to the equation — an element of pride and of curious interest in the turn of events. There was their boy, who was not dead after all but now nearly a man living with and bearing the name of perhaps the most powerful Pakeha in the country. It was a kind of distinction for the family. It even had an auspicious appearance to it, or the look of fate which should not be lightly interfered with. In the end something good might even come of it.

Finally, out of puzzlement, and deference to the mysterious ways of providence, and a kind of curiosity to see how the story would end, nothing was done about Ngatau Omahuru/William Fox at all.

There may, however, have been a response with an immense effect on the life of someone else. A few weeks after Tauke returned to Mawhitiwhiti with his dramatic news, another child was kidnapped thirty or forty miles away, in the newly settled district of north Taranaki, near a place called Lepperton. She was a little blonde girl named Caroline Perrett, mentioned earlier, who went missing near her house on the edge of the bush. Her father was certain that she had been snatched by a group of strange Maori who had been seen earlier in the locality. He hunted for her, unsuccessfully, until his death. Her family never forgot her. She was, however, not found for fifty years, by which time she had been twice married, was a grandmother, was hardly able to speak a word of English and had no recollection of her first life.

Why she was stolen has always been a mystery. Some Maori in Taranaki told me that it was because her father, who was making a road near the farm, persisted against all their warnings in destroying an ancient burial-site. But there were many Maori burial-sites disturbed in the nineteenth century and many tow-headed children around and nowhere else was such a penalty incurred.

Could her abduction have been a direct act of revenge for the kidnapping of William Fox, news of which had just reached Taranaki? Did some small renegade group pass by the Perrett farm and on impulse snatch the little blonde girl, just to even the score? The story of Caroline Perrett had a lot of publicity with a book published and a television documentary made just at the time I was in Taranaki in 1999. I discussed the story with Miri Rangi and we found that this explanation had occurred to both of us. 'You say A B C, we say A B C.'

The next year, Sir William and Lady Fox and their son left the country and went around the world.

There was now a new route for Antipodeans travelling to England. They could sail to California, take the railroad across the continent and then sail on over the Atlantic. This was a revolutionary advance – two hops across puddles and one over dry land – compared to the dreaded six-month journey the length of the Atlantic and the breadth of the Southern Ocean across the Roaring Forties. The Foxes arrived in San Francisco, a great Pacific port of 300,000 people – equal to the whole population of New Zealand – in mid-1875.

Everything was splendid and immense. They stayed in the Palace Hotel – their eyes popped at the sight of it; 'fourteen storeys, each fourteen feet high, beautifully furnished with lifts and every possible appliance'. They saw Yosemite, walled in by cliffs 'nearly two miles high in perpendicular height', and took the train over the Sierra Nevada in Pullman cars, with their sleepers and magnificent drawing rooms – 'not the tinkettle, ramshackle, miserable little omnibuses such as there were on New Zealand lines,' Sir William said in a scolding tone to his audiences back home, as though they and not he had had control of the matter. Why, if a man attempted to cross the continent of America in railway carriages such as those in New Zealand, he added, 'he would never come out alive'. The Americans were 'ahead of all the rest of the civilized world in the number and extent of their railways &c. I attribute their advance mainly to the fact that they have not gone in for mere money-grubbing but because they anxiously retained their civil and religious liberty.'

The Foxes went to Salt Lake City, Chicago and Boston, and ended up in Vermont and Maine. There they stayed for three months. The main purpose of the trip was not sightseeing but to advance the cause of Temperance. Everywhere he went, Sir William sniffed the breath of strangers and found proof of his theory of the evils of alcohol. He went down to Chinatown and peeped into an opium house to see the 'frightful effects which the opium eating exercised upon its victims'. He compared the effects of alcohol and opium and decided that brandy and whisky were infinitely greater evils. 'Yet Europeans stand aghast at opium but if they see a drunkard they simply say "The poor fellow is only on the spree."'

In Maine and Vermont, where there was an early experiment in prohibition, Fox 'saw not a single instance of drunkenness nor yet of sly grog selling, though I looked for opportunities and even tempted a steamboat waiter to supply me'.

'The state of Maine had closed no less than 3,000 public houses in one day. At first the new law was violently resisted. When the first cases were tried, the court was closed because the mob threatened to pull down the courthouse and maltreat the magistrate. But now the great majority of people concluded they were better off without strong drink, and one and all, with few exceptions, joined to abolish the liquor traffic . . .

'From being one of the most backward states, Maine had become one of the most advanced.'

Thus fortified in Maine, the Foxes sailed across the sea to do battle with 200,000 liquor traders in England, Scotland and Wales.

Sir William travelled around the country as 'honorary lecturer' for the United Kingdom Alliance, a prohibition organisation, and he went from one end of the island to the other and made innumerable speeches, and in some places he was cheered to the rafters and in others they sat on their hands, 'but the Cause is progressing steadily,' he wrote to his brother-in-law back at Westoe in Rangitikei.

Fox also went to his family home, to the other, first Westoe, in Co. Durham and took his wife to visit her people in Wiltshire. He stayed in London, and was greeted by the great figures of the day, especially those involved in the sacred cause of colonisation. 'I met the Duke of Manchester, Lord Denbigh, Sir G. Fergusson, Sir C. Clifford. They were all very polite to me and invited me to their houses . . .' One morning, near Paddington station, he ran into Alfred Domett who had returned to England for good, and who the day before had been with Browning who a week before had visited Tennyson. Fox was not the man to be overawed by the rush of literary wings so near. They exchanged compliments. Domett thanked him for the kind things which Fox had said about his poem *Ranolf and Amohia*, which is set among the geysers of Rotorua. This was feline on his part. Fox had publicly praised the 'splendor of the descriptions of the scenery and . . . atmosphere' but only after much preliminary mockery: 'Mr Domett, with a fervour of expression and a warmth of sentiment of quite 212 Fahrenheit, has endeavoured to clothe savage life and character with charms and dignity which it would be difficult to recognise in the realities of any Maori pa on the shores of Rotorua . . .'

Domett had his revenge. He praised some paintings, on show in London at the time, by an artist named Blomfield who had visited New Zealand. He specially commended an oil of Mt. Egmont, in Taranaki. This hit home. Fox was furious. Mt. Egmont was his own favourite subject and he thought of himself as a far better artist than Blomfield with what he denounced as 'hideous and pretentious' pink- and dun-coloured brushwork. And so there they stood, below the endless porticoes of Westbourne Terrace, exchanging compliments and secretly despising one another's aesthetic of the Maori world – a world which both of them, in their own way, had tried to wipe out. At this moment the two elderly gentlemen standing in Paddington's smoky winter sunlight seem to become ghost-like, for ever disengaged from even their own consciences.

Where was young William Fox, now aged fourteen, during all this? Was he there in Paddington at that moment? Did Domett look him up and down, or even pat his head? It seems quite probable that the boy might take a stroll with his father through the streets of London. But the fact is that we don't know. The records of the trip are limited. The Foxes, big fish in the pond of New Zealand, left no stir in their wake abroad. The former Premier of a small British colony meant nothing in an America of fifty million people, and not much more in London, capital of an Empire of 350 million and of hundreds of races and languages. The one or two newspaper reports that I could find about the trip were merely notices of speeches that Fox made when he returned to New Zealand. I began to suspect, in fact, that young William Fox had not gone on the world trip at all.

On this question, however, Miri Rangi was categoric: 'He went to England.' Certainly he left Wellington College at the end of 1874, and there is no sight or sign of him in the colony until the end of 1876, when the Foxes returned, and so we must assume she is right. 'He went to England.'

It is a miserly bit of information. One would have liked to know, for example, what it was like for a fourteen-year-old Maori boy travelling across 1875 America in the palatial 'drawing-room' Pullman car. And how did he, a son of the Mawhitiwhiti forest and Sarah Fox's only child, fare under the cool, interested gaze of her family, the Halcombes, who were rich landowners of Wiltshire?

There is no data. 'He went to England.'

Then I realised that I was looking at this in the wrong way. That abrupt sentence is in itself the information: fourteen-year-olds do not travel well. The costly experience is wasted on them. They have other things on their minds. They don't want to be in Salt Lake City or peering up at the pyramid of Cheops. They would rather be on the street-corner with other fourteen-year-olds, ruminating about, say, shaving, or the deeds of lordly sixteen-year-olds. When William Fox Omahuru, years later, back in Mawhitiwhiti, reported on his life and said 'I went to England', that was all there was to say. He had seen the great world early, and at the time it meant nothing to him.

And the world probably returned the compliment: a young Maori in 1875–6 would not have drawn a second glance in

London, where exotics of every race had been visiting for centuries. Three 'savage men from the New Found Lands' were seen about the court at Westminster in 1502. The first Polynesian, a lordly young Tahitian named Omai, was there in 1776 and was met by Dr Johnson: 'Sir, Lord Mulgrave and he dined one day at Streatham; they sat with their backs to the light fronting me, so that I could not see distinctly; and there was so little of the savage in Omai, that I was afraid to speak to either, lest I should mistake one for the other.'*

The first Maori was in London early in the nineteenth century and stood aghast at the size, noise and darkness of the city, at its multitudes of inhabitants, who apparently lived on thin air for where were their kumara gardens? But the single thing that most astonished him, in the tradition of the unpredictable outsider (like the Amazonian Indian in Manhattan in the 1940s who was impressed, above all things, by the number of brass doorknobs to be found there), was that he saw a man stumping down an alley on a *wooden* leg.

The age of these *frissons* was long past for both races. London knew all the prodigies that India and Africa could offer; and even in New Zealand young Fox had seen plenty of drawing rooms and steam engines. Perhaps the fog impressed him, and the grey sky, as low as funnel-smoke. One imagines him silent or monosyllabic, squirming with boredom, in the corner of the room under the potted palms, with, as usual, Sarah Fox his only ally.

From London, the family sailed to the Levant. They went to Beirut where they inspected a girls' school and to Egypt where they inspected the Sphinx. They climbed the Great Pyramid whose summit, according to Flaubert, who was there about the same time, was white with eagle droppings. They sailed on the Nile, saw Karnak, and Sarah Fox wondered exactly where it was

* James Boswell, *The Life of Samuel Johnson*, 1791.

that Pharaoh's daughter found the basket daubed with pitch among the bulrushes.

Then they went home. Back in Wellington, Sir William meted out the punishment due to his wife and son for their alliance. He sent the young man away.

10

Buller and the law

To put it bluntly, old William Fox threw young William Fox out. He had, of course, to do this cleverly, for his Maori foster-son was well known in town and could hardly be seen to have been driven penniless from the door. 'Doing good for the Maoris' was still a watchword in the colony; even 'clearing' an entire area of its Maori inhabitants was a policy which Fox described to his colleagues as being 'for the sake of the Natives themselves'. It would be hard to accuse him of racial prejudice while he had a Maori child bearing his own name and living under his roof, and in fact no one ever did. Even today Sir William is routinely described as a humane man and a 'philo-Maori', and one of the reasons cited is his adoption of young William Fox.

But Sir William was not to be deflected from his main purpose, which was to cause pain to his wife. The boy had to go, and a way was found: he was sent to Walter Buller and without any further ado or education was taken on as a clerk in Buller's firm and began his career in the law.

In the small colonial capital Sarah Fox probably saw her son again from time to time, perhaps only in the street, which would have caused her, one imagines, an equal mix of happiness and pain.

In other words Sir William's plan, as he might have said,

'worked to admiration'. His wife had been suitably rebuked and a thorn had been removed from his own flesh.

As to the thorn himself – things were not so painful for him. He bitterly missed Sara Fox – the only person he loved and who loved him – but he was now a broad-shouldered fifteen- or sixteen-year-old; the days of storybooks and cake-baking were over. And he was suddenly released from the tension and piety of the Fox household. The atmosphere at Buller's could hardly be more different. Buller was quite unscrupulous but was not a spiteful or jealous man; he liked company, new ideas, good food and wine. Even the house he was building at this time looks cheerful, a spanking new Greek-revival house, 'highly pretentious' some said, on the sunny side of The Terrace, two hundred feet above the town. It was still there among a row of turreted wooden mansions when I went to Wellington as a boy in the 1960s and, although they were now subdivided into flats, smelling faintly of gas leaks and face powder, above flights of narrow steps where, incongruously among the rubbish bins and gas meters, big tree ferns sprang up, they all seemed cheerful and metropolitan to me, their sagging windows glinting in the morning sun. My maiden great-aunts, when I visited them at the age of twelve, lived a few doors along from the former Buller house – mild and pious Aunty Mimi and wild Aunt Flora McDonald who was not really a maiden of any description, having once eloped to Australia in her youth (taking, according to one legend, the family's silver spoons down the ladder with her), and who was eventually to die, with a whoop of laughter halfway through calling out a funny story to someone in the next room. It was in one of these cheerful eyries above a bustling town, a mile from the sombre mansions around Parliament, that young William Fox now began a new life.

There was one other party who was pleased with the new arrangement and that was Buller himself. When Sir William offered to send the boy to him, Buller, with his wide-set eyes and great rayed-out whiskers, must have looked like the cat that got the cream, or rather one which has been offered full rights over the canary, and what a valuable little songbird this one was!

At that time, there was a fortune to be made for lawyers dealing in Maori land. Many millions of acres were being sold by Maori to whites, but before any sale, the Maori title had to be established by the courts. This did not only mean that the tribe must prove its ownership – which was complicated enough given the conflicting claims and histories to any tract of land – but often the share of each individual within the tribe was to be decided. This was a complicated and lengthy business, and it had Maoridom in a state of permanent upheaval, with large crowds attending court hearings in town for weeks on end. Here is Sir William Fox describing the scene in Otaki in the 1860s: 'I am writing with a perfect Babel around me so that if I am unintelligible to you, you will know the reason – the house is full of European lodgers, surrounded by crowds of noisy natives – there are 400 or 500 of the latter brought hither by this Land Court business.' Such scenes were being enacted all over the country, and they were unavoidable. A single Maori who wanted to sell his share in a block of land could initiate an investigation of title, and everyone else in the tribe would be forced to come to town and defend their rights.

At first many Maori had been eager to sell, and others were pleased at the idea of having a firmly established individual title. But by the late 1870s, disillusionment had set in. Court costs, crippling lawyers' fees (which was where Buller made his money), and the expense of the land survey often meant that by the time the title was established, the land had to be sold simply to defray the costs. Many Maori were now suspicious of the Native Land Court, of judges, of lawyers, even of the written word itself, a snare which often had them entrapped in debt and mortgages.

It was into this environment that Buller planned to introduce a representative of an unheard-of new species – a young *Maori* lawyer. William Fox, at sixteen, was of course not a lawyer, only a junior law clerk, but that was a fine distinction in Maori eyes: he emerged from a lawyer's office in a dark suit, he spoke English and understood the law, and yet he was Maori, he looked like them and spoke their language. Buller the Lawyer – *Pura Roia* – had already acquired a reputation for rapaciousness and his clients were shying away. The boy's presence in the firm could change that.

This was Buller's plan and it worked – again – 'to admiration'. Every morning Buller and his young clerk set out from the house on Boulcott Street (The Terrace mansion just above it was not quite finished) and walked down through the town to chambers. On the way Buller chatted in Maori – the boy's fluency in his own language was important for the success of the plan. In any case, Buller enjoyed walking along Willis Street, talking in Maori. He was fascinated by Darwinism, and he believed an inferior race was fading away before a superior one, according to scientific law. All the same he felt a kind of romantic regret about the transition, and at times he found he preferred Maori company to white in much the same way that he preferred the wild and unique creatures of the New Zealand forest, the sacred *huia* and the flightless night parrot, to the starlings and thrushes which the Acclimatisation Society were releasing into every wind. He did not know whether he agreed with Darwin's classification (Darwin himself being an early social Darwinist) of the Maori as low in the hierarchy of the races, above the naked Indians of Tierra del Fuego, but below, for example, the Tahitians. And what were the effects of hybridisation? To weaken both, or strengthen both or neither? Would amalgamation between the races save the Maori? Would dressing young William Fox in a dark suit and filling his mind with contract law and the rules of conveyancing change the nature of the 'struggle' between the races? What, in fact, was a 'race' anyway?

With these puzzles in his mind, the lawyer walked down Willis Street with his clerk, reached the cobalt-blue harbour which knowledgeable persons compared to Lake Como, turned left and arrived at the chambers of Buller, Lewis & Gully. Buller, Lewis & Gully was already one of the country's leading law firms and occupied a new two-storeyed neoclassic building standing between an ironmongers (with a life-sized iron statue of a lion on the roof) and Nathan's Emporium, the largest store in town, whose pediment was lined with twelve large Italianate urns. Beneath these symbols of force and wealth young Fox began his professional career in the law. In the first few weeks he may have been put to work as the office boy, a famous and pitied figure in the neighbourhood, because the second partner, Lewis, was a stickler for hygiene and the office boy had to swab the floors with carbolic three times a week; the whole street smelled faintly of carbolic, but the fumes clung to the office boy wherever he went.

William Fox was destined to rise quickly above this. We can follow his early career more easily than if he had been white, because Buller saved some of his ordinary and even trivial correspondence with his Maori clients, presumably as mementos of a vanishing people. They are written in Maori and are as dull and baffling as legal correspondence is supposed to be, but among their pages are references to William Fox, or Wiremu Pokiha or Wiremu Poki (his English name rendered into Maori), which give some idea of his progress with Buller, Lewis & Gully.

Some letters are to Buller himself and Fox is mentioned in an aside:

March 4, 1879.
To Buller, Lawyer,
My friend, greetings

This is a word to you to send me the watch you took away from here to be repaired by the watchsmith in Wellington. I gave the cost of the repair, 12 shillings, to Wiremu Poki, in Wanganui, at the time of the second trip he made to Wanganui for the sitting of the Maori Land Court this year 1879. Send it on the mailcoach; in fact if you are coming soon to complete the lease on Ruatangata and to bring the rental monies, you could bring it yourself. If you are not coming for a long time you could send it on the mailcoach this week to Turakina.

That is enough.

From your friend,

Karena Te Mana o Tawhaki

Others are about ordinary business matters:

To Buller, Lawyer,

My friend, greetings

This is a request to you that you make a formal deed for legal transfer of land and all stock and goods. A government agent has come to check the sheeps' brand. The mark on the cows is the same as the mark on the sheep. There are two carthorses, 6 hacks, two carts, 2 ploughs, 200 sheep. All these are held under the name of Taiwhaio Raratiki who with his younger brother owns all these things, etc., etc. –

On the bottom of which Buller has scrawled 'For W. Fox', indicating that he had already begun to put matters into his clerk's hands. By 1880, a third category appears, bypassing Buller altogether.

To William Fox,

Friend greetings,

Your letter arrived on the 1st of this month asking me to reply to your question of 1st of last month about my legal instruction to claim title to my shares in the land that have been dealt with by the Crown . . . Well, my friend, there is no land that belongs to me alone. The lands involved with the Crown title, there are many of us with a claim to these lands. They lie to south of the river at Turakina. No one would know how much land there is for each man . . . None of it belongs to one of us singly. I am chief of this hapu [sub-tribe] and of many hapu that you know of for Block No.3 and I don't want to sell any of this land.

Your loving friend . . . etc.

After two years with the firm, William Fox had made at least two trips to Land Court hearings in Wanganui, once apparently on his own. It was ten years since he had been in Cobb's Coach going in the other direction, a lost child among the Pakeha. And now there he was in a black suit, going along the same road, with a briefcase full of papers and the faint aura of celebrity about him . . . Mr Fox's son, Buller's clerk, the 'first Maori lawyer' . . .

Among Buller's clients were two men whose names he must have remembered. They were Pirimona and Herewini of the tribe Ngati Te Upokoiri, the two men who had caught him in the forest. It must have been strange for them as well to consider the facts. There was the boy whom Pirimona had snatched and Herewini had carried away, and now here he was again. He had grown up, been around the world, seen Boston, London and the Pyramid of Cheops, and now he was back and their comparatively humble affairs were in his hands.

Most of Buller's Maori clients were, naturally enough, from the lower central North Island, from Wanganui, Rangitikei and Manawatu, where he had worked as a magistrate and was widely known. By the late 1870s, the best plums had been picked in that section of the orchard. The real action in the land-market now was further west, in Taranaki, where the separation of the Maori from their land had been delayed by years of war. It was there that Buller turned his attention. And so the time finally came when young William Fox crossed a significant frontier.

One day he took the coach going west from Wanganui, across the Waitotara plains, through Whenuakura and Patea to Hawera, where he stayed the night, and the next day, probably on a winter morning in 1878, he crossed the momentous boundary between settler and Maori territory, the Waingongoro River.

This brings us to a point where it is best to admit ignorance; it is not clear even whether Fox is in a coach any longer, or on horseback, or even on foot. There had been a road built in the early 1870s, but its maintenance was sporadic, as was the coach service. No history has yet been written of the semi-independent Maori world in south Taranaki after Titokowaru's war and it is difficult to make sense of the patchwork of powers and loyalties. Some powerful Maori of the region were extremely friendly to whites, to roads, to coaches, to land sales; others were hostile. It is still more difficult to say anything about William Fox's state of mind at this juncture. Here he was – *home* again; he had crossed the river of his childhood, a river he undoubtedly splashed in as a child near the village of Mawhitiwhiti. He was home. But he did not go home.

Mawhitiwhiti was only a few miles north. The smoke from its fires on a clear morning could easily be seen from the road that Fox was travelling on. He must have known that his father and mother, Te Karere and Hinewai, and the elder brother he had once worshipped, Ake Ake, and his other brothers and sisters were only a few miles away. But he did not go near them. Hard-hearted or shy or perhaps simply feeling alien in these open plains scattered with clumps of forest and with herds of wild cattle, William Fox went on.

He was heading to a place called Parihaka, about fifty miles west of the river. Parihaka was a new Maori town built under the direction of two young chiefs named Te Whiti and Tohu, who had begun to attract a wide following among Maori for a new doctrine they were preaching: peaceful coexistence with the whites, but independence from their rule and, above all, an end to all land sales. It was a strange place for Buller's clerk to be heading; he was probably in search of a signature needed for some uncompleted land deal in Wanganui or Taranaki, and perhaps he thought that among the hundreds of Maori and whites, including interpreters and land officials, who went to Parihaka every month, one young Maori on lawyer's business could pass unnoticed. However, once at Parihaka, he was noticed by one person who knew exactly who he was, and who was to change the whole direction of his life. Before we come to that moment of recognition however, some further explanation of the state of affairs in the district is needed.

The confusion over land ownership in the territory that Fox was travelling through, which stretched for about seventy miles west of the Waingongoro, would be difficult to overstate. Simple malevolence could not alone have achieved the muddle. Squabbling between government departments, political instability (ministries rose and fell like dinghies in the surf), intertribal jealousy, simple forgetfulness and even mortality all played a part. Sir Donald McLean, who tried to untangle the mess, died – quite young – in 1876, leaving things more confused than when he started. If any reader is confused by the following brief account, they should not be too concerned: everyone at the time was puzzled as well.

To recap: during the first stages of the wars, in the early 1860s, the government decided to confiscate large areas of Maori land to punish those tribes which had been 'in rebellion'. When the wars finally sputtered out in about 1870, the tribes of south Taranaki were still in occupation of a great wedge of the 'confiscated' land and the government did not have the military strength or the will to evict them. For the next few years, the legal status of this territory changed with every wind. First, the confiscation was declared abandoned. Then it was said by McLean it 'would not be abandoned but would not be enforced'. Then McLean decided that it would be enforced, but only by recognising that the Maori were the owners. The land, in other words, was all to be taken from them but then all immediately given back; the Maori would get large reserves, under Crown grant, while compensation at market rates would be paid to them for the rest, which would then be sold by the government to white settlers.

But before this happened, McLean proceeded to buy several large blocks which were offered for sale by Maori owners; the form of conveyance was an ordinary deed of cession, and that meant that the confiscation must have been abandoned after all, for a deed of cession meant the land must have reverted to the original native title. To overcome this legal difficulty, a new form of transfer was concocted so that whites could gain possession of blocks of land. There was no deed of conveyance: instead the Maori owners of an area of land which they wanted to sell were made gifts or gratuities, known in Maori as *takoha*. A kind of mad informality now reigned: here, large sums of *takoha* were paid but no land changed hands; there, *takoha* was promised but never delivered over yet the land was taken by whites. *Takoha* as used by the government was a bribe, a sweetener, a sale-price; it was unaudited, and paid out by different officials – the Civil Commissioner, chief surveyors, agents of the Native Minister, even the Native Minister himself – none of them necessarily knowing what the others were up to. Sometimes it was paid to only a few of the owners of a block, sometimes to men with no rights in the property at all; it was paid in secret, it was paid in public, sometimes in cash, at others in 'tinned fruits and jam, and fancy biscuits, with mullet and salmon and lobster, plenty of good ale and wines and 3-star brandy . . . fichus, innumerable shawls, scarves and ribbon and feathers, French merinos and velvets, perfumery and trinkets, side saddles, riding habits and . . . reserved seats at the Star pantomime' and, in one case, in the form of 'counsel retained for Makarita when she was committed to trial for arson'.

There had been several attempts by the government to regularise the situation by one method – surveying the land in question, dividing it into Maori reserves and Crown land to be sold to settlers. This plan was met with the deepest suspicion by the Maori. In 1872, surveyors came across the Waingongoro River to begin work on the Waimate Plains but they were soon turned off. Further unsuccessful attempts were made in the following years. Of all the characters from English life who had presented themselves to Maori eyes in the last century – sailors, missionaries, judges, farmers, soldiers, coachmen, inn-keepers, bureaucrats – none cast a longer shadow before him than the surveyor armed with a theodolite. Wherever he arrived in a district, land in Maori ownership dwindled away. The theodolite itself was called *taipo* – a demon. (*Taipo* was an odd expression: the English assumed it was a Maori word, the Maori thought it was an English one. From what cranny the little dark noun first sprang will probably never be known, but its doubtful parentage did not lessen its force.)

Then, in mid-1876, the survey finally began in earnest. This was allowed by the Maori after repeated assurances that the most ample reserves would be made – all the *pa* sites and burial grounds, cultivations and grazing, fishing stations and river mouths were promised, plus an average of fifty acres per head, with compensation grants to be paid for the rest. After a small, token show of opposition, the Maori occupants of the Plains – about 80,000 acres out of the several hundred thousand acres in question – let the surveyors come forward across the river.

That was the situation that prevailed on the Plains when young Fox crossed them in mid-1878. In other parts of the Maori territory, *takoha* was still being paid, land was still being lost and Te Whiti's principle of peaceful coexistence and an end to all land sales was gaining adherents. Maori of different tribes – this mix itself a novelty in Maori history – had settled in Parihaka, some now landless, some 'loyalists' who had never been paid the promised compensation, some still landowners, and even a few whites (among the first residents was an Irishman named 'Plato' cast out by his own community). Once a month, on the eighteenth, thousands made their way to hear Te Whiti and Tohu speak.

The white authorities were in two minds about this phenomenon. On the one hand, Te Whiti was a 'singular man, a remarkable man' who had kept peace on the coast for years by his influence over the 'most turbulent spirits in the country'. On the other, they did not like the sound of his land policy. Officials complained that the nearer they got to Parihaka, the harder they found it to dispense *takoha*. 'Hold fast to the land,' Te Whiti said. 'Do not sell.'

It was at one of these great meetings at Parihaka that William Fox was seen by someone who knew him.

Here once again we are down to the bare bones of the story. All Miri Rangi could tell me was this:

'His brother Ake Ake saw him at Parihaka and he recognised him, but Fox would not say who he was.'

That is, he would not say who he *really* was. He did not deny that he was William Fox, a law clerk for Dr Buller. What he would not admit was that he was also someone else – namely Ngatau Omahuru, of Mawhitiwhiti, the missing child of the Umuatahi *hapu* (extended family) of the tribe of Nga Ruahine, Taranaki Whanui. In other words, he was Ake Ake's long-lost little brother.

So here is a strange standoff, perhaps down a side street at Parihaka, unobserved by others, the two brothers staring at each other with a peculiar mixture of emotions – joy, dismay, refusal

198

of acknowledgement and an intimation of the fatefulness that links blood relations. Ake Ake, by now aged thirty, was an impressive figure, tall, limber and sombre. His tremendous name, given to him at birth, Ake Ake Whenua – 'Forever the Land' – suited him, or perhaps we should say that he came to suit it, which is sometimes the way with names, and everything about his younger brother must have dismayed him – a land-dealer, no less, a money-grubber, a lawyer, a Maori who had become a kind of Pakeha in a fine suit . . . We do not know exactly how the conversation between the brothers proceeded but we know its outcome, for Ake Ake won the battle of wills, as is the elder brother's due. A month or two later, young Fox, who 'would not say who he was', is known to have made a visit to Mawhitiwhiti, and there, after ten years' absence, he presented himself to his mother and father.

It was a lamentable scene. Only a snatch of a sad and painful conversation has been remembered and was related to me by Miri Rangi. Its subject was Sarah Fox.

'She's my mother,' said Fox.

'No, *I* am your mother,' said Hinewai.

'She *loved* me.'

'*I* loved you!' said Hinewai, and as she spoke she hit her heart with a clenched fist. The gesture, which Miri repeated as she told me this, seemed to have come twisting and turning down through the generations.

'*I* loved you!' said Hinewai. And then she wept. Poor Hinewai, still an invalid, asthmatic and bronchitic, her son, the mischief boy, first missing presumed dead, then years afterwards reported alive, and now – here he was in front of her again, but once more turning away . . .

There was a cruel law at work here. The closer two people are by blood, the more any differences of culture loom between them. By this law of inverse proportionality, everything about the young man, down to the weave of his suit or his way with a

199

spoon, must have shown what a stranger he was. And how strange it all must have seemed to him. For a superior young person like himself, acquainted with the Palace Hotel and Paddington Station, the reed houses of Mawhitiwhiti, the open fires, the mud and bare feet and staring brothers and sisters and neighbours would have been a place where no compass worked as far as he was concerned, where, in short, he was lost. It is little wonder that he turned to the one certain fact of his (often lonely) last ten years – Sarah Fox. '*She's* my mother. She loved me.'

In the end the situation was saved by a practical consideration on the part of his father, Te Karere Omahuru. Te Karere was, on paper, a man of substantial property. There were at least six blocks of land which he or his wife owned or had an interest in,

ranging from a few acres forming a fishing station by the river mouth, to a vast block, 180,000 acres of coastal forest named Moumahaki – 'my rough raincape', Te Karere called it. These different parcels of land now languished in every state of title-confusion. Some had been officially confiscated and were apparently lost for ever. Two were reserves promised some years before but with no Crown grant to establish legal title. One was on land nominally confiscated but as yet unapproached by surveyors. One was a large block that had been wrongly surveyed. One was a block of land for which other Maori claimants had accepted *takoha* but which Te Karere had refused to sell. Everything was at sixes and sevens.

In several of these transactions his greatest enemies were not even the white surveyors, but his Maori neighbours. His main rival was a man named Katene. Oddly enough, Te Karere and Katene had one great thing in common: they had both lost a young son during the battle of the Beak of the Bird. The crippled boy who had his brains dashed out in the forest clearing, while young Ngatau Omahuru looked on, was Katene's son. But there was no bond between the two men. Wherever Te Karere turned, regarding land, Katene Tuwhakaruru was there before him. He was a mercurial figure, a great fighter and a turncoat who had changed sides three times in the last fifteen years. He was a firebrand on the Maori side in the early wars, then he joined the Pakeha and became one of their most trusted scouts and spies. Then he switched back and fought alongside Titokowaru, and now he was on the government side again, the right-hand man of the Taranaki Land Commissioner, Robert Parris, whose main function was to acquire land for white settlement, and of the leading 'loyalist' chief, named Hone Pihama or Ngohi, who dealt in land sales and gathered a rich crop of *takoha*.

It would be impossible in this book, or perhaps any book, to explain the property disputes simmering within and around

Mawhitiwhiti alone at this time. One example should be enough to relieve the reader of regret on this account. Here, just to let us skim above the treetops of one tract of forest, is an excerpt from a speech by Katene discussing a certain disputed reserve, named Tiritirimoana, in which he and Te Karere both had an interest.

> What I am about to say is to follow what has been said about these 10,000 acres. Tangiwa is the name of the kahikitea tree which is the boundary of the block. Te Uene is a *pa* in a clearing inland, belonging to Heke. This is an old boundary line. Araukuku is on one side and Okahu and Kanihi on the other. This was the boundary line decided by Major Brown and Pepe; it was to be the boundary of the 10,000 acres running inland. This boundary line is called Aowhenua. Waingongoro is on one side and Te Uene is on the other. We decided this and went into the question at Ngarongo. We all assembled there . . . I then heard what Major Brown had to say. I and Heke both spoke, and wished the boundary line to be taken back to Waingongoro, like the blocks for Araukuku. But the people for whom this reserve was to be made did not agree to it, because they claimed the land down to the river, and on account of their connection with Te Whiti who said all the land was to come back. We did not finish there but insisted that the reserve should be made. Then Major Brown spoke about the £1,000 *takoha*, which was to be paid to us. I then heard this money was to be paid to Okahu. It was for land the other side of the boundary I mentioned just now, from Onewaia to Te Uene, which was the inland boundary post. We were given notice that this money would be paid at Ngarongo. Some did not agree to take this money, but others did . . .

There are millions of words in the archives along such lines dealing with nineteenth-century Maori land, and none of the

202

above need concern us except, first, it shows how confusing it all was, and, second, that Katene as a matter of course thought that he could run rings around his contemporaries, whether white surveyors or his own neighbours, and that generally he was right. He certainly ran rings around Te Karere Omahuru. But now a new factor was entered into the equation: William Fox.

For Te Karere, it suddenly must have seemed that he was now able to turn the tables on Katene. He had not lost a son after all. His son had returned, and he was changed in ways that could not have been anticipated. He had become a kind of Pakeha.

And he was a *gentleman* (Maori were a snobbish race and watched with interest how rank functioned among the English). Strangest and most potent fact of all, he was *he roia* – a lawyer, associated with Pura Roia and Te Pokiha – Lawyer Buller and The Fox, that is Sir William Fox, two men whose names were well known throughout the Maori world. In essence, the boy had returned with two powerful fathers hovering behind him, and now, as far as Te Karere was concerned, he had three.

Buller certainly arrived in Mawhitiwhiti not long afterwards and met Te Karere. Within a few months, Te Karere had put all his affairs and lands into the hands of Buller and his son. His letters survive, again among Buller's private papers.

Mawhitiwhiti
November 25, 1878
Ki a Te Pura, E Koro, Tena koe
To Buller, Greetings Sir,
I still retain your love, as expressed in the word of God in the Bible you gave me, as food for my spirit, to enlighten my thought, to guide all my plans so that good may come to my own hapu, to Okahu. This is a hapu which has perished, that is, on its own lands. The lands have all been confiscated. Wanganui took the money for this land. My hand never reached out for a half share or a half share of land, never, not since the start of the trouble until now. It is only now I have begun to discuss land matters, because of your son . . .
December 7, 1878
I was standing naked and you clothed me, I was thirsty and you gave me drink, I was hungry and you fed me. I have sent the letter to Sheehan [the Native Minister] about the matters I have left with your son to be dealt with by you both and Sheehan, that is all . . .

December 14, 1878
. . . Buller, I will not forget my duty to entrust to you and to Fox the lands at Turangatapuae and Okahu . . . Oh Buller, you and your son should arrange this. I have asked those lands to be adjudicated by the Court, no matter whether leased

204

lands or lands which were confiscated after the war . . . The lands I left to him were Moumahaki, my rough raincape, so it could be dealt with quickly to assist us in the Court.

December 16, 1878
I am overjoyed to know the administration of all the rents, the timber interests, which are to be exchanged for interests in another block, is with you both, as well as the handling of rental monies, which provide the section of funds due to yourselves as sole administrators.

And so it went on, for two years or longer. Occasionally there were arguments and disappointments. Te Karere also wrote angrily to his son:

Mawhitiwhiti
April 25, 1879
Ki a Wiremu Pokiha
E tama tena koe
To William Fox,
My son, greetings
. . . I am fed up that the money has gone to Te Kaha and [Katene] Tuwhakaruru and they have settled on the land and built a house there I was sure the Court would get it right and settle matters according to the law. I will no longer look to you to help with this land which has been taken by wrong-doers. I will die upon the land here . . .

And he blamed Buller and young Fox for his defeats by his old rival:

My son, it is right for me to be sad that my land has been stolen away. My real regret is that [Katene] Tuwhakaruru has won. Major Brown and Williams are his backers. If Tuwha-

205

karuru was fighting on his own I could have prevailed but I cannot fight him and the Government . . . The length of your process was the problem, and the speed of Tuwhakaruru his weapon – quick money, quick discussion, quick title to land. The Government is behind him and does his bidding. Now I am crippled . . .

But he continued working with Buller and Fox who were his only allies:

May 21, 1879
To Buller,
Greetings
. . . Do not think I have become upset and am avoiding doing what we agreed. There is no doubt that I will get it finished whether or not the world was in turmoil. My love for you and your son will never cease, ever, until my body finally dies. I am fearful now of evil. I seek only what is good, peaceful existence and love one to the other . . .

Things might have continued in this vein until the family's legal position was settled satisfactorily or at least for once and for all. But early in 1879 a great crisis had begun to build up like a wave which was to sweep everyone in this story – Buller, young William Fox, Sir William, Te Karere, Ake Ake, even those figures from the dark past, Major Noake and John Bryce – along in its path. The crisis was generated around a single forceful personality, that of the young chief Te Whiti.

11

The fluff of the thistle

Long before this, in 1862, the year young William Fox was born, the people of the English settlement of New Plymouth to the north of Mt. Taranaki looked out one afternoon and saw an extraordinary sight. Rolling towards the town on the south road was a line of bullock-carts driven by 'fierce looking tattooed Maoris clothed with waist and shoulder mats and hair done up in the old-time top-knot' and containing a large number of white people, men, women and children, well-dressed in top hats or travelling gowns and carrying their baggage, all coming together out of forbidden or enemy territory.

The war, which had begun in 1860, had gone badly for the settlers. Military honours – or the death toll – were about equal for Maori and British, but a stalemate was reached. Around New Plymouth 189 farms were burned out and British Taranaki was reduced to the town of New Plymouth. British commanders could find no way to defeat the Maori who in twenty-four hours could build a fighting *pa* which might take weeks for the sappers to approach, and then abandon the *pa* on the night before battle. The Maori, for their part, could never overcome the global power of the British empire with its thousands of soldiers and marines and command of the seas.

Finally an uneasy truce was established. It was during this truce that the procession of Maori ox-carts and white passengers arrived on New Plymouth's doorstep. The whites had an interesting story to tell. A few days before, they had sailed from New Plymouth on the steamer *Lord Worsley* which about fifty miles down the coast ran aground. The situation was not a healthy one. A crowd of *waeromene* – 'wild men' as the settlers called their enemies – soon materialised on the beach. The passengers came on shore and were greeted calmly, but when one of them reached the top of the cliff he called back to the cook who was still on board, to throw all the ammunition into the sea, to stop it falling into Maori hands. Suddenly tempers flared and the shipwrecked crowd were surrounded by angry Maori. Then two chiefs arrived on the scene and threw their mantle of protection over the whites. One of them was named Eruiti Te Whiti. He had a bullock slaughtered to feed the whites, sent a message to town to announce that the passengers and crew were safe and organised transport back to New Plymouth. It was Te Whiti's men who, a day or two later, arrived outside New Plymouth, cracking whips over the oxen and bringing the whites home.

This was the first time that the existence, and the authority, of Te Whiti, who was probably at that time only thirty years old, came to the notice of people beyond his own tribal borders.

The safe return of the crew and passengers caused grave disappointment in New Plymouth. News of the maritime wreck had electrified the provincial capital. 'Much excitement and hope of a fight,' Arthur Atkinson, one of the leading settlers and a member of the 'Mob', as the Richmonds, Atkinsons, Hurst-houses and Carringtons called themselves, recorded in his diary. 'Everyone cheerful, as question about to be tried.' A military expedition was hastily organised but then the letter from Te Whiti arrived upsetting all the plans.

'Trial did not come off,' Atkinson noted, before going down to watch the arrival of the Maori drovers. 'It was curious to see these fellows whom we have been trying to knock on the head industriously for two years and who have tried with equal industry to knock us on the head, here in the midst of us. They have constantly denied our authority (i.e. of the law) and show no signs of any intention to abandon their old custom and before long we shall probably be at each other's throats again, but there was nothing like ill-feeling shown and everything was settled quietly.'

Atkinson was an eager reader – his diary records that that month he was 'reading *Origin of the Species* before breakfast' – and sometimes gives the impression of being rather sensitive, certainly more so than his warlike brother Harry, a future Prime Minister, or his fierce wife Jane Maria. When the 'Mob' had finally managed to engineer the war in 1860, Arthur wrote: 'After the battle I lay in the fern looking up at the constellation of Orion and his Belt, wondering, in the event of meeting death by the hands of the Maoris, which star I might be sent to next.'

Arthur was not sent to a star and even when the war went badly he and the other leading settlers could not be weaned away from their policy. Visiting New Plymouth, Bishop Selwyn pleaded from the pulpit: 'O earth! earth! earth! such has been our cry. The Queen, law, religion, have been thrust aside in the one thought, of the acquisition of land.' In Auckland, Selwyn tried again:

'He talked', Richmond's wife wrote to her husband, 'of a little island in the Western seas 1,800 years ago whose inhabitants were so fierce that strangers dared not trust themselves upon their coast, and so little valued even in the slave market at Rome they sold for the lowest price. He said God had waited 1,800 years for us, but that we, after less than fifty years among the Maori, were longing to fly at their throats and say "Pay me what thou owest", or "Let him die an easy death, that is the most he can expect".'

His words had no effect. Conceited and half-educated (a 'school attached to University College, London', is the highest seat of learning that can be spied among their biographies), 'the Mob' saw themselves as great radicals, leading the charge against the conventions. The most ferocious of them all, the feminist Jane Maria Atkinson, raged against the influence of the missionaries ('Government House is swarming with black suits and white chokers') and was all for war, whatever the costs: 'It might do us a great deal of good to have our homes burnt over our heads,' she declared. 'I don't know that anyone goes "the whole animal" to the extent I do on Native Affairs.'

During the worst phases of the fighting, the Mob did not lose heart. In July 1860, the English dead (led into action by a monocled dandy named Captain Beauchamp–Seymour, known in the navy as 'the Swell of the Ocean') lay so thickly scattered through a swamp at a place called Puketatauere that it was given a new name by the Maori meaning 'the place where the maize cobs are left to steep'. But the same week, an event took place in England which was to change the temper and increase the velocity of colonial expansion in New Zealand. This was the famous debate held in Oxford between supporters and opponents of Darwin's theory of evolution. As everyone knows, the debate was a triumph for the Darwinists and rationalists and a disaster for the Bishop of Oxford and his supporters. News of the contest did not reach the Antipodes for several months but when it arrived the accounts were keenly relished by the radicals. Of particular interest to them was the performance of a certain Admiral FitzRoy who took up the cause of literal interpretation of the Old Testament and came marching down the aisle of the hall crying, 'The Book! The Book!' He then made a speech stating that he had often expostulated with Darwin for entertaining views contradictory to the first book of Genesis.

FitzRoy was already notorious in Taranaki. He had been captain of the *Beagle* during Darwin's voyage, and had written and edited the first two volumes of the *Voyage of the Beagle*

210

(leaving the third to Darwin). In this he offered his opinion on the treatment and government of indigenous races by Europeans and his humanitarian views struck a chord in Whitehall at that time. FitzRoy, who had visited New Zealand with Darwin in the 1830s, returned there as Governor in the 1850s and it was FitzRoy who had taken the Maori side in the first land disputes between the races in Taranaki.

His defeat at Oxford on 30 July, 1860, must have delighted the Richmonds and Atkinsons. A new order was coming and the old order of 'sanctimonious' idealism was passing away. Whatever they thought privately of Darwin's Theory, it seemed to provide an unanswerable public justification for conflict ('struggle') and sustained the argument of the Richmonds and their supporters in England that 'war between the races must come sooner or later' (an idea so silly, said Hadfield, one might as well defend a murderer by saying that his victim was sure to die one day or other). And the Theory became a kind of burglar's jemmy to get at Maori land. When McLean proposed to restore some confiscated territory, Richmond jeered at this as an attempt to 'reverse the law of Natural Selection' and the principle of Survival of the Fittest.

Fittest for *what*? the more cautious settlers wondered, remembering the pillars of smoke rising from distant farms and the funeral carts rolling up and down New Plymouth's main street. Darwin himself, who was anti-slavery, passionately pro-North in the US Civil War and horrified by the repression in Jamaica, was cautious about the application of his theory to human races, for it was clear to him that mankind's environment is not merely physical but is constituted also by what he believes in. But the damage was already done; he had already written about inferior and superior human races and, in *Origin of Species*, he wrote:

From the extraordinary manner in which European productions have recently spread in New Zealand, and have seized on places which must have previously been occupied by the

211

indigenes, we must believe that if all the animals and plants of Great Britain were set free in New Zealand, a multitude of British forms would in the course of time become thoroughly naturalised, and would exterminate many of the natives . . .

Nothing, therefore, could stop the settlers from expanding the theory to include the two races. 'Liberation' of the settlers and 'extermination of the Maori' crept into the minds and newspaper columns of the colony as the inevitable effects of a scientific law.

Not long after the wreck of the *Lord Worsley*, a new Governor, George Grey, was sent out to try and solve the disputes between Maori and whites. Grey had already served as Governor in the 1850s and had learned the language, surrounded himself with Maori friends, compiled Maori poetry and legends. Now he was swept along in the new belligerent mood. He seized another disputed block south of New Plymouth, then invaded the Waikato and eagerly adopted Domett's plan for confiscation of millions of acres. The wars resumed in earnest.

Very little is known about Te Whiti's activities over the next seven years. The war began in Taranaki then moved off across the island like a brush fire, flaring up in the Waikato, in the Bay of Plenty, on the East Coast – where it turned into a Maori civil war – then back to Taranaki. Te Whiti was almost certainly present at one battle in 1864 but whether he fought or not or simply carried the *tokotoko*, a chief's staff, is not known. For the last four years of the fighting, however, Te Whiti took no part and retreated into territorial seclusion, in accordance with the message from his ally, King Tawhiao, head of a confederation of Waikato tribes:

Lay down your weapons. Be wise. I am going home to weep over my lost brothers. Though the whites exterminate the trunk, they cannot pull out the roots . . . Let no European

cross the border of this, our last free Maoriland. We want no
roads or schools from them. Let them do with their lands what
they will.

This seclusion was never to be permitted. It is a strange fact of
history that no matter how far the original inhabitants moved
away, the British newcomers, who often professed a desire to be
rid of the Maori, followed them. Te Whiti himself, years later,
once said to a government agent while passing through a remote
and uninhabited part of the South Island:

'Do not the Pakehas use everything?' he asked. 'Nothing is
spared by them. Here there are fine harbours and plenty of
lands, why don't you use them?'
I told him that the country was too high and rough.
'Yes,' he replied. 'If there were Maories living here, even as
rough and broken as it is, white men would come and dispossess
them. It is because there are no Maories living here in these horns
and bays of the sea, that you pakehas find this land useless.'*

But there was more to it than that. There was something else in
the attraction which the Maori world held for Europeans,
which, even from the early days of settlement, sounds oddly
like nostalgia for the Maori past. Jung has a theory that colonised
people begin to colonise the soul of their conquerors. To put it
another way, the Maori had been shaped for generations by this
country which was now to shape the English who had come to
settle there. If, in the nineteenth century, the Maori represented
the past to the settlers, they also represented the future.

And this attraction, like the force of gravity, worked both
ways. When the Pakeha arrived over the horizon, with his
innumerable possessions, his *things* – guns, watches, books – he

* John Ward, *Wanderings with the Maori Prophets, Te Whiti and Tohu*, Nelson, 1883.

213

in turn represented a mystery to the Maori – the wide world and all the events which the Polynesians had missed for several millennia. The Maori, despite their carved meeting-houses and jade clubs, were still living in the Stone Age. They had never seen metal. They had never seen a mammal larger than the low-slung Polynesian dog. They declined to believe in the existence of such a creature as a horse when it was described to them. When the first herd of cows disembarked on a beach in North Auckland, there was consternation:

> The Maoris . . . regarded them as stupendous prodigies. Their astonishment soon turned to alarm and confusion, for one of the cows that was wild and unmanageable, being impatient of restraint, rushed in among them and caused such violent terror through the whole assemblage, that imagining some preter-natural monster had been let loose to destroy them, they immediately betook themselves to flight.

Just as the Maori world was in a sense in the future of the settlers, the European world represented the future for the Maori. The stories, religious beliefs and the intellectual possessions of the newcomers were as sensational as their material goods. After the first missionaries arrived, there was a wave of voluntary manu-missions across Maoridom. When the freed slaves reappeared in their old homes up and down the country, as if back from the dead, and in some cases accompanied by their former masters, the new religion spread with them.

> If in 1860 [one European observer said] there was no hostility to the Queen, there was also little to the settlers. There was of course always a body of wild men who talked of throwing the Europeans into the sea, but they were heard with impatience. At one of the evening meetings which was held in a large house lighted up for the occasion, one of the advocates of a

general clearing-out of whites was pressing his views when Tarawhaiki walked quietly round and one after another put out the lights, till the place was in total darkness and the speaker in possession of the house was brought to a full stop.

'Don't you think you had better light up those candles again?' he asked. 'Most certainly!' replied Tarawhaiki. 'It was very foolish to extinguish them.'

The meeting at once apprehended the meaning of his words and the orator sat down amid roars of laughter at his expense.

That meeting was at Taupo in 1856. Several years later, when the wars were over, few Maori would have compared the Europeans to the light of a candle in a dark house. January 1869 was probably the darkest period in the history of the two races. Children were being murdered by both sides and hatred was everywhere.

It was in that month that Robert Parris, Civil Commissioner for Taranaki, rode down the coast and into Parihaka, the new town recently built by Te Whiti. The two men had not met for years, though they had not been far away; New Plymouth and Parihaka are about twenty-five miles apart. Parris, the chief land-purchase officer and one of the principal players in the purchase at Waitara, was greeted by Te Whiti with a memorable phrase.

'Let the great matters of difference which have separated us be settled,' he said. 'You have been lost to us and we have been lost to you.'

Te Whiti was born in, probably, 1832, a date with which most of the authorities agree, although not his own tombstone which gives his birth as 1817. The discrepancy sums up the state of information about his early life. As a youth he came into contact with Christianity through one of the freed slaves mentioned above. When the Rev. Riemenschneider, a German Lutheran,

215

landed on the coast in 1846, he met Te Whiti with the words: 'I come in peace and bring you God's Word.'

'Yes, we know that Word and greet you in peace,' the young man answered. The young Te Whiti sought out the company of Europeans, had a prodigious memory, was a 'smart athlete', and lost a middle finger in the millstones while grinding wheat at the Lutheran mission. Some report the finger was on his left hand, others on his right. During his life Te Whiti was interviewed by dozens of journalists and officials, and was seen by thousands of Maori and whites who flocked to listen or watch. Perhaps it is a sign of his forceful personality and oratory that no one noticed his age or which finger was missing. How he gained his authority at an early age, his working relationship with Tohu, the differences between them (sometimes their followers clashed) are all unclear. The biography of Te Whiti has not been written; when it is it will be by someone, presumably a Taranaki Maori, with access to the oral tradition, including his speeches and the songs composed by and about him. In the meantime, we have to rely on often hostile official and newspaper sources. By 1870, on the seventeenth of every month, the anniversary of the beginning of the wars, thousands of people were coming to Parihaka to hear Te Whiti speak.

He was a marvellous metaphorist. His main message until about 1877 was always the same: *Do not sell your land*. The sale-price was like honey deposited by the bees high in a tree. To sell was like felling the tree to get the honey. 'Then there would be great trouble and death among the bees. Some would wander away and be no more seen; others would stay around their old house and perish miserably.'

Or, to sell was like hanging the land on the forehead of a strong man (the government) who could never be approached again.

Or: *E kore e piri te uku ki te rino, ka whitia e te ra* – 'Clay will not stick to iron when the sun shines.' Iron was the white man, clay

216

was the Maori who sold his land, and the moisture that stuck the two together was money. But when the sun shines, the clay dries and falls to pieces.

Ka whitia e te ra . . . 'When the sun shines . . .' Sunlight always stood for the same thing: clear, dry reality when the illusions vanish, when the hangover comes, when the children are crying and the land was gone.

'The tribes are like the fluff of the thistle. When the sun shines, you know it is dry.' There seems at first to be something missing from this sentence, and then you realise there is an undescribed gesture . . . up and out went Te Whiti's hand, invisible thistledown was blowing in the wind.

Two thousand Maori watched every gesture. *They* were the fluff of the thistle. They were, almost literally, in the palm of Te Whiti's hand. He was the greatest orator of the day. 'I do not know a single member of either branch of the Legislature who combines to anything like the same degree his graceful attitude, earnest expression and easy eloquence without a hint of declamatory rant,' wrote S. Croumbie-Brown, an English correspondent who had covered the US Civil war, been a confidant of Ulysses S. Grant, was disliked by the local journalists ('he is either a disguised Duke or undisguised snob') and who was in time to play a role surprising for a journalist and become a minor but crucial figure in the events about to unfold in Taranaki. 'Having heard Te Whiti addressing his people, it is not hard to comprehend the secret of his great power over them.'

Te Whiti refused to be photographed and would not agree even to a pencil sketch being made of him. Many European visitors to Parihaka therefore offered their own descriptions: 'He is one of the most prepossessing natives I have ever seen. Through his features the intelligence of the man beams out. His complexion is very light, his hair dark, streaked freely with grey, and his features mobile and expressive when at rest. His face is very sad with a look of meditation. In conversation his

217

face becomes animated, his eyes sparkle and his smile wins one's good will at once. He is very fond of controversy, especially on Biblical subjects, and possesses a good stock of general information, showing that he is a reader of the newspapers. When addressing the natives, one loses all consciousness of his insignificant stature in watching his face. His address is then commanding, his eyes flash fire, and his voice is impressive.'

Even Titokowaru fell under Te Whiti's spell. At one of the early meetings at Parihaka, Titokowaru and his men came down from the hills, firing their guns in the air. Te Whiti stopped speaking and went towards them.

'Titokowaru the man is welcome,' he said. 'But when Waru the man comes to Parihaka, Waru the warrior must stay at home.'

Titokowaru indicated his armed men behind him, and called: 'Who is behind *you*?'

Te Whiti answered: 'God.' Titokowaru laid down his guns and, not without occasional misgivings and rebelliousness, submitted his *mana toa*, his prestige as a fighting chief, to the *mana* of Te Whiti.

Even the land officer Robert Parris – 'always in such a fearful hurry and bluster, a worshipper of power and a grinder of the person in a low position', as one of his employees called him – could not help being impressed by his greatest obstacle. Te Whiti was 'a fanatic imbued with peaceful desires,' he wrote, 'who would set the country ablaze if that way disposed,' but he added that there was no sign that he was so disposed and the force of his personality was unmistakable. 'Your Whanganui natives came to Parihaka,' Parris told a colleague, 'breathing that [they] would confute Te Whiti and annihilate his influence, but they were like innocent curs barking at the moon and soon retired into the shade.'

If some thought he was a fanatic, and others worried about his hold over Maori tribes along the whole west coast, Te Whiti was seen by most people in and out of government as a peace-maker, a 'singular' and 'amiable' man whose influence was benign.

This perception began to change in the year 1878, when the question of forcible confiscation returned. The man who raised it again was John Ballance. He was no longer the editor of the *Wanganui Evening Herald*; he had gone into politics, risen quickly and was now Colonial Treasurer. From the outskirts of Wanganui on a very clear day it is possible to see Mt. Taranaki ninety miles away to the west, a triangle glittering above the lowlands. Perhaps it was this sight that reminded Ballance that there was unfinished business between Maori and white. He began to promote a plan to survey and sell the Waimate Plains by force, which would put half a million pounds in the treasury.

Te Whiti's attitude to confiscation was complex and, like a lawyer's list of arguments, contradictory. First he argued that since his and the adjacent tribes had never signed the Treaty of Waitangi, they had never become British subjects and therefore could not be punished for 'rebellion' by loss of land. Then he claimed that he had never been in arms against the Queen, so that the confiscation did not apply to him. Thirdly, that the confiscated land had never been conquered in a fair fight, so to speak, and had not been occupied by the whites. Fifteen years had gone by. How, by the stroke of a pen, or the whim of a Treasurer, could it suddenly become white-owned? Fourth, he pointed to the promises from McLean that the confiscation would not be enforced.

Despite these arguments, it is clear that Te Whiti was prepared to accept confiscation even at this late date, on one condition – that 'adequate' reserves (the figure generally bandied about was between a quarter and a third of the territory) were set aside for the Maori. The government made promises to this effect. When the surveyors finally appeared on the Waimate Plains, Titokowaru, whose land lay directly in their path, put the whole matter in Te Whiti's hands. 'Enough blood has been shed for that land,' Te Whiti said. 'Let no more be shed.'

This was in the spring of 1878, at the same time as young William Fox was reunited with his family.

For seven months the surveyors came on, working closer and closer to Maori settlements, cutting through gardens and trampling crops, running a line right to Titokowaru's door and making sectionalised blocks suitable for sale to white farmers, with no sign of the promised communal Maori reserves. No one has ever found an explanation for these actions. Finnerty, the chief surveyor, was said to be a 'particularly stubborn' man, but the fact that he repeatedly flouted the instructions of the Native Department raises the suspicion that he was working secretly with some element in the government, perhaps led by Ballance, that did not want peaceful accommodation with the Maori.

In late March 1879, on Te Whiti's orders, the Maori on the Plains surrounded the surveyors, packed them, their instruments and camping equipment on to carts, and conveyed them all to the far side of the Waingongoro river.

After the surveyors were evicted from the Plains, Te Whiti was demonised on all sides. He was no longer the man of peace, according to the Native Minister, John Sheehan, but a false prophet or a 'believer in his own fanaticism' who 'for years past . . . has been prophesying the disappearance of the Europeans . . . like a "swish" from the face of the country.'

Sheehan knew this was not true and he carefully concealed from Parliament the record of a long conversation between Te Whiti and a special commissioner named Mackay who was sent to report on the crisis. Mackay's telegram, describing his interview, has been described as the most accurate and revealing record of Te Whiti's view that the government ever received. It was suppressed since it showed that Te Whiti was eminently sane. It also reveals that he had a sense of humour – a rare thing in a fanatic and, presumably, in a false prophet as well.

Te Whiti: Tell me plainly what you want.

Mackay: I want you and the Government to come to an amicable arrangement about all the confiscated lands. I fear that if you persist in stopping the survey evil will arise, and I wish to see the matter settled quietly.

Te Whiti: The land is mine. I do not admit your right to survey it. My blanket is mine: do you think it right for you to attempt to drag it from my body and clothe yourself with it? If I tried to tear your coat from your back you would resist me and you would not be to blame for doing so. What right have I to take your coat forcibly from you?

Mackay: I do not ask you to give your blanket to me, and you remain naked. I say, spread the blanket . . . and let you and the Governor sit down on it in friendship.

Te Whiti: That will not do. You want to cut my blanket in two. It will be too small for me then. I have already given up enough land to the Governor and he should be satisfied with all the country he has between Waitotara and Waingongoro. Pull off your trousers; give me one leg and you keep the other. You hesitate. Do it at once; let me have one leg; you can keep one leg of your legs in, and we shall walk about together. Do it quickly!

Mackay: . . . The Government will persist in the survey.

Te Whiti: The land is mine; you neither conquered it nor do you occupy it by force . . . As you came along, Blake, did you show Mackay the line cut through the cultivations at the door of Titokowaru's house?

Captain Blake: Yes, we saw that.

Te Whiti: Where, then, is the piece to be retained by the Natives? . . . You say, let me and the Governor sit down on the blanket together. The Governor will not do that; he is dragging it all away for himself . . . You will do us a great wrong, and you ought to be ashamed of it, oppressing a people because they are smaller in number than yourselves.

221

Even at this point, it was clear from the record that Te Whiti was ready for compromise. 'With an eager expression' he then asked whether Mackay was authorised to offer him a part of the land. Mackay said he could not make a definite proposal but that he would return to the government and 'if there is anything of importance to communicate, we will return to see you'.

Here again a puzzle arises. Plans were in fact drawn up in Wellington, with several thousand acres marked out as reserves, but no one was sent to Parihaka to inform Te Whiti.

After waiting two months, Te Whiti produced a master-stroke which was to make him famous throughout the country and further afield. It was a Sunday morning towards the end of autumn. Calm reigned on the farms across white-owned Taranaki, some of which had been in European ownership for almost twenty years. Seven miles out of New Plymouth, Mr William Courtenay of Oakura awoke to the fact that something unusual was afoot on his land. In the early light he saw fifteen or twenty strangers moving across his land. Human beings rarely, if ever, 'rub their eyes in disbelief', so let us say simply he could not believe his eyes. The unknown strangers, all Maori, had come with horses and ploughs and they were calmly turning one of his grass paddocks into plough-land. Courtenay rushed to town and telegraphed the Premier: 'Five ploughs and 20 hostile natives are ploughing my best field . . . If the Government do not remove them at once I will shoot their horses and the natives also.'

The same scene was repeated across Taranaki. Over the next two months, on dozens of white farms from Pukearehu in the north to Hawera in the south, ploughmen appeared before dawn and worked until dusk. They descended on the land around a constabulary post; they carved up the front lawn of a leading Hawera settler. Although it was agreed that they were 'very civil and dignified' and no settler was ever threatened, the anxiety and anger of the farmers rose.

222

Te Whiti remained calm. Even if both Maori and European together tried 'to create a war, it would be in vain'. He was ploughing the *puku* – the vital parts – of the government, he said, in order to strike deep at European passions and emotions. There was a simple reason for it all: 'I am cutting a furrow to the Governor's heart.'

The government felt the furrow more deeply than it cared to admit. It became clear early on that the ploughmen were not 'wild men' trying to evict the settlers and take back the farms. They were in many cases loyalists or neutrals who had lost their land in the first round of confiscation and fifteen years later were still landless and without the compensation that had been promised them.

How can we trust your promises to us when we see the effect of the promises made even to your friends? That was the point of Te Whiti's *coup de théâtre*, illustrations of which were already on their way by sea to London and soon to appear in the pages of the illustrated weeklies. The ploughmen, like those in a medieval woodcut, look oddly remote from all the world's affairs, although the picture shows them surrounded by crowds of

223

policemen, settlers and seated Maori, all in a field under the snowcapped mountain.

The settlers formed volunteer units, and began drilling and building blockhouses. Near Hawera a hundred armed vigilantes descended on one ploughing party and carted them across the Waingongoro Bridge, where Maori gathered on one side and the settlers on the other. Harry Atkinson – the brother of Arthur, and now the local member of Parliament, told the *Taranaki Herald*: 'He hoped, if war did come, it would mean the extermination of the natives.'

'Perhaps', wrote the *Patea Mail*, 'the present difficulty will be one of the greatest blessings ever New Zealand has experienced for without doubt it will be a war of extermination. The time has come in our minds when New Zealand must strike a blow for freedom, and this means the death-blow to the Maori race.'

To appease the settlers, Major Noake was brought back and put in command of the local military district. He at once set about 'increasing rather than decreasing excitement in the district', according to his former commander, Colonel Whitmore, who was now in the government.

After two months of crisis, and the arrest of about two hundred men – the first of whom to be tried received a year's jail for 'maliciously breaking the soil of a certain field, to the value of five shillings'; the rest were held without trial – the government conceded there was some justice in the Maori case. 'It turns out that from the White Cliffs down to Waitotara the whole country is strewn with broken promises,' the Native Minister, Sheehan, told Parliament in July.

This seemed to point towards a compromise, but the government's only action was to pass a bill allowing Maori prisoners to be held without trial. Apart from that, the ministry was in any case beyond making plans: it was collapsing in on itself. Once more the spotlight settled on Sir William Fox. He was elected leader of the opposition and in his speech, described by a historian twenty years later as 'perhaps the most merciless ever heard in the House', he moved a motion of no confidence. The main issue was the crisis on the West Coast. Fox attacked Sheehan for 'shaking his fist in Te Whiti's face', but his main objection was to the sexual conduct of the Native Minister. Fox, a great puritan who disliked sex as much as he did alcohol, was outraged at the stories about Sheehan, a smooth-talking Catholic lawyer with a penchant for pretty Maori girls. 'You cannot travel into any part of Maoridom . . . without hearing tales which make us blush for our country . . . You may track the progress of the Government through the districts in which they have travelled by the foul and foetid odours they have left behind.'

A few days later, the government fell. At Te Whiti's order, the ploughing ceased. The new government's first act was to announce that a commission of enquiry would be held into 'the existence and extent of all alleged unfulfilled promises in regards to land'. In due course, Fox was appointed to head the commission of enquiry, with Francis Dillon Bell and a Maori chief named Mohi Tawhai sitting alongside him.

This was intended as window-dressing to soothe public opinion at home and abroad. The new ministry was, in fact, of more ferocious temper than the old one. It included the bellicose Harry Atkinson, a new Attorney-General named Whitaker, 'cold, subtle, shrewd', and a Native Minister who had never held a cabinet post before. He did not believe that any promises had been broken or, if they had, he did not care. He denounced Te Whiti as a man 'far gone in insanity'. His answer to the question of disputed Maori land was simply to take it all by force if necessary and settle the coast with a 'close population' of white farmers, and leave the Maori whatever reserves the government pleased. His first parliamentary bill extended the imprisonment without trial of the ploughmen, whom he soon had secretly moved to South Island gaols.

The Native Minister's name was John Bryce.

Many of the Maori population were incredulous and alarmed. Was this the same Bryce they had heard of, Bryce-*kohuru*, Bryce the murderer, they asked. It was. To the Maori on the coast, the two faces of government, represented by Fox and by Bryce, now looked towards the West Coast with the same expression, empty and menacing.

But then Sir William Fox, as contrary as ever, changed his mind. Once in the role of commissioner, his vanity and elder statesman's ambition led him to believe that it had fallen to him alone to solve the West Coast issue. In any case, he could not bring himself to play the role of second fiddle to a man like Bryce. If anyone was to deal with Te Whiti, whom he acknowledged was 'a remarkable man', it should really be another remarkable man – Sir William himself.

And there was another factor which affected Fox's view of Te Whiti – the single unvarying spectre in Sir William's mind, the bottle of liquor that was always floating before his eyes. His passion for teetotalism had, if anything, increased in his old age. Since returning from his lecture tour to Britain, for instance, there had been only one social gathering at Westoe – a picnic on the lawn in 1877 for five hundred Total Abstainers who drank squash and played Quoits, cricket and something called the 'Jolly Miller'. 'At five o'clock,' the local paper reported reverently, 'the company withdrew. By sundown, Westoe had returned to its normal air of quiet.'

Social events at Parihaka were not quite so grisly, but grog-sellers were expelled from the village and if there was drink it was distributed free with the food on the *marae*. At Parihaka, as Sir William noted, there were none of those 'sickening sights, so shameful to ourselves, of a crowd of Maoris of both sexes filling the purlieus of a publichouse in a state of wild intoxication . . .

'Te Whiti . . . has so often shown a strong moral sense and ever laboured to elevate the character of his people,' Fox added, and nothing would do more to reconcile him to the settlement

226

of the country than the 'certainty that the advancing wave of civilization would not bring with it . . . the curse and destruction [of drink]'.

On 20 January 1880, the Commission of Inquiry into alleged Grievances of Aboriginal natives in relation to certain Lands taken by the Crown was established. The first hearings of the Commission opened on 11 February 1880.

A few days earlier, however, Bryce had moved hundreds of armed men over the Waingongoro River and on to the Waimate Plains, on the pretext of 'repairing the road'. 'Even though the bayonets of the soldiers blind your eyes with their brightness, do not flinch,' Te Whiti told his audience at Parihaka on 18 February.

'Old things have been swept away and new things are coming . . . What if the Government takes the land? The Government have nothing but their guns. We can only look on and laugh.'

On 13 February, as the Commission began its hearings in the little town of Oeo, and the soldiers built watchtowers and blockhouses, a comet was reported in the papers. In the night sky, one correspondent wrote, it appeared to be 'descending directly on to the Waimate Plains'.

12

'Gone to the devil'

The West Coast Commission opened in the Town Hall of Hawera for a reading of its terms of inquiry in English and Maori and then immediately adjourned. The first real hearing came a week later, in the little settlement of Oeo – a dusty hotel, two small houses and a woolshed – twenty miles down the coast from Parihaka and one day after the meeting there.

Te Whiti, when he heard where the commissioners were, smiled and said: 'Yes, they are there to catch the Maoris going home from Parihaka. They don't know how to catch them any other way.'

About two thousand people had gone to the great meeting at Parihaka that month. On their way home, one newspaper reported, 'natives approaching Oeo were one by one stopped by Mr Parris and Mr Williams who begged them to come before the Commissioners. The natives laughed and passed on, not a single one going to the deserted hotel.'

This was not quite accurate: the hotel was not completely deserted. There were several of the best-known loyalist chiefs present and a few plaintiff waifs and strays, including one Maori who had run away to sea as a boy, 'gone to see London', and fought for the English in India and China, and who now wanted some land to call his own. Te Whiti dismissed such applicants. The Commission was gathering chaff, he said. He himself had already bagged the wheat.

Among the chaff were William Fox junior, and his father, Te Karere Omahuru.

Throughout all the recent upheavals – the eviction of surveyors, the ploughing demonstrations, the appearance of Bryce's 'road repairing' army – young William Fox had kept up his new relationship with his family, partly as long-lost son, partly as legal adviser. The family was affected by the growing turmoil around Te Whiti, though less than many in the district. Te Karere was more interested in his legal battles with his rival, Katene Tuwhakaruru, than the events across the plains, and in his letters to his son he made only one fleeting and somewhat inscrutable mention of Te Whiti: 'We are all waiting for Sheehan's army to destroy Parihaka. Listen, when that day comes, Te Whiti says that will not be a battle between mortals.'

There was some division of feeling in the family. Ake Ake, one of Te Whiti's supporters, was at first involved in the ploughing, but he then fell ill and thus failed to get himself arrested and deported. Young Fox himself had by now visited Parihaka again and met Te Whiti, who was interested in the young man from two worlds, representing the things Te Whiti most abhorred – land sales and lawyer's snares – not to mention the man whose name he bore, Sir William, 'that fox, who confiscated the land and made promises which were broken'. (Te Whiti himself also had an English name, Edward, in his youth, but a decade before had returned to his birth name, Te Whiti o Rongomai, which means 'the shining flight of the god Rongomai whose symbols are comets and meteors'.)

Te Whiti took the visitor aside and spoke to him privately: 'You should be working for your own race,' he said. 'Stand by your own people.' But Buller's clerk remained unmoved, which shows some strength of character, for few people could resist a personal appeal from Te Whiti, and he went back to his business in the office in Wanganui. But the two seem to have remained on friendly terms. In mid-January, just as the army was massing, a certain Mrs Bartlett who ran a hotel at Opunake ten miles around the coast from Parihaka made a visit there. She received 'quite an ovation from the Maoris', according to the newspapers, as the first white woman to visit the town. (The Wanganui paper actually said 'the first woman', but perhaps it was a printer's error.) Te Whiti came out to greet her, called for an interpreter and then he 'had a long *korero* [talk] with her, saying she had nothing to fear. He was father of all in the district and wished to live in peace with the Europeans . . . He said there would be no fear of any fighting taking place, for the Europeans and the Natives were to live peaceably together. The English, he knew, were a very strong people, much stronger than the Maoris, and could crush the Maori to the ground if they chose, but he knew they would not do so.'

This *vignette* is interesting in itself, but also because Mrs Bartlett and her companion, a young telegraph clerk from Wanganui named W. F. Gordon, who was one day to become a leading local historian, came to Parihaka armed with a letter of introduction from Gordon's friend, young Fox, who by now was known as William Fox Omahuru.

The hearings lasted about two months and the commissioners, with a baggage-train of stenographers, secretaries, translators and surveyors (Sir William was convinced that half the trouble had been caused by informal promises never written down or recorded in an orderly way), wandered in a great semicircle around the mountain from Hawera to Oeo to Hawera to Waitara to New Plymouth to Hawera to Patea.

On at least two occasions Sir William announced that the Commission would go to Parihaka. Te Whiti, it was known, was eager to see them there. But both times, Bryce complained and put a stop to the plan. Sir William disliked staying in hotels in the small colonial towns, their public bars below him filled with roistering settlers and Maori, and it is entertaining to think of the ageing knight, kept awake at night by the row below his window in the streets of Waitara or Hawera, thinking wistfully of being abed in quiet and sober Parihaka.

On the other hand, the further the commissioners kept away from Parihaka, the more eminent and numerous were the Maori claimants who appeared before them. Te Whiti, it appeared, had not bagged all the wheat. But the underlying problem with the whole enterprise began to emerge. Although the terms of the inquiry were extremely broad – to look into *any* grievances regarding the land – Fox absolutely refused to allow the validity of the confiscation itself to be questioned. Thus an unspoken range of injustices rose around the little courthouses and town halls where the Commission sat, but they were not to be looked at or mentioned. Whenever anyone tried, Fox cut them off or treated them to a speech in the annoying metaphorical style many whites imagined was irresistible to Maori taste. One chief named Ngahina, for instance, whose village of Pokaikai had years before been attacked at night, during a truce, by Colonel McDonnell, and who had already had lands confiscated at Waitotara, Whenuakura, Patea and Tangahoe, demanded to know why, twelve years later, he should now learn that thousands more acres were still to be taken from him on the north side of the Waingongoro.

'What does it signify to the Europeans that a few years pass over?' asked Fox. 'It does not signify whether it takes a short time or a long time, because the English people is like a river which is always flowing. It is quiet and it is deep, and it flows from its source to the sea, straight on; and when people put a dam in it, unless the dam is for some good purpose, the water goes over it and presently carries it away. Whereas the Native people is like a sieve with small holes in the bottom of it; it looks for a moment as if it were full of water, but if you look at it next day you will see that the level is lower, and the following day the level is still lower, and the next day lower still. And where is the river that is to pour to fill it up again? We listened patiently to what Ngahina said, but he must understand that it is nonsense about all the land on the other side [of the Waingongoro] being left for him and his people.'

William Fox Omahuru appeared at three of the sessions in different towns, on occasion spoke on behalf of his family and at other times on behalf of all the people of Mawhitiwhiti. He was at pains to point out that they had been more sinned against than sinning, and they had gone over to Titokowaru during the last war in fear for their lives, given the uncertain temper, even unstable mind, of Colonel McDonnell who had led the massacre at Pokaikai. 'They were living peaceably but Colonel McDonnell took them as prisoners,' young Fox told the commissioners. 'After that another European was killed by Titokowaru's people and McDonnell began to think that these things were committed by the friendly Natives who thereupon became afraid and fled to Titokowaru in the night-time . . .'

The atmosphere in the court remained rigorously formal. Young Fox did not, at this point, describe his own subsequent fate before the commissioner, who knew it perfectly well. But everyone in the courtroom was aware of it, and the newspapers picked it up and ran the story about a 'bright, intelligent young native, a clerk in the office of Buller & Lewis' who had spent most of the day speaking before the Commission and who, long ago, was 'captured with two other native boys. Two of them blubbered a good deal and their captors silenced their cries by braining them against the nearest tree. The third, an attractive-looking youngster, was taken away uninjured. Sir Wm. Fox obtained him from the natives, adopted him and reared him up, so that the young man is now in a fair way of becoming the first lawyer of his race.'

The jocular note – 'blubbered a good deal', 'brained them

233

against the nearest tree' – had crept into the newspapers in the last few years and was quite different from the tone, however hostile, towards the Maori a decade before.

In the final hearings, a subtle new tension was in the air. The Commission had now moved to Patea, south of the river, the old headquarters of Major Noake, and, in this district, the legal position regarding land was slightly more complicated. The first wars had taken place, all the land was confiscated, then reserves were given back to the tribes. Titokowaru's war then broke out, and when the Maori returned some years later they found that now their reserves had been taken as well. In the words of one chief, Taurua, 'I saw that European houses had been built on that land, and that their grass was growing there . . . I now request you,' he concluded, 'to give me back my land.'

In other words, there had been a second confiscation, and one that was entirely illegal. No Act of Parliament had been passed to allow it. Throughout the Commission hearings, Sir William had repeated endlessly that the original confiscation legislation could not be overturned, but now, all around him, were complaints that a crucial component of that law – the awarding of reserves – had in fact been overturned. And the man responsible for this was none other than Sir William Fox himself, who had been Premier at the time. It was his foster-son who, in all the confusion, put his finger on the legal question.

'Taurua,' he said, 'was taken prisoner from here to Otago. I was taken to Wellington . . . They were taken on account of their having been in rebellion, but I was only a child when I was taken. I saw in the *Gazette* the appointment of this Commission to inquire into the grievances of the Natives in this district and to fulfil the promises made by Government, in order that peace should be established between the two races. I have claims myself in this land; it is not that I am speaking solely on account of myself. I am speaking for the whole of my tribe. It is quite true, as stated by Taurua, that this land was returned by Mr Richmond to him and his tribe. Mr Richmond said that no Europeans would be settled on this block of land':

> *Sir William*: That is quite true; we are aware of that; but the second war swept all those promises away.
> *William Fox*: I have acted according to the *Gazette*. Mr Richmond's promise to Taurua was not made verbally only; it was put in writing.
> *Sir William*: We know that, but the war swept away all promises, written and verbal, to those who joined in it.

Young Fox rose to speak again. He had only one question:

'I wish to know whether the confiscation of 1863 or 1864 is in force now, or whether the insurrection of 1868 did away with it?'

It was a crucial point. How could the insurrection of 1868 sweep away half the confiscation legislation while the other half remained in force? The two Foxes, one who had broken the law and the other, his own son, who had suffered because of it, must have looked at each other at that moment like two strangers. But then the moment passed, or at least so far as we can tell from the transcript, which was later edited by Sir William before publication. It was in the interest of neither of them to fall out. Young Fox still expected some gains from the Commission with reserves in other districts, and Sir William still wanted his Commission to succeed. At that point of the story, they had a common enemy, and that was John Bryce.

It may seem incredible in the modern age, but the West Coast Commission, which began its hearings in February, issued an interim report in March, a full account of the origin of the troubles in July and its recommendations in August. They were remarkable documents, considering the two authors. The word

235

'shame' tolls through them like a bell. The commissioners were ashamed at the treatment of the Maori, at the broken promises, the provocative behaviour of surveyors, the reliance on bribery and spies, the disdain and inconstancy of ministers, the refusal to consult Te Whiti.

'We have so disheartened our steadiest friends among the tribes by our rashness and pusillanimity that they are afraid to tell us what they wish or even to point out the land that ought to be reserved to them . . .' read one report.

'The spectacle of these four chiefs trying in vain to get the paltry dole of land which had been promised to them . . . is sad enough. When it is remembered that one of these chiefs was Te Puni, the earliest and truest friend whom the English settlers ever had, the story ought to fill us all with shame. We could not bring ourselves to believe that such a thing could be; nor was it till after repeated applications to the Native and Land Department that we could be persuaded of its reality', said another.

'We cannot say', wrote one newspaper, 'that it is the most disgraceful of all chapters in that history of disasters to aboriginal races. But it is a chapter not at all creditable to the European race, and it is creditable to the Maori.'

The Commission's recommendations, so far as they concern us here, were simple: to redeem the old promises made over the years, and, above all, to ensure that extensive reserves were made and marked out for the Maori owners, before the next and final acts of confiscation were made.

In the last sentences of their final report, the commissioners seemed to shake their heads over the policies of Bryce. 'This West Coast question will never be settled except by some arrangement with Te Whiti. To fill our gaols with prisoners, not for crimes, but for a political offence in which there is no sign of criminal intent is a most harassing and perplexing process. There is no statesmanship merely in acts of force and acts of repression. In what manner Te Whiti should be approached is a matter for Your Excellency's Advisers: we only venture to suggest that no time should be lost in doing it.'

Approaching Te Whiti was just what Bryce planned. While the commissioners toured the province and the comet slowly faded from the night sky, the Armed Constabulary pushed on digging trenches and building blockhouses. At each step taken by the commissioners, Bryce outflanked them with new provocations or repressive laws. When the interim report was issued, the road-builders marched north and built two stockades almost at the door of Parihaka. Two days after the second report came out, the Native Minister introduced new legislation, the Maori Prisoners Act, providing for further detention without trial of the ploughmen. When the third report came out, more fierce laws were passed, which the former Premier, Grey, denounced as 'a warrant for the arrest of any Maori for any offence or for no offence at all'. There was strong opposition in the House to these laws – 'a disgrace to the Statute Book', 'utterly unworthy of Englishmen', a blot on the escutcheon of the colony, and so on, but in the end, party politics prevailed and the laws were all passed.

On the ground, however, Bryce's deeds were failing to have the desired effect. Te Whiti announced that he *wanted* the road to be repaired, and sent several cartloads of food to the soldiers as a sign of hospitality. The soldiers in turn wanted to treat their Maori visitors to a pint of beer each, but the latter declined. Instead, the army band issued forth and played 'several airs for the amusement of the Natives, who frequently exclaimed "Ka pai pompom!" – "What a fine thing, this band!"'

'Your tribe (the Constabulary) are *rangatira* (men of standing),' one Maori said. 'Why are you working on the roads, surely a job for *tutua* (low-born men)?'

This was not at all what Bryce had had in mind. But eventually he found a possible source of strife. A month before the second report of the Commission appeared, the new road

237

was approaching the gardens which spread for several square miles around Parihaka. Hursthouse, who was the surveyor and engineer in charge, had been ordered to make the road as straight as possible, but this would have meant cutting through dense forest. Instead he ordered the soldiers to break down the fences around the Maori gardens and began driving the road through.

Dillon Bell had warned that if a road was put through cultivations, it must be fenced on each side to stop livestock wandering in, but this was not done. In the morning, the army returned and found the fences repaired and the road blocked. They broke them down again. The Maori rebuilt them, the soldiers broke them down. This continued for days, and it was just what Bryce had been looking for.

At first the contest of wills was not dangerous: there was a certain amount of shoving and shouting but it was not altogether ill-natured. The colonel in charge telegraphed Bryce to say the Parihaka men 'seemed very reasonable' – they wanted gates across the gaps in the fences as they would be sowing the next day. 'I agreed not to let the pigs into the sown paddock tonight and to report to you.'

Bryce refused to authorise gates and, four days after the Commission published its second reports, he ordered any men repairing fences across the road to be arrested. Fox and Bell had warned against mass arrests for political offences: 'the worst of it is that it does not advance the one thing that is really wanted – peace upon the Coast.' It was becoming clear that not only was peace not the thing that Bryce really wanted, but that it was one thing he really did not want.

It was now that Te Whiti's second *coup de théâtre* began.

Day after day, he sent men down to the gardens to rebuild the fences. 'They . . . came . . . knowing perfectly well that their attempt to re-erect the fence would prove a mere demonstration – a demonstration repeated forty or fifty times at least.' Some 'had prepared themselves for arrest by washing themselves and putting on their best clothes and when taken they held out their arms to receive their manacles.' On one occasion at Pungarehu, three hundred men and boys descended on the roadline, dug up the road, sowed it with wheat and put up a fence.

'Their appearance when digging in such an immense body is spoken of as very remarkable when viewed from a distance,' one paper wrote. 'They looked like an immense swarm of bees moving with a steady and uninterrupted movement across the face of the earth. As each portion was finished, they set up a shout and a song of derision,' which could be heard 'miles away'.

At the beginning of September, Bryce himself arrived at the scene and the mood immediately became darker and more violent. He had just armed himself with yet another piece of legislation under which anyone erecting a fence could be jailed for two years with hard labour. Watched by two thousand women and children at Parihaka, the men marched down the road and straight to the fences:

2 September (*Hawera Star*) 'Mr Bryce was present. A scuffle broke out and as expected the constables had the best of it. Claret was freely distributed. The natives were very sulky . . . The Native Minister congratulated the police.'

4 September (*Wanganui Evening Herald*) 'Some of the natives got rather roughly handled in consequence of their troublesome and provoking behaviour and it would astonish many how well the men kept their temper under very trying circumstances . . . 59 were arrested and placed in an iron building.'

They appeared in the District Court in New Plymouth and all received the maximum two-year sentence of hard labour. There were now hundreds of men in gaol. The demonstrations were carried on by old men and children. Every day forty or fifty of these *morehu* – the remnant – arrived at the gardens, and on some occasions another party of over a hundred small children, who were known as the *tatarakihi* – cicadas – came out to traverse the road through the cultivation, 'warbling, like a flock of blight-

239

birds, a chant taught to them by Tohu', according to the commissioner Robert Parris who saw them pass.

The blight-bird or silver-eye is a tiny bird – a newcomer to the country, as it happened, having been blown 1,300 miles across the Tasman from Australia – which moves in flocks at about waist-height over the fields and through the forest. Perhaps it was the sight of these children, building their tiny fences of fern across the road, which began to force a change of mind even in the hardline newspapers. Was it better, the *Patea Mail* demanded of Bryce, 'or cheaper or easier to take Maori fencers prisoners and keep them in gaol for a year or more than to set your 800 unarmed idlers to work putting up fences where the highway has cut through native plantations?'

The government too, under pressure from Bell and Fox, had had enough. Bryce had demanded a march on Parihaka itself, but this was refused and he was ordered to stop taking prisoners. He handed in his resignation as Native Minister.

From all these latest events, which again turned the country's attention to Parihaka, William Fox Omahuru had, as usual, kept aloof. Since the Commission hearings he had returned to his work in Wellington, with occasional trips to Wanganui, and to see his parents at Mawhitiwhiti.

Then, during a trip north to Taranaki in late September 1880, he disappeared.

He was last seen in Wanganui and should have returned from there to Wellington. Buller, understandably, was annoyed and then concerned. Where was his valuable songbird, the bright and intelligent youth on whom many Maori clients of Buller, Lewis & Gully now relied? To find out what had happened to him, we have to go back to 3 September, the day on which John Bryce had arrived to oversee the arrests of the fencers.

It was Miri Rangi, sitting in her front room with the shades half drawn, who outlined to me what had happened. That day,

Fox's brother, Ake Ake, was one of the demonstrators who came down to the fences. He had, as we know, once been a warrior, one of Titokowaru's leading young fighting men, but like Titokowaru he had accepted Te Whiti's philosophy of non-violence. When the constables came for him across the field, he did not fight them off and he did not run. He stood there and let his hands be tied – whether behind his back or in front of him is not clear. But then, instead of being marched to the 'iron building' mentioned in the newspaper, he was thrown to the ground and dragged across the stubble.

The verb Miri Rangi used for 'drag around' was *totoia* – by chance the two long 'o's of the Maori word make it sound close to the English 'torture', which is precisely what it seems to have been. At the end of the procedure, Ake Ake was badly injured and covered in blood.

How, one thinks, could such a thing happen? In the first edition of his *History of New Zealand*, Rusden openly suggested that John Bryce, as a young man who worked as a 'cowboy', had acquired his reputation for cruelty by 'throwing stones at the eyes of the patient cow'. A tethered cow being tormented . . . Years pass, and now it is a man who is tethered before him . . . The suspicion must arise that the treatment of Ake Ake Omahuru took place not despite the presence of the Minister of the Crown, but because he was there.

As Miri Rangi told me this story, the room became very still and seemed to become darker, as if for a moment we were in a place where there was starlight.

'Sometimes,' Miri said after a pause, 'we still cry about what happened.'

Among the emotions I felt were dismay and a kind of anxiety – the anxiety of the excluded. This was caused by Miri's use of the word 'we'. All my life I had belonged to another 'we', the majority who had been kept in the dark or who had deliberately kept themselves in the dark about their history. The jovial euphemisms of the newspaper reports now seemed obviously and deeply suspect: 'Some of the natives got rather roughly handled . . .' 'Claret was freely distributed.' And there was a further piece of evidence, odd and compelling, to ensure that no one could think the story was a piece of wartime propaganda. After this incident, Ake Ake's name was changed. For the rest of his life he was known in the family circle at least as 'Aki 'Aki, or Haki Haki, which means 'covered in scabs'. It is just a little pun that has twined its way around the story, perhaps intended to defuse the pain of the event. But time has left this play on words alone for over a century; if it had sprung up around a lie or an exaggeration, would it have lasted all these years?

In 1937, a local Taranaki historian named Houston went to visit Mr Ake Ake Omahuru at his home along the Hastings Road outside Hawera. He found an old man, nearly ninety, 'grey and very bent', who had been 'wounded in the arm at Pungarehu'. It is unclear from Houston's notes whether the injury was merely reported to him, or if it was a disability still evident – the result, for example, of being dragged across a field while bound at the wrists. Ake Ake, Houston reports, still wore the white plume of the albatross, a sign of adherence to Te Whiti's doctrine. He was 'very polite – carried out a short form for us – but unwilling to talk'.

If the story shocks us now, imagine the effect it had on young William Fox. According to Miri Rangi, Ake Ake was too badly injured to be taken to gaol with the other arrested men. Even if Fox did not see him immediately, he must have heard of his injuries when he went to Mawhitiwhiti in October. When he was a child he had hero-worshipped his elder brother; in the last two years, however, relations must have been strained between the follower of Te Whiti and the lawyer working for the Pakeha. But now everything changed. Now, what was young William Fox to think? Or worse still, he must have wondered, what had

242

his brother, the sombre hero of his childhood, been thinking as he was being dragged over the stubble by the white men?

At the end of November, Buller finally received a letter from the young men's father.

> To Dr Buller, my friend, greetings my dear friend. Do not be saddened by the length of time that Pokiha [Fox] is here. His delay here is caused by illness. He had a serious sickness when arriving here from the South. This is why he has been detained here by me. When he is well he can return. I will relay word of his recovery to you and send him on his way. He has not yet been able to attend to my affairs, because of how sick he has been. That is enough.
> From your dear friend,
> From Te Karere Omahuru.

Young Fox may indeed have been ill – possibly even as ill as his father said – but two months passed and there was no word from him.

Bryce had withdrawn his resignation as Native Minister, but now it was Sir William who was firmly in charge of policy. Change was in the air. There was a new Governor on the way, Sir Arthur Gordon, a Christian humanitarian – or, that is, a 'gospel-grinding nigger-lover' with 'wild democratic theories' according to some settlers. But Parliament and public opinion had also turned against Bryce and were backing the commissioners. Fox was appointed to a new one-man commission to carry out his earlier recommendations and to define the reserves which he insisted were the key to the whole matter.

There was now also foreign opinion to consider. Te Whiti had secretly written to a British MP, the celebrated or notorious radical, Charles Bradlaugh, who took up the case. (He had hired someone to translate the letter a few months before; there is a possibility that it was William Fox Omahuru.) Suddenly the plight of hundreds of Maori prisoners detained without trial, and in some cases dying in detention, became the subject of urgent inquiries from Whitehall; the matter was raised in the House of Commons and in the British and European press.

Soon the prisoners began to come forth from their South Island gaols, bringing with them the usual reports of ill treatment that emerge from such places. They sailed north on the *Penguin*, the *Stella* and the *Hinemoa*. Arriving in Wellington, on their way home to Taranaki, one group was visited by the Premier who 'enquired kindly into their condition'. Meanwhile it had been decided that the Governor himself should meet Te Whiti and soon his aide-de-camp was on his way to Taranaki. On Christmas Day he arrived in Parihaka in full dress-uniform and handed a letter from the Governor to the chief, offering to meet Te Whiti and discuss matters.

Te Whiti is said to have smiled at the size and grandeur of the envelope, but after hearing a few words, he stopped the interpreter. It was too late, he said. *Kua maoa te taewa*: the potato is cooked.

The potato is cooked! The words flashed around the colony. What did Te Whiti mean? Everyone had their opinion: A feast was being prepared for the Governor. The pear was ripe. Readiness was all. 'It means nothing at all,' the *New Zealand Mail* announced: 'it is senseless gibberish.' Even today analysis worthy of Levi-Strauss is applied to the remark. Raw food retains its life force, cooked food is dead and *tapu*. He, Te Whiti, had lost his life force, his *mauri*, and how could it be restored to him? The phrase was doubtless pregnant with these senses – it was a very old proverb (the actual translation being 'the kernel of the tawa has been steamed') – but the superficial meaning was quite adequate for the occasion. He, Te Whiti, was surrounded by fire. There were blockhouses and soldiers all over the

Parihaka block. At that very moment, five thousand acres of his ancestral lands, containing his best gardens and ancient cultivations, had been surveyed and were about to be offered for sale to settlers. 'The cooked potato cannot discuss!' It is absurd, in other words, for a potato to discuss its situation with the flame. In any case it was too late. How can cooked food become raw again?

Furthermore, he added, if the Governor wished to know more, 'he must come to the pot where the cooking was being done.'

This was precisely the situation that Fox had warned about again and again – that Te Whiti's land should not be surveyed and sold to white settlers without his own reserves being marked out and given to him. But Fox was now in Taranaki. He set up his office in Hawera and in mid-January he made his first brief visit to Pungarehu, the army post two miles from Parihaka, to explore the district and begin his work of defining the reserves.

There was still no sign of young Fox. Buller finally confided his concerns to Sir William who set about a new task with his usual energy. He soon tracked down the absconder.

Hawera
31 January 1881

My Dearest Buller
On Thursday last I sent Hadfield [one of his interpreters] to Pungarehu to look for William Fox Omahuru. Next day I got a telegram from him that WFO had gone to Mawhitiwhiti – I took a buggy and went there, but he had gone back to Kaupokonui *en route* for Parihaka. A Boy was just going to the former and I despatched a note by him. Yesterday Hadfield returned without having been able to find him. This morning I shall send letters to him to be delivered by Mr Carrington who is at the Camp near Parihaka.

Hadfield saw WFO's father at Parihaka – he understood

from him that he was *en route* for Wellington and he did not seem to expect him back at Parihaka . . .

Magnificent weather up here – but lots of dust when it blows.

Yrs faithfully,
William Fox.

But the very next day there was a development:

Hawera

1 February 1881

My Dear Buller

Since my last note W. F. Omahuru turned up here and I got hold of him and had a serious talk with him. The result I am sorry to say is not satisfactory. He was reticent, not to say sulky, said that his father told him to stay with him to look after his interests and would not say whether he meant to go back to Wellington or not.

I read him the greater part of your letter to me and gave him a good deal of advice and warning, but am much afraid that life in the bush has too many charms for him.

The Australian niggers say 'too much whitee man no good blackee man' – and I fear the Maories have the same sentiment, and look upon such civilization as we give them as no improvement but rather the worse.

I know it will be a great disappointment to you, as it is to myself, if this poor boy goes back to the blanket [?] and its surroundings but I fear he will not be persuaded.

He has gone back to Parihaka to see his father and promised to let me know the result. But I fear it is of no use my attempting anything more. He promised also to write to you.

Yours faithfully,
W. Fox.

Within forty-eight hours came the denouement:

Hawera
3 February 1881

My Dear Buller,

I saw Omahuru riding on the Waimate Plains this morning. I asked him whether he was going back to Wellington; his reply was he did not think he should go back 'at all'. Another illustration of Cuvier's apothegm that 'it takes 40 generations to make a wild duck a tame one.'

I fear his decision is final and you will see him no more in your office.

I regret not only the act, but the way in which he has done it, exhibiting no feeling of gratitude or consideration when so much has been done for him.

I am getting on first rate with my claimants, but I hear nothing of the Treaty of Waitangi – not even an allusion to the scarlet blankets. That venerable document is left to Mr Bradlaugh and Mr Agricola Sherrin to vex their souls withal.

Yours faithfully,
W. Fox

Reticent, sulky, this poor boy, no feeling of gratitude . . . as usual in his writing – though not his speeches or actions – Sir William struck a tone of fluent and mild regret. It was sad in its way, but, after all, what had happened? A wild duck had flown away, back to the wild . . .

Soon some of the newspapers got wind of the story.

'This native . . . well educated and versed in English law and with a decided talent for that profession . . . has abandoned everything and surrendered himself body and soul – to Te Whiti,' wrote the *Taranaki Herald*.

'He is now at Parihaka living as the other natives are living there. From this it is very evident that it is impossible to civilise the natives and that it is only a waste of time and money in attempting to do so.'

'There is a melancholy story running around the colony about a Maori lad Sir William Fox saved from death and Dr Buller half trained to the law . . . who has relapsed into the barbarism of his forefathers,' said the *Wairarapa Standard*. 'The holy wish of the *Taranaki News* is that he may blot himself out of existence.'

But young Fox had no intention of blotting himself out. He was soon in the papers again, far more of them and this time at greater length. At the monthly meeting at Parihaka in March, in front of an assembly of several thousand Maori and a hundred or so Europeans, the young man made a speech. This in itself was unusual. Every month at the great meeting or *hui* Te Whiti spoke at length, and then Tohu, but as far as newspaper and official reports indicate, no one else spoke. Once, Robert Parris (who was now appointed to assist Sir William in the new commission and was accused by many of hoodwinking Fox and feathering his own nest) leapt to his feet as soon as Te Whiti had finished his address and tried to speak.

'Do not speak now, speak tomorrow,' Te Whiti ordered.

'No one can answer for tomorrow,' said Parris. 'I cannot say how long I will live . . . perhaps tomorrow will never come.'

'Very well,' said Te Whiti. 'Speak on the day that never comes.'

Te Whiti's speeches were reported widely, and often wildly, in papers across the country, and he complained that his real message was misunderstood by the journalists who heard it:

'When I speak of the land, the survey, the ploughmen, and such small matters, the pencils of the reporters fly with the speed of the wind, but when I speak of the words of the spirit, they say this is the dream of a madman! They are so greedy for gain that nothing seems to concern them unless it is in some way connected with the accumulation of wealth.' And it was not only his underlying

248

message but his use of language and the Maori tradition of rhetoric that was beyond the reporters. Despite that, for month after month, across the columns of the country's two hundred or so papers some version or other of Te Whiti's words appeared.

Tohu got far less attention, being, in the European view, a less impressive speaker, and, in any case, it was generally thought that he simply repeated what Te Whiti had said.

Now there came an unprecedented event – a speech by an outsider, not even twenty years old, and with the reporters closing in to listen.

It was partly a comic turn, a boy's speech, boastful and excited, and the crowd, which listened to Te Whiti in rapt silence, greeted Fox's speech with cheers and hilarity. This was a version which several papers ran:

> These words I speak in obedience to Te Whiti who has asked me to tell you my thoughts . . . Fox is *pouri* [dark of heart] because I, the young chief, Wiremu Poki, have abandoned him . . . Am I not his namesake? I am to tell you why I left. I was getting weary of the evil customs of the Pakeha, indeed it was time to go, or I might have become as they are, so much have I learned thanks to my education.
>
> Another reason why I left my benefactor I will tell you. In the candour of my heart I really believed that Fox was the *pohe* [boss] to conduct this work [the Commission], though I know it was me whom he depended on for the results, but I found out that Fox was not leader at all, that Parris dominates him, even as Te Whiti dominates Parris.
>
> So when I saw that Fox, the *Roia Nui Whakaharahara* – the great lawyer of high-standing – was not a hundred-year-old rata, but only a cabbage-tree . . . the fog that had obstructed my sight and troubled my mind rolled back and light displaced the darkness. After that, could I have remained to be deceived. Never! [Immense cheering]

It is straight talk, though, to say that Fox was kind to me –
although he never once gave me sixpence to buy a glass of
beer. But why was he kind?

The lawyer I was placed with was kind too, exceedingly so,
and often gave me a shilling. But why were they or any other
Pakeha kind or affectionate? I will tell you, as I too am a
lawyer and I have found the Pakeha out.

Listen, when you receive kindness from lawyers, and
Pakeha are loving to you, be on your guard. That love is
bait to entice a little fish, as by that means they will catch a big
whapuku [groper], and so *two* fishes are consumed by the kind
and affectionate Pakeha. [Great cheers and shouting] And if
they could catch a *tohura* [whale] by impaling the groper on a
hook, that whale too would be gulped down. [Renewed
cheering]

Oh yes, I know, but '*No whia, koke* [No fear].' [Frantic
applause]

Those are my thoughts. I have told you one of the reasons for
which I deserted the Pakeha and came back to you. My love for
my people and land will never pass away, as true as that I am a
lawyer. No teaching will change my nature, but the Pakeha
will not see that an albatross cannot be changed into a crow.

The speech or excerpts from it reached the readers of many
newspapers. 'This young native', a Wellington paper observed,
'does not seem to be impressed with a high idea of our morals. It
shows how little good may be accomplished in educating a
Maori.' The full speech – with a good deal more about Parris's
control over Fox – was printed in the *Patea Mail*, which Sir
William himself must have seen. It is hard to imagine his shock
and rage. He was publicly accused by his own son of incompet-
ence and deceit. He was, what? a cabbage-tree and a 'log on the
drift and an object of pity'. The warlike *Patea Mail*, no friend to
the commissioner, had some fun at his expense:

250

While Sir William Fox has been 'settling' the native difficulty, his foster-son deserted him, having flung away his fine clothes and adopted the Maori blanket, *à la* Te Whiti . . . His speech must have a sad interest for Sir William Fox, who has failed even to 'settle' this one Maori youth.

Another paper, the *Wairarapa Standard*, had a different angle:

We know the lad very well and feel no sorrow in the case. Even Sir William can be consoled . . . Did our readers ever hear of Antony and Cleopatra? Do they remember what Plutarch says about Antony's flight – that a lover's soul lives in the body of his mistress.

In other words the young lawyer has a Hinemoa in his eyes at Parihaka, and some good may be expected from a man who goes to the devil after a woman – although Sir William would not.

Hinemoa is the name of the girl in the most famous of all Maori love stories, a kind of *Romeo and Juliet* in which she runs away to find her forbidden lover and swims a lake at night, guided by the sound of his flute. The *Wairarapa Standard*'s correspondent was a white named Thompson, married to a Maori woman from Taranaki; he spent a lot of time at Parihaka and there is no reason to doubt his story. Now William Fox, or Ngatau Omahuru or Wiremu Pokiha, or Wiremu Poki – by this point of his life he was trapped in a haze of different names – was for the first time in his life free of them all. At the age of nineteen he was in the state of simplicity – a lover. The identity of his girlfriend is unknown. Miri Rangi had not heard this part of the story.

Fox was not the only young lover at Parihaka that night. A Maori prisoner, recently released from the South Island gaol, had eloped from New Plymouth with a 'white maiden, the eldest daughter of the late Mr W. Sturmey'. This caused unhappiness

251

in New Plymouth: 'A well-known manufacturer of ginger beer galloped to Parihaka with a letter to Te Whiti demanding the surrender of the fair absconder . . . The fair Hebe, however, kept aloof from all Europeans and was not to be seen although the Natives acknowledged she was there. She concealed herself in one of the *whares* with a strong guard of native women to prevent intrusion.'

There was an abundance of food at Parihaka that March but, above all, melons were in season. Of melons there was an immense supply. There was a row of melons a chain long and seven feet high. Melon rinds and melon seeds were everywhere underfoot. People slipped and slid all over the place. That night at Parihaka, after all the speeches and discussions, the papers said, 'the greatest hilarity prevailed amongst the young people'.

Among the audience at Parihaka who heard the 'young chief, Wiremu Poki', was an unexpected figure: Walter Buller. What exactly Buller was doing there is not clear. Probably he hoped to swoop down on his valuable clerk and carry him back to the Wellington office. There is no indication of his reaction to young Fox's speech, but he probably enjoyed it enormously – especially the parable about the gulping down of whales, for he was now in possession of great wealth which often has a strange effect on the conscience. 'A whale? Excellent!' But perhaps I am exaggerating his shamelessness. At any event, he left Parihaka without his clerk, although they maintained contact and a few months later William Fox Omahuru seems to have visited his Wellington office again on family business. In the meantime, he stayed on in Parihaka or at least came and went frequently. He became Te Whiti's chief translator and interpreter and was often at his side when white visitors arrived. He was given a room as an office and was evidently valued for his legal skills and his acquaintance with the official world or the workings of the official mind. As a joke his office was called '*our* house of

252

parliament', which may not sound particularly funny but for several years the very word 'Parliament', referring to the legislature in Wellington, had been heard with detestation in Parihaka. Nothing of good had ever come from there.

However, the political atmosphere continued to improve. The country believed the Taranaki problems were on the point of disappearing. The Governor went on a tour of the South Island and found, even in the small towns, a 'keen interest in the Native question'.

'At Ashburton, the Caledonian Society did justice to the bravery and intelligence of our Maori fellow subjects,' the *Lyttleton Times* reported. 'They recognised that their rights have been ignored and wished for cordial understanding between the two races instead of a legacy for our successors of bitter hatred and deadly feud.'

Bryce had resigned again and this time his resignation had been accepted. Fox was fully in charge and at work in Taranaki. Te Whiti had signalled that he would accept a compromise: confiscation with ample reserves. The Governor was watching closely. There was now no impediment on the road to 'cordial understanding' between the two races.

Within a few weeks came one of the strangest twists of the whole story. It became evident that Sir William Fox had, without explanation, reversed his policy towards Te Whiti and suddenly turned his back on a figure he himself described as 'that strange man who undoubtedly has kept the peace for us for many long years and who even now seems determined that there shall be no bloodshed'. It was only a few months before that Fox had said the West Coast question would 'never be settled without some arrangement with Te Whiti' and that he must be 'invited to concur' with any settlement.

The invitation never came. Fox carried on assigning reserves all over the confiscated land, but not at Parihaka. He went south and began work on the far side of the Waingongoro where there was no urgency at all. He arranged matters with Titokowaru on the Waimate Plains, even going to visit the old warlord himself, the shadowy arch-demon of his own speeches for years, and he took Lady Fox along with him, as to a tea party.

But to Parihaka, where the best arable land was being surveyed for sale, and where Hursthouse was pushing on with military roads, Fox would not go. When a British MP named Brogden, who 'had heard a good deal about Te Whiti in England', and even the Duke of Manchester, who was Fox's personal friend and mentor, came to New Zealand and went to meet Te Whiti, Fox would not accompany them.

The provocations continued. On the Parihaka land, the whole of the seaward block was already up for sale and no reserves had been marked out: it was clear that Fox had abandoned his promise that ancestral cultivations were not to be taken under the

confiscation. He was soon to announce that even the main reserve to be allotted to Te Whiti would, in fact, be held by the government and leased to white settlers; the lease revenue would by handled by the Public Trustee and drip-fed to the Maori owners. The Maori estate of thousands of acres of mountain forest, plains and beach was to be reduced to an inland town, its inhabitants living on handouts and surrounded by white farms.

In April, at the next meeting, Te Whiti was in an unusually downcast mood. It was a dreary autumn day with intermittent heavy showers. The evil, Te Whiti said, that rested on the Maori did not belong to the present but belonged to the past. Both the land and its inhabitants were created, but while the land would remain, men were struck down. He had little to say, he added, the rain so depressed him. The times were dark and he could throw no light on them.

'The rain coming on heavily, the meeting broke up,' the colonial press agency report concluded.

No one has ever explained Sir William's change of mind. Historians talk simply, if wearily, of the 'dichotomous Mr Fox' who always changed his mind anyway. The general assumption has been that he had simply decided to end the financial burden of keeping an army on the coast and to bring things to a head by provoking Te Whiti to war.

There is one slight figure in the midst of these dark times who has been overlooked . . . the runaway, the young lawer William Fox Omahuru.

It may seem fantastic to suggest that an elderly statesman, a Royal Commissioner, would reverse public policy because of an absconding foster-son. But we cannot forget what Fox's own contemporaries thought of him. 'The essence of undying vindictiveness.' 'Crabbed, spiteful and envious.' 'A Hotspur of opposition,' one of his friends, a politician named Gisborne, said. 'Aggressiveness was the law of his nature, he was always eager for the fray.'

It is true that Fox always needed an enemy to hurl himself against. Now that his earlier foes – Grey, Bryce, 'that cur, Ballance' – had been reduced, perhaps only Te Whiti could supply the deficit. And Te Whiti had committed at least one personal offence against Sir William. He had won over a certain 'bright and intelligent Maori youth', who was now living at Parihaka, making outrageous speeches, greeting visitors at Te Whiti's side, and whispering in his girlfriend's ear. And this boy, after all, was Fox's own creation. He had obtained him, named him, brought him up, shown him the world, sent him to Buller, made him a star in the Commission hearings. There is even some suggestion that he intended to grant the youth extensive reserves and then, as his legal guardian, lease out the lands and manage the profits. The *Patea Mail* accused Fox of this three times and the charge was never rebutted. Whatever the truth of that accusation, Fox had nonetheless been made to look foolish and Te Whiti had won the boy to his side.

Once again the voice of Gisborne comes back to us: 'He had at his command eloquence and humour . . . and was normally good natured, but often too bitter, too violent, too fond of personal denunciation. And he rushed from one view to the other so wholeheartedly, it became extreme.'

Te Whiti, that 'remarkable man' had now become a personal target of Fox's, and battle plans began to be drawn up.

Sir William did finally make a visit to Parihaka. Here is a description of the place by a British correspondent writing for *The Graphic* in 1881. 'Parihaka, the principal Maori stronghold in New Zealand, is an enormous native town of quite an imposing character. I never before saw such numbers of Maoris. It was such a picturesque sight, such gay colours, fine-looking men and pretty girls.'

But when Sir William arrived, early in 1882, it did not look like that at all. Half of the houses had been demolished. The *wharenui* or meeting-house had been laboriously pulled down. There were no pretty girls. There were no young lovers slipping over on melon rinds. Te Whiti was gone. Young William Fox was gone. Even Ellen Sturmey, the girl who eloped from New Plymouth, was gone. She had been marched back to New Plymouth under military escort. The place was semi-deserted. It was a mass of grey and brown shadows. We know it looked like that because, when he arrived, Sir William took up his position on a small conical hill on the edge of town and took out his watercolours and painted the scene of his triumph. His picture survives. It is in a file in a library in Wellington and you are allowed to examine it if you put on a pair of white cotton gloves.

13

When a body meets a body

The lands of Te Whiti, the Parihaka block of about 80,000 acres, were divided for the first time in history into two parts, by the new military road in 1881. Between 10,000 and 15,000 acres on one side – the 'seaward block' – contained the best arable land and was more or less open country with a few stands of trees and scrub. On the other side of the road the forest was thicker, becoming extremely dense the further inland you went.

It was the seaward block which had been surveyed by June 1881 and was now being put on sale. No one, however, had officially informed the Maori owners that this land no longer belonged to them. In July, the midwinter month, Te Whiti sent people over the road to begin clearing and fencing their cultivations in preparation for the spring planting. Robert Parris was sent to tell them that they were now trespassing on Crown land. Parris was ignored by the gardeners and was soon sent by Fox to some other part of the province. Eventually, as the cultivation continued, an armed force was sent in and ordered to prevent the Maori from taking possession of 'Government land'.

It was here, among the high hummocks of the seaward plain, that the third act of Te Whiti's drama opened.

It is strange country even today, covered with dairy farms and dotted with suburban-looking farmhouses. As you approach

Pungarehu on Highway 45, hundreds of low conical hills, about 50 ft. high on average, rise on all sides. These hills were formed, according to geologists, by bubbles in an ancient lava-flow. Over time the lava was covered with trees and grass. It is a suggestive and emblematic landscape – as you go across it you feel you could be moving among the arrested waves of a sea: even today, any object on one of the summits of one of these low hills – a black-and-white cow, a pine tree, a concrete water tank – acquires a formal and impressive air, as if it has been placed there for a good reason by a painter of the Flemish school.

In 1881 the biggest army camp in Taranaki stood on one of these hills at the Pungarehu crossroads. To the west it looked over the seaward block to the coast and inland to Parihaka about a mile and half away. Three other forts stood a few miles to the north and south. August came and went and the strange, low key confrontation continued. Gardens were cleared, fences were built, troops pulled them down, the fences were restored. Tempers flared, threats were made, but there was no actual fighting, and nor were there any arrests. The presence of Governor Gordon and fear of British opinion prevented a return to the tactics of the previous year. Fox, who was the only man empowered to end the new crisis, stayed away. But in government circles, out of earshot of Gordon, plans were being laid to bring about a crisis.

There was now little love lost between government and Governor. Some of the settlers affected to despise Gordon as a bohemian for despite the fact that his father was a former British Prime Minister and he himself had been a page to the Queen, it was a well-known fact that he had once worn a floppy straw hat in public, and he never could get all his waistcoat buttons into exactly the right buttonholes. For his part, Gordon turned away in distaste from the new class governing the country. In the past, he wrote privately, New Zealand had had 'more gentlemen in public life than any other constitutional Colony', but now Parliament was composed mainly of 'drunken, ignorant, corrupt boors'. He was still more shocked by the new generation in the Church of England. 'From none do you hear more bitter and savage anti-native talk than from the clergy . . . Hardly the smallest vestige remains of Bishop Selwyn's work. The Bishops who have taken [his] place . . . are men of quite another stamp – not gentlemen, not learned, not active, and I am almost tempted to say not Christians, so bitter and narrow are they in their sayings and doings.' Gordon was not a man who could be transformed, like his ill-named predecessor, Sir Hercules, into a puppet of the government. Their new plans to bring matters to a head with Te Whiti were therefore carefully concealed from the constitutional head of state. Then Gordon made life easy for them by deciding to leave the country for several weeks. He wanted to go to Fiji, where he had previously been Governor, to oversee an important court hearing. He asked his ministers whether there was any impediment to this. Why, no, on the contrary, said Hall. The Governor steamed away on the SS *Emerald* on 13 September.

Instantly the authorities swung into action. Within a day, the government sent more soldiers to Taranaki and a bill enshrining Fox's plan to keep control of the 'inalienable' reserves was presented to Parliament. On 14 September, the House voted an extra £84,000 to the military. A message written on the sixteenth was sent to Governor Gordon: 'As to the state of things at Parihaka . . . Mr Hall and Mr Rolleston agree in thinking the appearances do not indicate serious mischief.'

Te Whiti and Tohu knew what was coming. On 17 September at the Parihaka meeting, Te Whiti warned his audience. 'All the evil that has existed over the land is now upon us. All the talk today is of fighting, and now nothing is left but to fight. The peace that has existed has passed away; there is no peace now . . . Both sides, take up your weapons . . . Goodness is the only weapon which will be victorious, and good will rule the world . . .'

There was a flurry of excitement when this speech was reported; some papers, leaving out the last sentence quoted here, said that here finally was a declaration of war. 'Pakanga, pakanga, pakanga . . . strike, strike, strike. All our talk today is of fighting . . . If when the pakeha comes on the land . . . they bring guns, bring your guns . . . fight and kill,' was one version that was published. Other papers and the government interpreter gave a whole spectrum of interpretations, generally less inflammatory, and within a day or two a second speech by Te Whiti was being reported, 'giving the real meaning of his speech'. The dispute was over the land. *His* weapons with which he would strike and strike and strike were planting, fencing and good words.

But the Taranaki settlers were in a state of high excitement, and 'persistent efforts were being made to work up a Maori scare' reported Croumbie-Brown, the correspondent for the South Island paper, the *Lyttleton Times*. New Plymouth was about to be burned down. The Maori were fortifying the slopes of Mt. Egmont! Settlers on the Waimate Plains (now surveyed and sold) should expect to be murdered in – as usual – their beds, on a word from Te Whiti. On 21 September, Parliament voted a further £100,000 in defence funds. The new Native Minister, Rolleston, however, was still waylaid by doubts. The son of an English clergyman and in his own words a 'terrible radical' while up at Cambridge, Rolleston prided himself on intellectual rigour and a scrupulously maintained conscience. He sent his interpreter to Parihaka to report on the situation himself. The young man, Riemenschneider, was the son of the Lutheran missionary who had first met Te Whiti in 1846. Te Whiti had known him since he was a child and talked to him freely. He was *pouri* [dark-hearted] that reports of his speech should have alarmed the settlers, he said, for he would stick to his doctrine of peace. The only way in which he would strike was in cultivating the lands of his ancestors. 'As to blows – never.'

Riemenschneider then toured the cultivations and, when he returned, Te Whiti asked him whether the work of the hoe and the spade looked like mischief. 'Let us put an end to these reports. As to fighting, it is absurd. You ought to know me better than to ask me such a question . . . Is it likely after all these years of peace that we should take up arms again?'

'He pointed out that the Maori people were crushed and no helping hand was held out to them. Turkey had nearly been crushed by Russia and in her extremity England had come to her rescue . . . Why had the Governor rushed off and forsaken his sucklings? He would have liked to have seen him, not his subordinate who came in a soldier's stripes.

'He desired to know where Sir William Fox was and expressed his regret at Sir F. Dillon Bell having gone, for Sir William had a halter round his neck and was not free to do as Sir Dillon Bell would have . . .'

'Towards evening,' Riemenschneider continued, 'the fencers returned. Te Whiti, noticing their gloomy looks, asked them if they had returned with a clear conscience, or if they had behaved insolently to the Pakeha during the day, because, he said, "if you break the rule, I shall hear of it."

'They looked crestfallen.'

All these notes made by Riemenschneider were carefully inscribed by the Native Minister into his personal diary. They proved one thing. Te Whiti had not changed. He was saying the same thing now as he had said ten years and perhaps twenty years before. The two races must live together. 'Even if a million Pakeha came to this district, they would not be opposed.' If either Maori or white tried to make a war, he, Te Whiti, would prevent it. 'If war came, we would laugh at it.'

At least forty of his speeches, one a month for over three years, were reported in the national press and the message did not vary, although their emphases, brilliance, and the quality of the translations, do. Here for the record is a version of just one of them – given at Parihaka, as it happens, on the same day Fox made his there. If readers object to being asked to read what appears to be a sermon, and one translated into a heavy Victorian style of English at that, they must remember that it is not really a sermon at all, or at least not only a sermon, for although there was the strong presence of a mystic in Te Whiti, he was a mystic firmly on the ground and attempting an extraordinary political feat – to forge a permanent and not merely expedient peace between two of the most bellicose peoples in the world, the English and the Maori.

He begins by comforting the first of the returned prisoners, some of whom were suffering the psychological effects of imprisonment.

Whatever befalls a man, suffering and death are his ultimate fate. It was so of old, it is so now and will be in the future. So do not think that we alone, the small people of the island [the Maori], are the only ones who are to suffer, that we alone do wrong, and that the great and strong of the land [the English] are right, for it is not so. For all people inherit suffering, whether good or bad. The fact of your having suffered imprisonment neither proves that you deserved it, nor that your works are bad. Nor, because the great of the land have escaped, has that proved that they are good . . .

It is not right that fear of war, or imprisonment, should be made master of the world, and that the great and strong, by coercion, should become masters of creation. It is not right that the men of the island [Maori] should be made slaves to fear of war, anger and vexation or that the land should be relinquished from that cause. If it happened to be the case that the world had been created in a feeling of anger and vexation, then it would be right that these moods should continue to rule the world, and conclude all things. But no, the world was created through love and all things made upon the face of the earth were created out of affection and love. Therefore, I say, since things commenced with love, our affairs should continue by love, through to the end. I will not allow strength, unhappiness, anger, war and tumult to finish the things that we are engaged in . . .

Struggle, war, quarrels of all kinds . . . no good has ever come from them. Therefore I implore this gathering not to allow war, or the fear of war, to become masters of the land. Do not engage in the first, and be patient, so that there is no excuse made for it . . .

My words are not unimportant for they concern the whole world. The old bad way of settling questions of land is to be abolished; the land problems will be settled by love. The things which I propose are entirely new. Until now, all quarrels have been settled by a strong hand, by war and bloodshed, struggle and unhappiness of all kinds, innumerable evils, and the vanquishing of the weak. Now let us take no heed of the evils brought into the world by Adam, but look further back and see that the heavens and the earth were created out of love. It was when man grew envious and angry that land questions came to depend on the fighting strength of the disputants.

By quickness and strength in movement does the fish find for himself a calm and stormless haven when the hurricane troubles the ocean, and in the same way does man find for himself a new home in a distant land. Under all your tribulations, let the great men of the island see your calm and peaceable behaviour, your patient and cheerful state of mind, gathered here in my presence on the *marae*.

Those who despise you for your quiescent and uncomplaining attitude will do so because of the novelty of such behaviour. Nothing good and lasting has ever been accomplished by might, strength, war. If there had been, then there would be a good reason to laugh at us for our patience under wrong and spoliation . . . Quarrels, fighting, fear of war, and war itself – these from now on shall not be allowed to dominate the land.

But remember – the work is not yet complete, which shall finally accomplish the permanent peace. The shark is hooked and dragged into the canoe and the fisherman beats him and throws him into the bottom of his boat, but although quiet for a time, he is not dead. But when struck a well-directed blow on the snout and the froth gathers about his lips, then with a quiver of his tail he expires and not before. The men upon the land [Maori] shall only find deliverance from strength and war by a true, disinterested and perfect love. God will not allow the land and men to owe dependence to war but to love alone. The leaders of the great people, the brave and strong in battle [the whites], are raging with passion, because of their importance, to bring matters under the dominion of war.

Rolleston, the classics scholar – and it would be interesting to know what he made of the speech above, its allusions and imagery (*the froth on the lips of the shark!*) – was a troubled man. Not trusting Riemenschneider's report, he went to Parihaka to see for himself, but found it all as described. He toured the ancient planting-grounds, now declared government property, and scolded those Maori he found there. He saw 'a man and a woman weeding. I told them their labour was in vain. Their crops would not be allowed to grow mature, the fence would again be removed. After this, the man would not speak but the woman said: "Why cannot we cultivate together?"'

He saw another couple at work. Did they not know they were trespassing? Did they not understand they were now on another man's land? All she knew, the woman said, was that it was the melon patch for next March. He went to see Te Whiti and told him that land must be surrendered and the blanket must be shared. Te Whiti 'took my hat in his hand and said, "what is the good of a hat if it is cut in two?" '*

Rolleston went away, still troubled. In a phrase, he could find no fault in the man. But the Cabinet wanted a report from him blaming Te Whiti as a stubborn fanatic. Rolleston's wife also nagged at him to support his colleagues, especially Bryce, whom she admired and had dubbed 'Sir Bryce'. For days, Rolleston dithered with his conscience and then, suddenly, there was no time for that luxury any more. News reached Wellington that the Governor, having been sent a message from his private secretary that 'war with the Maori was now regarded as almost inevitable', was steaming at full speed back from Fiji on the *Emerald*.

Now things began to speed up on land as well. John Bryce arrived in the capital with the look of a man whose hour had come. Telegrams flew between the new Premier, a man named Hall, in Wellington, Fox in Taranaki, and Whitaker, the Attorney-General – that 'cold shrewd subtle man, careless of means, and careless of consequences' – in Auckland. At half past five in the afternoon, when official hours were past, the acting head of state, Chief Justice Prendegast, summoned members of the Executive Council to Government House. The meeting opened at 8 p.m. At 8.15, Rolleston signed a proclamation which berated the people at Parihaka for 'making themselves poor by contributing to useless expenditure on feasts', for listening to the sound of Te Whiti's voice which unsettled their minds, for assuming a 'threatening attitude' which caused apprehension among the settlers and for compelling the government to incur great expense on the armed constabulary. All aliens or non-residents were ordered to leave Parihaka. (This was at Sir William's insistence. 'Send the aliens away' was the first

* Account from Rolleston's unpublished diary, Alexander Turnbull Library.

267

piece of advice he sent to Hall.) If Te Whiti did not accept the 'ample reserves' intended for him within fourteen days, the lands proffered would 'pass away from them forever' and he and his people would be responsible for this and 'for the great evil which would fall upon them'.

Hall told Fox that he did not expect Te Whiti to accept the ultimatum, in which case a large military force would be sent in, Te Whiti and Tohu arrested, their adherents dispersed, and the government would then 'make roads straight through the inland block and probably sell portions of it'.

After signing the proclamation, his last act as Native Minister, Rolleston resigned, and Bryce was reappointed to the office. About the time Mr Bryce was being sworn in, the *Emerald* was rounding the heads out of Cook Strait and she dropped anchor in the inner harbour, in sight and almost in earshot of the town, at 10.15 p.m. By then lights were on in the Government Buildings and the printing presses were running. Gordon, however, knew nothing about this and decided to sleep on board that night. At midnight a *Gazette Extraordinary* was issued, sent to the newspapers and the proclamation was telegraphed across the country. At 4 a.m., Bryce was already on the road out of town with the *Gazette* in his pocket, on his way north to Wanganui and from there to a final rendezvous with Te Whiti. That, however, was fourteen days off. The real reason that the new Native Minister hurried away in the dark was that he had no wish to meet His Excellency when morning came.

The proclamation did not officially reach Parihaka until three days later, when two civil servants, Bryce's secretary, W. J. Butler, and the translator, Wellington Carrington, arrived on a Saturday afternoon and asked for an interview with Te Whiti. By then Te Whiti knew its contents. Late the night before an unidentified British army officer arrived at Parihaka. The town was mostly asleep but he was met by or taken to see young

William Fox Omahuru and told him of the proclamation. Fox left him in the meeting-house and went alone through the dark streets to Te Whiti's house to give him the news. In the morning, the officer had gone. No one knew who he was or why he came but it seems to have been a friendly act; he may have been a certain Captain Dawson, who in the days to come was to perform another act friendly to Parihaka, and one more critical to the outcome of events there.

In an official report, Butler described the meeting with Te Whiti that took place the following afternoon:

'Te Whiti greeted us in the most friendly manner and after some ordinary conversation I handed him the Proclamation. After carefully examining the address he handed it to Rangi who read it aloud in perfect silence to about the middle of the last paragraph when Te Whiti said, "That will do, read no more."

'After a short silence, I said "Have you any message for me to take?"

'Taking the Proclamation in his hand, he said "No, this does not admit of any reply. An officer slept here last night. These are not new words; they were uttered some time ago in the House by Sir William Fox who said the Maories were to be deprived of all their land."

'Te Whiti's language was temperate throughout, without the least sign of temper. There was a weary and careworn expression on his face as we left.'

If the proclamation was met without 'the least sign of temper' in Parihaka, there were stormy scenes in Wellington when Gordon came ashore in the morning and learned he had been outfoxed by his ministers. They claimed to have been in complete ignorance of his imminent arrival: 'When he appeared in their midst, they expressed great surprise to Gordon – but not to each other', as one historian put it. There was an 'unpleasant scene' in the Executive Council where Gordon demanded to know how circumstances had changed to justify the new policies. The Chief Justice, Prendegast, emerged from the meeting 'ashen and fuming'. Gordon then tried to have Prendegast's actions invalidated since he himself had been back within territorial waters when they were taken and he appealed to the Colonial Office. The reply went against him, for reasons that seem occult even by Whitehall standards: a Governor sailing away from a colony remained in charge until the ship left territorial waters. Sailing back in again, he resumed his powers only when he touched dry land.

'The cruellest and most ridiculous Proclamation that has ever emanated from the Government printing office was on Wednesday last got ready for transmission to Parihaka,' said the *Lyttleton Times*. 'The stronger side informs the weaker that if, within fourteen days, its proposals . . . are not accepted, it will be made landless and homeless forever . . . The Natives are the owners of much of the soil. It is not for the Government to tell them they shall have this or that. It then informs them with marvellous effrontery that unless they accept the offer they are to be without land at all . . . Any war that follows must be an unjust war, involving this country in the crime of bloodguiltiness . . . We are for force because we are strong.'

This was exactly Gordon's view, and he enclosed them with his Despatch to the Colonial Secretary. This habit, of adding newspaper statements, which amplified his own views, to his official papers enraged the colonial government, but it was one which would one day bear fruit.

Outflanked, contemplating a war or massacre to be carried out under his own hand, Gordon considered resigning, but he knew that would simply reinstate Prendegast who, as Attorney-General, had declared that the rules of civilised warfare did not apply to Maori and, as Chief Justice, ruled that the Treaty of Waitangi was a legal 'nullity'. Gordon decided to stay on and he experienced the ignominy of the highest office: it was 'I, Arthur

Hamilton Gordon' who was required to sign the warrant calling up thousands of members of the volunteer corps, and he could only watch from a distance as plans were laid to arrest Te Whiti for 'uttering seditious words', while Bryce was given 'a large amount of discretion' in the expected assault on Parihaka. The seditious words in question were from the speech of September. *Pakanga, pakanga, pakanga.* 'Strike, strike, strike.' Te Whiti had in fact been translating the advice of Sir Donald McLean ten years before: 'Be strong in planting. Let your battle be with the soil.' Te Whiti's town was to be attacked because he had quoted a former and much admired Minister of the Crown.

When Gordon's warrant to bring under compulsory military law the various volunteer corps from New Plymouth, Patea, Wanganui, Rangitikei, Nelson, Thames, Wellington and the Wairarapa was published, a storm of protest broke out across the country. Other towns complained that they were being excluded from the 'warm work' being planned at Parihaka. A young woman poet, Jessie Mackay, satirised her neighbours in the southern town of Timaru:

A voice from the North — 'Who will come to our aid?
Who will face the dark Maori with bright gleaming blade?'
Loud are the shouts that the far echoes fill,
As the brave Timaruvians answer 'We will!'

But the brave Timaruvians did not notice her mockery. Volunteers were streaming towards Taranaki by train and ship. In Wellington 'the measured tread of armed men awakened echoes in the Empire City. Citizen soldiers breathed out threatenings and slaughter against the "enemies of the Queen" as they marched to the steamer to the air of "Let me like a soldier fall".' In Auckland, the 'train swept slowly out of the station amidst the enthusiastic cheers of an immense multitude . . . the

271

ladies used their handkerchiefs till they were wet and flourished them till they were dry.' In Marton, the volunteers 'marched for the railway station, headed by their fine brass band playing the favourite air "The girl I left behind me" . . . Children were held up for a farewell kiss from their fathers; many a maiden might be seen turning away with the handkerchief to her eyes. At last the train started, and a thrilling cheer rang out from hundreds of throats . . . All along the line people of both sexes and all ages were seen gazing with eager eyes . . .'

It is hard to understand the change in the public mood by November 1881. Gordon said he thought ninety per cent of the white population supported the attack; it was probably less, but there is no doubt that a change had taken place. It would be easy to blame the press which, with a few exceptions, was against Te Whiti, and many editors, with a journalist's natural scepticism towards high-flown language, took a delight in displaying the 'gibberish' and 'goody talk' of the 'Prophet'. By the time his words had passed through several hostile frontiers – from Maori to English, from the *marae* to a news report – his speeches had often taken on a hair-raising appearance. But can that explain the wharves black with people, the flowers and the bands, the eagerness at the thought of war against a race who were now outnumbered twelve to one? Here is one young volunteer, a recent migrant, Edmund Goodbehere, writing from one of the camps on 1 November:

> Dear Mamma,
> Four o'clock in the afternoon, lying on dry fern a most luxuriant bed after the watches. We had a most enthusiastic reception at the stations on the line and hundreds lined the streets at Wanganui to see us march through. Inspected by Major Noak [sic]. The dock was simply packed with people who cheered us lustily and showered bouquet's [sic] upon us. I should think there were three or four thousand present among whom were Miss Gregory, Miss Halcombe, the Atkins and all the Halcombe children of course.

The Halcombe children were the nieces and nephews of Lady Fox and foster-cousins of William Fox Omahuru. It is strange to think of them cheering and showering bouquets on the men marching off to what was being described as the 'extinguishment' of Parihaka, where their former playmate was living.

On the same day as Edmund Goodbehere wrote from his camp at Rahotu, Te Whiti addressed a final meeting five miles away at Parihaka. There were no matters to discuss, he said. All they had to do was stay firm, and watch the right. 'The south wind knows where it comes from and where it goes. Let the booted feet come when they like . . . The canoe by which we are to be saved is forbearance. Let us abide calmly on the land . . . Be firm, that the world might be informed and hear the good word. There are thousands in the world aiming at good, and all nationalities are anxious to meet . . .'

There were two-and-a-half or three thousand present, including many Pakeha. Among them was W. F. Gordon, the telegraph clerk who had befriended young William Fox when he was a law clerk working for Buller in Wanganui. As he strolled about the town, Gordon saw him again. 'He and I were good friends,' he wrote in a letter some years later, 'and I was pained to find him at Parihaka . . . He was sitting down with the Prophet and politely excused himself from taking a stroll round with me, as Te Whiti was curious to know what the remarks were, that many Pakeha Visitors made when they visited Parihaka that day! I take it he repented his action that day, which no doubt greatly displeased Sir William and Lady Fox.'

It is not, in itself, an illuminating report; Gordon had a genius for being in the right place at the right time but not understanding what he saw when he got there. But the encounter is interesting all the same: it was the moment before the hurricane struck, and gives us the last clear sighting of William Fox Omahuru for many years.

Most of the 2,500 colonial soldiers on active duty around Parihaka were in place several days before the ultimatum expired on Saturday 5 November. The Native Minister Bryce took personal charge of operations and rode about the countryside reconnoitring the ground – the hillocks, gardens and clumps of forest which stood between Pungarehu camp and Parihaka. On Thursday, Bryce and his military escort were seen on the outskirts of Parihaka. A Maori policeman was sent out to invite them into the town. Bryce declined, but promised to pay them 'an informal visit on Saturday'.

On Saturday morning the camp was roused before dawn. For some reason the *reveille* took place in silence. No bugles sounded; the NCOs went quietly from tent to tent rousing the men. At 6 a.m. the Armed Constabulary marched out of Pungarehu. They were joined a mile down the road by the Volunteer Corps who had marched north from Rahotu four miles away. At 7.15 a.m. the first columns of the combined forces were sighted by those watching from a low hill in front of Parihaka. They were advancing east with the rising sun in their eyes, and with a band playing 'When a body meets a body coming through the rye'.

About half a mile from the town, the troops halted and separated. Bryce had imposed a news blackout the evening before and any reporters found on the road or in the surrounding terrain were to be arrested on sight. The Volunteers took the left with the intention of encircling the town and flushing out any skulking newspapermen. At 8 a.m. the main body, composed

275

mostly of regular forces, then continued their march down the road to Parihaka.

But as the Volunteers circled out through the scrub, someone else had preceded them that morning:

> . . . like Indians on the war-path we slunk along under cover, for fresh horse-tracks were seen everywhere and we feared the patrols of our hostile friends. It was one of those beautiful mornings that our favoured clime enjoys, but the diamond drops of dew upon the fern, so pretty in the distance, are drenching upon near acquaintance. The hoary head of old [Mt.] Taranaki rose before us in all the virgin beauty lent to it by the new born day . . . Our pilot, known as the hero of the Queensland and South Australian boundary line expedition of a few years back, took us through fern and forest safely up close to Parihaka before the dew began to dry upon the leaves. At seven o'clock the strains of the band were heard playing the armed force out of Pungarehu.

There were five in this advance party. Two of them were guides: Captain Dawson, an ex-Imperial officer (and possibly the man who took the news of the proclamation to Te Whiti), and a surveyor named H. Vere Barclay. The other three were journalists – a reporter from the *Lyttleton Times*, an agency reporter named Humphries, and a special correspondent for the *Lyttleton Times*, S. Croumbie-Brown, the 'disguised duke or undisguised snob', the personal friend of Ulysses S. Grant, and the Edinburgh *Daily Review*'s correspondent during the US Civil War.

Croumbie-Brown had been covering the Parihaka story for about two years and in that time had undergone a personal transformation. At first he had written in a jeering tone about the 'Prophet' and offered his services to the government as a spy in Parihaka and on one occasion he even supplied a map showing the best approach for a military attack on Te Whiti's citadel – the very attack he was now trying to circumvent. He later attempted to become a negotiator between Te Whiti and the government, boasting that he had 'gained ascendancy over the mind of Te Whiti'.

As time went on it appeared rather that Te Whiti had gained ascendancy over the mind of S. Croumbie-Brown.

He began to see the land question in a new light and his reports became increasingly hostile to Bryce and his policies. The two men became engaged in a bitter public feud. When Bryce banned newsmen from the scene of the invasion of Parihaka, it was Crombie-Brown, above all, that he had in mind.

Croumbie-Brown was extremely proud of a gift which Te Whiti once gave him. It was a shark-tooth pendant which Croumbie-Brown wore as a 'breast-pin' – presumably what we would call a tiepin. On several occasions he reminded his readers of this exceptional object and of the fact that for many miles around he was recognised by the Maori because of it. They called him Mako-Taneha – 'Shark-man' – as also did Te Whiti, who in general had a low opinion of journalists and journalism, but here made an exception.

At the sound of the military band playing, and realising that the Volunteers were fanning out in the scrub below them, Croumbie-Brown and Humphries hastily descended from their hilltop and made their way into Parihaka itself, while the other three men stayed hidden in the bushes on the hill to watch the army's approach.

Walking around the town, Croumbie-Brown said he found a 'prevailing sadness, as though they felt a great calamity was approaching . . . It was saddening in the extreme; it was an industrious, law-abiding, moral and hospitable community calmly awaiting the approach of men sent to rob them . . .' Tohu came to meet the newsmen and welcomed them; like Bryce, he understood the importance of eyewitnesses. The visitors were offered a place sitting on the *marae*, where most of the community were now gathered, but they chose to hide inside a cookhouse, a reed-walled *whare* standing beside the crowded *marae*. It was through the latticed walls of this building that much of the information we have of events that day was filtered.

The *marae* was packed with about 2,500 people who had assembled there in the early hours of the morning.

While the army was still out of sight of Parihaka itself, the band stopped playing and there was silence over the countryside, broken only by the baying of dogs at the approach of the column.

At its head was the commanding officer, Colonel Roberts, on a black horse and Bryce on a white horse. On foot, walking beside Bryce, was Rolleston. Behind them was a special squad of ninety-six men, picked for size and strength and armed with revolvers, and with axes for 'close work'. Then came Armed Constabulary, infantry, mounted rifles and further detachments of volunteers. About four hundred yards from the village, the army halted for about ten minutes, and then the special advance squad were sent forward to the entrance. At the first sight of the soldiers a great cheer rose from the gates of Parihaka. This was the *tatarakihi* – Te Whiti's cicadas – two hundred children who came running out to meet the soldiers. The boys lined up across the road, and began to sing and perform *haka* or action songs. Some way behind them were girls with skipping ropes and bread; five hundred loaves had been baked during the night for the visitors.

The advance guard marched on the children, then wheeled away at the last moment, unsure how to proceed. Bryce then ordered a cavalry charge, but the *tatarakihi* sang on as the horses thundered towards them.

'Even when a mounted officer galloped up and pulled his horse up so short that the dirt from its forefeet spattered the children they still went on chanting, perfectly oblivious, apparently, to the pakeha,' one old soldier, Colonel Messenger, recalled years later.

'I was the first to enter the Maori town with my company. I found my only obstacle was the youthful feminine element. There were skipping-parties of girls on the road . . . I took hold of one end of [a] skipping rope, and the girls at the other end pulled it away so fast that it burnt my hands. To make way for my men I tackled one of the rope-holders. She was a fat substantial young woman, and it was all I could do to lift her up and carry her to one side of the road. She made not the slightest resistance but I was glad to drop the buxom wench. My men were all grinning at the sight of their captain carrying the big girl off . . .'

Bryce and Rolleston marching down the road, with an army and indeed a nation behind them, were in deadly earnest. The night before there had been an extraordinary scene at Pungarehu camp, worthy of Cervantes but in fact described and published by John Bryce in a letter to a newspaper in his retirement. It was a conversation between Bryce himself and Rolleston. By now Rolleston, plus his conscience, was completely under the thumb of his wife and had turned himself into a kind of squire to 'Sir Bryce'.

I spoke seriously to my friend [Bryce wrote] and begged him not to go in with us [to Parihaka]. He became very sad and said, 'You are captain here and if you order me to go away I will go.' I replied that I could not do that, but for anything I knew to the contrary, he might be killed the next day. 'And you,' he said, 'what of yourself?' 'Ah, that is another matter, I shall be where my duty requires me to be.' 'So shall I,' he said. Then I used my last argument and declared that if anything happened to him, Mrs Rolleston would have good cause to reproach me. His voice was slow and emphatic as he replied, 'If anything happens to me Mrs Rolleston will be grieved, but rather than see me in these circumstances evade a danger which you are to incur, she would prefer to see me dead at her feet.' We went on to Parihaka next day together . . .

It is difficult to see how either man could imagine they would be in danger. Parihaka was unfortified, unarmed, thoroughly pre-inspected and surrounded; Bryce's motives for writing this apparently ludicrous and emotional account years afterwards must be regarded with suspicion. At the same time it is certain that there was danger waiting at Parihaka the following morning – for those in the town. Two or three unimpeachable authorities indicate that if there had been any Maori resistance or even a sign of resistance, every man, woman and child would have been 'put to death'. 'If one rifle had gone off by accident, a general fusillade would have soon reduced the village to a shamble', the captain of the arresting party wrote later. The stakes, as the army rounded the bend of the road, were extremely high, whether it was a matter of being killed or becoming mass killers.

They were met with a gleeful shout from children, singing, skipping ropes, loaves of bread and a rope-burn, and even the regular soldiers were grinning at their captain. 'If war comes, what can we do but look on and laugh,' Te Whiti had said. That particular prophecy had already come true. Croumbie-Brown had at this point crept forward from his hiding-place and watched about two hundred boys dancing the haka and singing songs at the invaders. 'It was mere child's play to break through these,' he wrote. Captain Messenger confirms the fact.

But in a sense they have never broken through. Bryce's reputation was never to get over this moment. Whatever was to happen next, this was the abiding image of the day, and when you first read about it, at least if you are a New Zealander, you feel as if you are remembering something. Bryce, his army and the children, they are all still there, on the bend of the road outside Parihaka.

Croumbie-Brown retreated back inside the town and took up his view through the walls of the cooking *whare*. The Constabulary came into the town at about 8.45 a.m. Bryce, Rolleston, Colonel Roberts and staff took up a position in the graveyard, which lay on a slight rise near the gates. At 9.40 a.m. Major Tuke and W. J. Butler went to the edge of the *marae*, now silent and densely packed, and read the Riot Act, the major in English and Butler in Maori. The Riot Act provides that if twelve or more people unlawfully or riotously assembled do not disperse within an hour of the reading of it by a competent authority they shall be considered felons. Croumbie-Brown takes up the story:

> . . . the Maories paying not the slightest attention but main-
> taining a dead silence . . . The whole assemblage sat with eyes
> fixed on Te Whiti. His slightest variation of countenance was
> reflected in the faces of all, and any words that he addressed to
> those close to him were whispered from one to another until
> they reached the uttermost circle of the densely-packed
> meeting.

At ten o'clock, ninety-five hand-picked men armed with loaded revolvers and carrying handcuffs marched further into the *pa* and took up a position beside the crowd.

Tohu spoke briefly: 'Let the man who has raised the war finish his work this day. We will wait where we are . . . Even if the bayonet be put to your breasts do not resist.'

Peering through the walls of the hut with the journalists was a third white man. He was a former government agent and now freelance journalist named Thompson who was married to a Maori woman, and who had also fallen out badly with Bryce and Sir William Fox. He was the friend of young William Fox who had told the story about the boy's love affair which had attracted him to Parihaka. Thompson was a fluent Maori speaker and he whispered a translation of Tohu's speech to Croumbie-Brown.

After that another silence fell. 'Until 10.50 a period of deep suspense followed,' the *Lyttleton Times* reported. Bryce, on his white horse, standing in the graveyard, was described as looking 'exceedingly anxious'. Rolleston smiled throughout as if it was all great fun. The volunteer corps were stationed on hillsides and hillocks to the west, north and north-east of the village.

Croumbie-Brown described this silent hour as most exciting.

At 10.50 the bugle sounded 'advance skirmishers' and the Volunteers came down from the higher ground. The arresting party marched nearer the dense mass of people on the *marae* and Hursthouse, the interpreter, acting on instructions, ordered Te Whiti to 'come and stand in the presence of Mr Bryce' in the graveyard.

Te Whiti replied that he would stay with his people. 'He had nothing to do with the fight of that day. He was prepared to see Mr Bryce if he had anything to say to him. For his part, he had nothing but good words to say to Mr Bryce.'

Bryce replied, in a tone 'considered harsh by those who heard it': 'I feel inclined to humour your wish to come and see you. Make a good road, therefore, for the passage of my horse through your people and I will come to you.'

Te Whiti: 'But some of my children might get hurt.'

Bryce: 'No, this is a quiet horse.'

Te Whiti: 'I do not think it good you should come on horseback among my children.'

Bryce: 'The days for talking are over.'

Te Whiti: 'When did you find that out?'

Bryce: 'Since this morning.'

Te Whiti: 'Then I have nothing more to say.'

At 11.30 a.m. Bryce ordered Colonel Roberts to have Te Whiti and Tohu arrested. Colonel Roberts repeated the order to Major Tuke. Major Tuke addressed the men, cautioning against excitement, but adding that if any Maori flashed a tomahawk to shoot him down instantly, and then ordered Captain Newall to arrest the men. Captain Newall then ordered Sergeant Silver and a constable to arrest Te Whiti and, if they used handcuffs, to 'clinch them tight'. Sergeant Silver and the constable stepped into the crowd and the crowd made a way through for them.

Te Whiti and Tohu were not handcuffed. Before they were led away, Te Whiti told the crowd: 'Be of good heart, and be patient . . . Be steadfast in all that is peaceful.' Tohu said: 'This is the doing of war . . . Do not be sad . . . We looked for peace but we find war. Be steadfast and of large heart. Keep to peaceful works. Do not be dismayed; do not be afraid, but be steadfast.'

'Even in that hour of trial, Te Whiti was every inch a chief,' Captain Newall later wrote in his diary. 'His grizzled hair and beard and smiling handsome face created anything but an unpleasant expression . . . His utterances were gentle in the extreme. Tohu's voice reminded me of nothing so much as a ship's cable when the anchor is dropped.'

As Te Whiti was led away, Croumbie-Brown heard a woman near his hiding-place begin to cry. Another woman said to her: 'Why are you sorry? Look! He is laughing as he goes away with the Pakehas.'

14

The next comet

Te Whiti and Tohu were taken to the nearby army camp on 5 November 1881, and held there for seven days before being transferred to the New Plymouth common gaol, awaiting trial for sedition. The trial date was set for the following May, and during this period of six months, apart from a preliminary hearing in the Magistrates' Court, the two men might as well have vanished from the surface of the earth.

Back at Parihaka, once the two chiefs had departed, something very odd happened. Over the next three weeks there were to be deplorable events in the town and beyond, but for sheer oddness the next hour stands alone. In short – nothing happened at all. Everyone remained where they were. So we have this: 2,500 adults sitting silently in the *marae*, about twelve hundred armed men surrounding them, the children, now silent, still at the gate, Bryce sitting on his horse watching the crowd. One chief spoke just after Te Whiti left, urging the people to remain calm, 'even if we are all arrested on the land that has come to us from our forefathers'. After that – nothing. No one moved or spoke.

What was Bryce thinking while he watched the crowd from the graveyard for fifty minutes? Was he hoping for some sign of resistance to justify the presence of his army? Even if he had given up hope of a deadly fusillade, he must have expected something to happen, or at least some course of action to occur to him. But nothing happened. One of the things that most infuriated the authorities was Te Whiti's claim that he was the decisive figure in a drama no one else understood, and that the fate of the relationship between the two races rested with him:

'War shall have no sway . . . The old evil has lost its power. Take no heed of the thunders and lightning and rain [the army]. Listen everyone. *The bell did not start ringing today, it has been ringing for two years past and now a keeper has been appointed to the door to refuse entrance to those who come too late. I am speaking to people of both races.*'

Now this outrageous figure had been removed. And, in his absence, no one knew what to do next.

After an hour Croumbie-Brown and Humphries emerged from their hiding-place: '. . . if anything in connection with one of the saddest and most shameful spectacles I have witnessed could be ludicrous it was the expression on the faces of the authorities when they saw that their grand scheme for preventing the Colony from knowing what was done in the name of the Queen at Parihaka had been completely frustrated,' Croumbie-Brown wrote. 'Not an action escaped observation; not an order was unheard.' Bryce, Rolleston and the staff abruptly departed for Pungarehu and the volunteers withdrew some distance, putting a cordon around the town. The people remained on the *marae* until the moon rose over their houses.

The next day, the dispersal and destruction of the town of Parihaka commenced. A proclamation was posted ordering all those from other areas to leave Parihaka at once. The rain came down and a gale blew; the volunteers' camps around the town were a sea of mud, the Maori residents stayed indoors, the proclamation flapped in the wind unread. On Monday a six-pounder Armstrong cannon ('the bulldog that bites' as the soldiers called it) was mounted on the hill behind the graveyard (now named 'Fort Rolleston') and under this gun and surrounded by troops the Maori, who had gathered again in the *marae*, were given an hour to disperse. One Nelson paper reported that the volunteers amused themselves by aiming silently at individuals in the crowd and flourishing their bayonets. No one moved. Only one group left Parihaka in the following twenty-four hours – the well-known chief and former parliamentarian Wi Parata departed for Wellington with a number of his friends to see the Governor. The next day, the identification of the different tribes and their dispersal 'at the point of the bayonet', the press agency said, was to begin.

But first, there came a diversion. This was Sir William Fox's doing. During the invasion of Parihaka he had stayed in the distance, monitoring events from Rangitikei and urging the Premier by telegram to 'send the aliens home, taking care they do no mischief on the roads'. Once again his obsession with 'the outsiders' at Parihaka, including his own foster-son, was evident. In a speech two days before the attack, he elaborated on the Parihaka problem. 'Te Whiti was a most remarkable man, but in his late proceedings he had been pushed on by outsiders who had no right to be at Parihaka at all – men who had not the bone of an ancestor in the land and no claim whatever to it. The Government were acting most righteously and if war ensued the Maoris would have only themselves to blame and their blood would be on their own heads. [Applause] But too much sensation was being made about the troubles. The constables would simply take the Maoris by the scruff of the neck and put them out of Parihaka.'

In the following week, Fox had a further suggestion. He wired the Premier again: 'There is considerable feeling on the coast that if stranger natives are compelled to leave Parihaka they might scatter and attack country settlers . . . Do you not think it prudent before they are dispersed to seize all the arms and ammunition at Parihaka from both residents and strangers?'

Then a third consideration came to mind. If the 'stranger natives' were expelled without their arms (mostly fowling pieces) and then arrived at their home villages, scattered across Taranaki, it was possible they could rearm there. It was decided that every Maori house in Taranaki was to be raided for arms.

Operations at Parihaka were suspended for a day or two while Bryce, Rolleston, Atkinson and columns of troops fanned out across the country. The extraordinary scenes of government ministers personally smashing down doors and breaking open chests – even in long-friendly Maori settlements – will not detain us. It may be coincidence that the first name, in a list which the papers published of villages thus visited, was Mawhitiwhiti.

The destruction of Parihaka was then resumed. Collaborators were brought in to peer into the faces of the crowd and identify the 'aliens' – people from outside tribes – who were then taken off under armed guard. By the twelfth of November less than a hundred had been taken away. As they left, their houses were demolished.

The runaway bride, Ellen Sturmey, was discovered and marched off home in the midst of the New Plymouth Foot Rifles. The press reported however that she was 'tired of living among the Maoris,' and that, 'as usual in matrimonial squabbles, there were plenty of tears, but her husband told her to put her boots on and be off.'

Night raids began through the town, with troops breaking into every house, marking those that were empty for demolition in the morning. Syphilis is reported to have made its first appearance in Parihaka following these raids.

A new technique was applied: More than a thousand women and children were herded away and lined up before a colla-borator from Wanganui named Utiku Potaka, who, said Bryce later, had 'the eyes of a hawk'. 'The process is strangely like draughting sheep, today the Wanganui ewes were culled,' one paper reported. Mistakes were made. Families were separated, women and children sent on forced marches in the opposite direction from their homes. 'I think it may be necessary to destroy every *whare* in the village if the Maoris hold out,' Bryce telegraphed Premier Hall, to justify his actions. 'Well, I have ordered them to return to their homes emphatically enough, and apparently I might as well called [sic] from the vasty deep.' This was an interesting sentence, not just for its bad grammar: always eager to show his own learning to his better-educated collea-gues, Bryce had misquoted Shakespeare's 'I can call spirits from the vasty deep.'* In a Freudian slip, Bryce placed *himself* in the vasty deep, the deadly place of refuge, according to the New Testament, for those who 'offend against these little ones'. *It were better for him that a millstone were hanged around his neck and he cast into the sea than that he offend against these little ones.*

By 21 November, 1,507 people had been sent away from the town and their houses destroyed. Often they put a brave face on their departure, performing a *haka* to those left behind. But one Maori, watching the separation and deportation, the falling houses and the crying children, was overheard by a reporter from the Nelson newspaper: 'It would have been better,' he said, 'not to have been born.'

Three weeks after the invasion, the population had been reduced to about five hundred. A new road was built inland behind the town cutting through cultivations. Acres of gardens and crops had in any case been destroyed to discourage reset-tlement. In one of his final acts, Bryce, who now named himself Minister of War, had the great Parihaka meeting-house dis-mantled. 'It was a great job to get it down as it was very substantially built,' he telegraphed the Premier. 'But put 100 stout men behind a rope and something has to give.'

★　　★　　★

* *Glendower.*　I can call spirits from the vasty deep.
　Hotspur.　Why, so can I, or so can any man;
　　　　　　But will they come when you do call for them? (*Henry IV, Part I*)

In the last week of November Sir William Fox finally came back to Taranaki. He went to Oeo, the little town down the coast from Parihaka, where he had opened the hearings of the West Coast Commission not quite two years before and where he was now going to meet the Native and War Minister Bryce. As he rode west on the single narrow road that linked Oeo to the south and east, the Royal Commissioner travelled against a tide of hundreds of Maori men, women and children, walking east. These were Ngati Ruanui and Nga Ruahine, young Fox's tribe, which had made up one of the largest groups at Parihaka. They had been marched to Oeo under armed guard, some in handcuffs, and there left to their own devices. At least five hundred of them had camped there for several days and then in large parties or small had begun to straggle home to their raided villages. Among them – possibly – was young Fox, and – possibly – the Royal Commissioner and his foster-son came face to face.

It is here, on the narrow Oeo road, that, surrounded by question marks and *possiblys*, the story of the two William Foxes comes to an end. They may have met or exchanged glances – there is no evidence either way – but they must have been aware of each other's presence. The former Premier who even in old age liked to ride a 'tearing beast' was a famous sight in Taranaki and not easily missed. And he, for his part, knew exactly who Ngati Ruanui and Nga Ruahine were, where they had just come from, where they were going, and why, and he knew of one young man who was likely to be among them.

There is no sign that Sir William and his son ever spoke or communicated again. When the Royal Commission published its recommendations on Maori reserves in 1882, a number of claims were refused, but 'particularly a claim by Wiremu Omahuru . . . based on some alleged promises made by Sir Donald McLean'.

When the people of Mawhitiwhiti finally reached their home village at the end of the week, they did something that seems quite natural after their three-week ordeal under Bryce. They got drunk. In fact, they got roaring drunk. The local white settlers, who had been among the most fervent for the destruction of Parihaka, now changed their minds; it occurred to them that they may have made a terrible mistake. 'Over 300 Natives have arrived at Mawhitiwhiti and others are following,' a paper reported on Saturday.

SUNDAY EVENING: An enormous quantity of beer and spirits have been broached and a perfect Saturnalia is now going on. Numbers of Maories continue to come in and a feeling of uneasiness exists in Normanby lest, maddened with drink, they should commit excesses. The town is absolutely unprotected; both the Waihi and Normanby redoubts have been abandoned by the Constabulary. Nothing could more markedly prove Te Whiti's influence for good than the fact that at Parihaka those very people now drinking to excess and indulging in other immorality were kept under the strictest restraint.

28 NOVEMBER: The Maories are now coming into Normanby in hundreds from Mawhitiwhiti and preparing for a continuation of their debauch in a paddock about a hundred yards from the Normanby Hotel. An ox and numerous sheep have been killed and the supply of drink is unlimited. I anticipate that before night the scene will be a shocking one. The Maories appear perfectly reckless in their drinking, and many are very sullen towards Europeans.

LATER: The Maories have camped for the night in a paddock close to the township. This afternoon they danced the haka wearing only a shawl around their loins. A number of Europeans were present, including a few females. Beer was handed about in buckets . . .

291

At this point, among buckets of beer and shawls and a few European females, oblivion descends. That was the last scene to which we can track William Fox with any confidence and there must be some doubts about his presence at the party or his state of mind if he was there. How much at home he would have felt at 'a perfect Saturnalia' in a dark paddock near the Normanby Hotel is open to question. In some ways the young man with his haze of names around him never successfully completed the transition back into the Maori world.

When he described seeing William Fox sitting with Te Whiti before the invasion of Parihaka, the telegraph clerk W. F. Gordon said that he believed that Fox later 'repented his actions' – that is, his support for Te Whiti, which 'no doubt greatly displeased Sir William and Lady Fox'.

Gordon was not a reliable judge in this or in many other matters. Insatiably curious, which gives him some value as an eyewitness, he was also something of a buffoon and was certainly regarded as a pest at Parihaka where he constantly kept trying to snatch a portrait of Te Whiti. In the same week that young Fox made his speech on the *marae*, Gordon was vying for attention with a performance of his own on the mountain above. 'Mr W. Gordon gave a cornet recital . . . at an elevation of 6,000 ft.,' the New Plymouth paper reported. 'The pieces played were the National Anthem, the German "Fatherland", the "Marseillaise" and "Yankee Doodle". The recital would have been on the summit but a thick fog enshrouded the musician. The sound of the cornet awakened singular echoes among the rocks and brought down a quantity of loose rock from precipices above. We believe that never before has "God Save the Queen" been played at such an altitude.'

W. Gordon may have been enshrouded by fog more often than he realised. There is no doubt that Sir William was 'greatly displeased' by the actions of his foster–son, but there is one sign that suggests Lady Fox actually approved of her son's departure to Parihaka. In 1881, that same year, she published a pamphlet entitled 'To the Mothers of New Zealand'. It is an odd, droll, harmless little thing – and poignant in a sense, for it is a tract on childcare from a woman who had limited experience in that field.

'Never threaten children when you do not intend to punish them,' she writes, for example. 'I lately heard a woman call out to her child "Mary Jane, come into the house or I'll kill you." Mary Jane did not come into the house, and her mother did not kill her, but what better was either mother or daughter?' The pamphlet also contains a poem that opens with a quotation from a figure with whom Sarah Fox from time to time identified – that daughter of the Pharaoh who found one of the enemy's children, one of Hebrews' children, in 'an ark daubed with slime and pitch' among the bulrushes.

The Mother's Charge
'Take this child away, and nurse it for me, and I will give thee they wages.' – Ex.ii.9.

'Take this child and nurse it for Me,'
Thus the kindly princess spoke,
As the lovely weeping infant
In her breast soft pity woke . . .
Let no harsh nor hasty spirit,
Rudely crush the tender shoot . . .
'Take this child and nurse it for Me:'
Think – within your loving arms,
There may lie the mighty statesman,
Or the orator that charms . . .

Ornate and sentimental, the sole published work of Lady Fox sank at once from public view. I found what I suppose is the only extant copy in the archives of a library in Dunedin, almost within sight of the harbour causeway where many Maori prisoners were sent by Sir William and set to hard labour. But reading these lines, published the same year as Fox ran away to Parihaka and made his speech, it is hard to avoid the impression that their author, timid and pious as she was, delivered one veiled rebuke to a certain harsh and hasty spirit, and, more than that, she thought that her only child, whom she undoubtedly loved, might become a leader of his own people.

But young Fox was not to become a great statesman or orator. The 'bright and intelligent' child had been given another destiny

which was unusual and precise: to be fought over. Several times in his life, up till the age of twenty, this happened to him. He was not to become a leader or even a symbol but he invited symbolical associations. Perhaps all children do, their gaze is less cryptic than adults' and offences against them cry out to heaven. In that sense, he did have a certain power to lead. Herewini, Buller, Richmond, Sir William Fox, Lady Fox, Te Whiti – all these people the small and insignificant person of William Fox Omahuru set thinking, and set against one another. His photograph led me, for instance, a hundred years later, towards this story of Te Whiti, and he led Sir William and Te Whiti not just towards a story, but deeper and deeper into their own one, which from now on goes on without him.

But not without this postscript: After coming back from Dunedin, I saw Miri Rangi and happened to say I had found a poem by Sarah Fox. She wanted to see it, and I showed her the few lines above which I had copied out.

'But this is a great *taonga* [a treasure],' she said.

'Is it really?'

'Of course it is,' she said, and she asked me to send her a copy of the complete poem running to about forty lines.

'I'll translate it and turn it into a *waiata* [a song]. When we open our new meeting-house, we will sing this Sarah Fox song.'

And so one day soon the words of little timid Sarah Fox will be heard again, although in a form and place she would never have dreamed of, at Aotearoa Pa, not far from the dark field where the people from Mawhitiwhiti came home and got drunk many years ago, and perhaps even beyond there, on *marae* across the plains of south Taranaki.

On 12 November 1881, Te Whiti and Tohu were taken at 4 a.m. under the guard of the Taranaki Mounted Rifles from the blockhouse at Pungarehu camp to the common gaol in New Plymouth to appear that day before the Resident Magistrates'

Court. Word of their transfer must have leaked out; as they left Pungarehu, Te Whiti's son was seen waiting at the camp boundary and Te Whiti was allowed a 'brief interview' through the fence with the boy, who burst into tears.

Only one remark about Te Whiti's imprisonment in the army camp has survived. A journalist who spent some time at Pungarehu listened to the soldiers talk. 'Te Whiti's influence seems to be felt by all who approach him,' he wrote in the *New Zealand Herald*, 'and the roughest men say, with curious unanimity, that he is a gentleman.'

On the bench in the New Plymouth Magistrates' Court sat the magistrate and eight justices of the peace in two rows. Te Whiti was charged with being a 'wicked, malicious, seditious and evil-disposed person' and with:

> Wickedly, maliciously and seditiously contriving and intending to disturb the peace of Her Majesty's subjects, and to incite and move to hatred and dislike of the persons of Her Majesty and the Government, and by inciting members of Her Majesty's subjects to insurrections, riots, tumults and breaches of the peace . . . on 17 September did wickedly, unlawfully and maliciously declare . . . the false, wicked, seditious and inflammatory words . . . 'Naku te whenua. Naku nga tangata. Ko te tino pakanga tenei o tenei whakatupuranga . . .'

This sentence was tentatively translated as 'Mine is the land, mine the people. Here we have the great struggle of this generation.' The committal hearings then immediately descended into force. The three government interpreters all gave different versions of the September speech, none could agree on its implications, one gave two different versions of one phrase, all agreed that they had not heard Te Whiti's own explanation on the evening of 17 September. A dispute then broke out between the interpreters and one of the sitting JPs, namely Robert Parris, the Land Commissioner: it turned out that no one had ever shown Te Whiti or anyone at Parihaka any map or plan explaining what land was to be reserved for them.

'The government informs the public that for two years the Natives have persistently refused the reserves pointed out to them,' wrote the *Lyttleton Times*. 'And it turns out that no reserves have ever been pointed out to them.'

Te Whiti, on the third day of the proceedings, made a short speech. He said that he and his people had been told that after confiscation all their land belonged to the government. 'It is very little I have to say. We have been staying on the land ever since the war was over; we have been cultivating the land; we have not put food in to cause a quarrel . . . It is not my wish that evil should come to either of the two races; my wish is for the whole of us to live happy on the land. I have not wished to do evil or kill up to the present time. My wish is for the whole of us to live happy on the land. That is my wish. That is the way I have addressed the Maori people. That is all I have to say.'

The prisoners were then 'committed to the common gaol of New Plymouth, there to be safely kept until . . . delivered by the due course of law.'

The trial was set for 1 May 1882. It could clearly never take place. The prosecutor told government ministers that the case for sedition was weak. Furthermore, the High Court judge who was to hear the case had already made clear his view of the events at Parihaka. Three days after the invasion, Judge Gillies, addressing a Grand Jury in another case being heard at New Plymouth, said he would be wanting in his duty if he ignored the extraordinary circumstances in the district, where large bodies of armed men had assembled on active service. 'The employment of armed force was only justifiable either . . . in repelling armed

297

aggression, or in aid of the civil arm of the law, when that arm had proved powerless to enforce the law's mandates; *in any other case the use of armed force was illegal, and a menace, if not an outrage, upon the liberties of the people.*'

It was clear to the government that Te Whiti, Tohu and Mr Justice Gillies must never meet in court. Several months passed. In April 1882, five days before the case was set to open, the two chiefs were suddenly transferred to the South Island city of Christchurch. There the quarterly sessions were safely over. Bryce and other ministers had some breathing space. They used it to bring in a new law which would allow 'two aboriginal natives named Te Whiti and Tohu' to be held indefinitely without trial. No information was laid before the House to justify the bill. An amendment to allow Te Whiti and Tohu to appear at the bar of the House was defeated.

The Governor exploded against this. It had, he wrote back to London, 'probably no precedent in Parliamentary history . . . No such legislation against individuals has been resorted to in England since the attainder of Sir John Fenwick, nearly 200 years ago; no such legislation has been even attempted since the Bill of Pains and Penalties against Queen Caroline; but even in the worst days of English history the right of self defence has been unchallenged.'

Bryce also produced an Indemnity Bill by which he himself and those acting under his orders at Parihaka were 'freed, acquitted, released, indemnified, and discharged of, from, and against all actions, suits, complaints, informations, indictment, prosecutions, liabilities and proceedings whatsoever.'

This time, there were many voices raised in Parliament against the bills. 'Here is Te Whiti, a man without a particle of [English] literary culture or historical knowledge, and yet by the sheer force of his intellect and tenacity of purpose, by his honesty and purity, he is able not only to defy but to a large extent defeat the Native Minister and the brute force which was brought to bear against him,' one MP thundered. 'This Bill, bristling as it does with injustice from the preamble to the close, is an insult to every sentiment of freedom in which Englishmen have been cradled. The very fact of its being brought in is a confession of weakness . . . The Native Minister has no particular liking for Maoris; but the midnight proclamation, the hurrying to and fro in hot haste before His Excellency the Governor could reach these shores – all these things were very curious . . . I express it as my conviction that the driving of the natives from Parihaka, the demolition of their houses, the wanton destruction of their crops, amount to a gross outrage, a cruel and arbitrary outrage upon justice . . . and humanity.'

A dozen other speakers rose to condemn Bryce and the provocations he had offered the Maori of Taranaki. Party politics being what they are, however, even some of those who spoke against the bills voted for them; they passed with a majority of two to one. Meanwhile the government ensured by a secret arrangement that Gordon's despatches to London, which laid all bare to the Colonial Office, were not laid at all before the House of Commons. Te Whiti and Tohu, despite the protection of the British constitution, were left hanging in the wind.

Christchurch, however, the cold autumnal city where they arrived from Taranaki in their convict uniforms, was a world completely unfamiliar to men like Bryce. Wealthy, liberal, snobbish and cultured, it was the city of the *Lyttleton Times*, of Croumbie-Brown's reports, of the famous 'philo-Maori' Fitzgerald, of Samuel Butler: on the western horizon stood a row of snowcapped peaks among which Butler had dreamed up *Erewhon*, in part an attack on racist settlers. It was the city where the mordant poet, Jessie Mackay, quoted earlier, was making her name. She had already turned her attention to the invasion of Parihaka:

Yet a league, yet a league,
Yet a league onward
Straight to the Maori *pah*,
Marched the Twelve Hundred.
'Forward the Volunteers!
Is there a man who fears?'
Over the ferny plain
Marched the Twelve Hundred

'Forward!' the Colonel said:
Was there a man dismayed?
No, for the heroes knew
There was no danger . . .
Dreading their country's eyes,
Long was their search and wise;
Vain, for the pressmen five
   Had, by a slight device,
    Foiled the Twelve Hundred.

Children to the right of them,
Children to the left of them,
Women in front of them,
   Saw them and wondered . . .
When can their glory fade?
Oh! the wild charge they made!
   New Zealand wondered
Whether each doughty soul
Paid for the pigs he stole,
    Noble Twelve Hundred!

Sir Arthur Gordon, who had 'met one or two nice people' in
Christchurch, had gone to live there — as far away as he could
decently remain from the ministers of his own government
whom he abominated. Under the stone spire of its cathedral,

Christchurch had retained, more than anywhere else in the colony, a memory of the idealism of the founding years. Some of the reasons for this were not especially noble. The vast blue plains on which the city stood had never been home to more than a few hundred, perhaps one or two thousand, Maori; the entire South Island, a land the size of England, had been bought from the Maori for a song, for a farthing an acre – and even where there was fraud (and there was) the voices of Maori complaint were so faint, and intermarriage in any case so nearly an accomplished fact, that they could be ignored, and Christchurch felt virtuous.

In defiance of Bryce, the city therefore decided to lionise its two visitors, the prisoners Te Whiti and Tohu. The governor of Addington Gaol had them fitted out in tweed suits and on the first night sent over a dinner of tinned lobster. The Resident Magistrate swooped on the prisoners and took them under his wing and out of the gates to show them the sights. Crowds, curious and friendly, appeared wherever they went. Te Whiti especially was taken with the river. Christchurch, having showed Te Whiti its wonders – the steam tram, the iron foundry, the locomotive workshop, a boot factory where they were led into the presence of the Leviathan Sewing Machine – was surprised when Te Whiti, asked what impressed him most, answered: 'The river.' He stood in long contemplation of it. Quite different from the twenty-four torrents rushing down the sides of Mt. Taranaki, the river in Christchurch, named the Avon, rose a few miles away in the middle of a level plain and wound endlessly through the town, always ahead of you, around every street corner, clear, fast and placid, filled with the shadows of English trout, and set between rounded banks of green lawn and lined with Church of England institutions, churches and schools and shaded by English willows and oaks. (As a Catholic boy growing up in Christchurch, where Catholics felt somewhat excluded from the mainstream, I remember thinking of the Avon as a distinctly *Anglican* entity.)

Bryce was shocked at the liberties extended to the two Maori chiefs. He complained to the Minister of Justice, who reprimanded the magistrate. A new arrangement was made. A special warden was sent to Christchurch to take charge of the prisoners. He was an employee of Bryce. Once more, Te Whiti and Tohu were Bryce's personal prisoners. But Bryce had also been taken aback by the evidence of popular support in Christchurch – at that time the colony's largest town – for the two men. He himself only really knew one electorate – the still bloodthirsty populace of Wanganui. (At a banquet in Wanganui, where Bryce had said that 'every man, woman and child at Parihaka' could have been put to death, the remarks was greeted with an ovation.) Bryce was a bully, or worse, and a coward, but he was also a practical democratic politician. He knew the importance of public opinion. For all his bravado he was somewhat shaken by the attacks on him in the press and in Parliament over his Indemnity Bill. He was unsure now how to deal with the prisoners. A regime of privation was now politically impossible. A plan to send them into exile – into real exile, that is, out of the colony altogether – was considered, but there was only one place where the government had power to sent them, and that was to England. Jocular reports floated up to the surface of the local press:

> Sir Wm Fox has had a long interview with Hon. Mr Bryce and has offered and accepted the post of Showman to Te Whiti at a handsome salary. They will start for England in a few days. The Govt. will net a large sum by exhibiting Te Whiti. A squad of the Royal Rifles accompany Sir William as doorkeepers, money-takers, etc.

But it did not take long to see the dangers that lay in that direction. Te Whiti in England, taken up by a Bradlaugh, or by supporters of Selwyn, who luckily was dead but who still had

302

numerous and powerful friends, was a dangerous prospect. The colonial government was shameless; it was afraid of nothing, neither its own opposition, its Governor, or the Colonial Office, but it was terrified of English public opinion.

All these things considered, it was decided that the 'silken captivity' of Te Whiti and Tohu would continue for the meantime. Their new warden was named John Ward, a dull, boastful man who had fought in the wars in the 1860s, spoke Maori, was about to bore Te Whiti with his theories on culture, evolution and 'the battle for life', and to listen at keyholes and gloat over his prisoners, but who was by and large no more dangerous than a big police dog that has not been ordered to attack.

The new plan was to awe Te Whiti and Tohu with the might and wealth of the European race and then attempt to win some sign of submission from them. They were taken on a railway trip for miles across the plains waving with golden corn, and they were led up the bell-tower of the new cathedral, which had been designed by Gilbert Scott and consecrated, with great ceremony, the same week Parihaka was attacked by Bryce. It was 6 p.m. on a winter evening when the prisoners reached the cathedral. The organ was playing. Te Whiti put his finger on the keyboard and played the bass note. It was dusk when they reached the balcony on the belfry; they were not greatly impressed with the prospect of the dim and scattered city, but were pleased that they could just make out, three or four miles away, the bare plain of the Pacific Ocean, over which lay the road home.

Various interludes followed. Ward was pleased to note on one occasion that the 'prophet [Te Whiti] trembled' when a loco-motive came thundering down on him. Once, a silly woman rushed out of a crowd and shook Te Whiti's hand; she had an electric battery concealed in her sleeve. Te Whiti gasped when he felt the shock and muttered that changeling word neither English nor Maori, *taipo*! – 'goblin!' This also gratified Ward.

They were taken to the Christchurch Exhibition where a crowd of three hundred or four hundred followed them, and they had to escape into a pavilion where an 'armless woman served, knit and wrote,' and where they were then shown 'Bismarck', the Learned Pig, playing euchre. One afternoon they visited the statuary room at the Christchurch Museum where they saw casts of the naked Mercury, Hercules, Venus de Medici, Andromeda and others. Te Whiti was fascinated by the presence in the room of European ladies.

'Ward, are these women not ashamed to come and look at these statues? I know Maori women are not fastidious, but I thought the European ones so very chaste and proud they could not have viewed such objects.'

He then addressed the ladies in Maori. Their responses most consisted of bewitching smiles and whispers 'Oh, what a nice man he is' and so on.

Happily they could not understand his homily. Te Whiti told them to go and get married at once, so that they would not need to spend their time in a museum looking at nude statuary.

In the meantime, at Parihaka, Te Whiti's followers made attempts to meet again on the *marae* on the eighteenth of each month. Bryce ordered more houses torn down. Sir William Fox had still not found time to survey the reserves intended for Parihaka but he had them reduced by five thousand acres, as a punishment for those who had refused to listen to the 'midnight proclamation'.

The quarterly session of the Supreme Court opened in Christchurch in early June 1882, but on that date Te Whiti and Tohu had been removed to the alpine town of Queenstown, where they were gravely impressed by the presence of a steamship on a lake so far from the sea and where Tohu seems to have fallen in love with a lady at, or perhaps the lady of, the hotel where they were staying. It was not until 14 June that the prisoners were informed that there was to be no trial. Butler, Bryce's secretary, presented this fact to them as a great concession, as a mark of friendship, from a government which now wanted to 'assist' the prisoners and treat them as 'gentlemen'. Bryce was smarting from the press opinion that he had been 'defeated' by Te Whiti, who had 'taught him a lesson in dignity', and he was determined to find some formula which he could present as submission on the part of Te Whiti. If he accepted the reduced reserves on offer, and promised to hold no more meetings at Parihaka, he and Tohu would be set free.

> Te Whiti: The Government assist me? Faugh! [The notes are Ward's] I want no assistance from the Government. Let them do what they like.
> Butler: You are very foolish. The Government want to make friends with you, and if you do not grasp their proffered hand . . . you will both be kept in captivity.
> Te Whiti: I do not care [about that]. You can do what you like. I want none of your 'love'.
> Butler: Very well. You will be kept prisoners and sent to Nelson.
> Te Whiti: I do not care. I have nothing to do with that. It lies with you.
> Butler: No. It lies with you, Te Whiti, but your heart is hard and you won't listen.
> Te Whiti: Never mind my heart. Let the talk cease.

On 26 July, the prisoners were back in Christchurch and Butler, who had brought the proclamation to Parihaka and stood beside Bryce at the invasion, now arrived there to renew his case.

Te Whiti: I came here to be tried. Why not try us and kill us now?

Butler: You are not to be tried, or killed. You are hard-hearted, Te Whiti. We wish to treat you as gentlemen.

The two prisoners were then sent to Nelson. This was a town with a very different atmosphere from Christchurch. Nelson had once been the home of Domett, and a stamping ground of the Richmonds and Atkinsons, some of whom, as the *Lyttleton Times* noted, always came into view just before racial trouble or war broke out in New Zealand, 'like the petrel on the ocean at the approach of a storm'. The attitude in Nelson towards the prisoners was cold. There were no visits from scholars or Maori linguists or friendly magistrates.

Butler once more arrived and renewed the siege:

Butler: My friends, I go to Wellington tomorrow. Have you looked over the house here and are you satisfied with it? Or is there anything else either of you would like?

Te Whiti: The house is a house. We have nothing to do with it.

Butler: Yes. Well, have you thought over what we were all talking about in Christchurch and Oamaru? . . . If you both will give up your old practices and live as good quite men, a Crown grant for your lands will be made out and you will both be brought back at once to Taranaki.

Te Whiti (excitedly): What land? What land?

Butler: The land reserved for you and your people.

Te Whiti: Where is the land you (the Government) have stolen!

Butler: The Government have stolen no land from you, Te Whiti; but some of the land you speak of is settled upon, and the Government hold some.

Te Whiti: Who told the Europeans to settle upon it, and who

gave any of it to the Government?

Butler: It was taken by the Government, as well you know, in payment for war expenses.

Te Whiti: And this land, who is now giving it back?

Butler: The Government, at the request of the West Coast Commissioners.

Te Whiti (in derision): The Commissioners! They *are* Commissioners! (Excitedly) Did not those men [Fox and Bell] say that all the land was to be taken, and none given to the Maories?

Butler: No. They said you were to have plenty of land and . . . that yourself and Tohu were to be considered favourably, as they (the Commissioners) loved you both very much.

Te Whiti: No, that's not correct. They said that all the Natives were to be driven away and the land swallowed up by the Europeans.

Butler: No, no. Te Whiti, you are wrong about what you say in reference to the Commissioners. They expressed very great love for you in particular and your people as a whole and wished even more land than this mentioned to be returned to you.

Te Whiti: It is all my land, and the Government have stolen it, and drove my people away. I am here.

Butler: No, they did not drive your people away. They are all there. Only the strangers were sent back. All your children are there. And what has happened is your fault. As a sensible man, you know that.

Tohu (laughing): Did not the Government come to my place with all their soldiers and drive the people away, and here I am. Who did all this? Why, the Government, who you say are so kind and full of love. What is this house? Why, a prison. Let the talk cease.

Butler: The Government never brought up their soldiers to your place until you forced them to do so by your foolish conduct, but they want to forgive, and bury the past. If you agree to cease and give over the foolish work you have been doing, you will be brought back and more land given to you than you know what to do with.

Tohu (energetically): This talk is nonsense. Who raised the fighting spirit between the Government and me? Not I.

Butler: Yes, it was you.

Tohu: Well, why did the soldiers not fight if they were ready?

Butler: If only one shot had been fired that morning, at Parihaka, all you Natives would have been killed. But the Government don't want this . . . The Government say 'We must protect the Maories . . .'

Te Whiti: I expected to be tried . . . I want to be tried. It is no use coming to me now with this food [kind words] of the Government after all the wrong done. Why did they not offer it before?

Butler: It was offered to you always, but you put away the food from you always.

Te Whiti (very excitedly): That is wrong. It was never offered as I hear it today. It was always 'War! war!' . . .

And so Butler went away, and the two remained as prisoners, and Ward watched them – especially he watched Te Whiti – and wrote his diary. 'Is it not disgusting to see a man, so obstinate and pigheaded as he is?' The rain fell. The atmosphere was depressing. The only news to reach them from the outside world was what Ward chose to translate from the newspapers.

Tohu especially found the constraints of the house wearisome. One day he announced he was going for a walk. Ward said he was too busy to accompany him and that he therefore must stay at home. Tohu ignored him and set off down the road. Ward rushed after him. Two middle-aged men grappled in the open air. Te Whiti came out and calmed them down and they returned to the house, but the local chief of police was called and the house arrest was from then on enforced more strictly. The incident weighed heavily on the prisoners.

Some hope may have entered their minds in August when a deputation of three Maori chiefs arrived in England to petition the Queen for redress of Maori grievances. Te Whiti, ever since writing to Bradlaugh, had conceived the idea that some protection for the Maori might be found in England. The chiefs' petition complained about the government's attempt 'to enkindle strife' at Parihaka, 'to capture innocent men . . . seize their property . . . break down their houses' and begged that Te Whiti might be set free. Lord Kimberly, the Colonial Secretary, fobbed them off with an audience with the Prince and Princess of Wales and had the petition referred back to the New Zealand government, to Whitaker and more precisely to Bryce, Minister of Native Affairs and of War. The chiefs stayed on a few weeks in England, two of them visited Lichfield Cathedral, before sailing home.

'On arriving at the Selwyn memorial,' the *Lichfield Mercury* reported, 'both visitors were marvellously affected. They stood gazing through the ironwork, weeping bitterly. On entering within the chapel containing the monument, they gave way to expressions of delight . . . they noted the determined lines on the bishop's face, spoke of his iron will, and his kindness and firmness. They were particularly pleased that he is laid on what is a New Zealand mat, adding that it is right that it should be so . . .

'There was something particularly touching in the visit of the Maoris. Their visit here is a last resource, a final effort on the part of a doomed race. Bishop Selwyn's devotion to the Maori cause is well known, and possibly, had he been living still, the deputation would have excited more attention; it would at least have compelled a measure of respect, which the visitors have so far failed to excite. It may be reasonably hoped that the Colonial Government will speedily consider the alleged claims of the Maoris.'

This was reprinted in New Zealand papers at the end of September, two or three days after the row between Ward and Tohu, when the two men were scarcely speaking, but Te Whiti and Tohu must have already known of the failure of the August deputation which would have been reported by telegraph at the time.

A week later came more bad news. John Bryce had just returned from a triumphant trip to Parihaka. 'Native matters are considered in a very satisfactory condition,' the official sources reported, and the resident population – now reduced to about three hundred – were described as 'thoroughly pleased with Mr Bryce'.

Bryce rode over the old cultivations to see for himself that there was no 'undue planting' – that is, putting in spring crops which might produce a surplus for summer visitors and to make sure there were no strangers at work there. The new chief, named in the papers as 'old Tummake' (probably Tumuaki, meaning chief or leader) assured Bryce that all the meetings had stopped and that strangers were not welcome: 'There has been enough trouble from strangers.' Further afield, those deported from Parihaka had been offered work by Bryce. If they are hungry, he said, 'I propose to give them road work at low wages, taking care not to pamper them.'

There exists a memorial of Bryce's visit to Parihaka in early October. Among his party (Bryce enjoyed taking his friends and cronies along on his ministerial expeditions) was a photographer who, just before nightfall, set up a plate camera on the edge of the village and shot a picture of Parihaka with the Great Comet of 1882 appearing above snow-clad Mt. Taranaki in the background.

This comet had first appeared in early September. It had grown steadily in brilliance for three weeks until it was visible in the

310

daytime and at night outshone Venus. It was at its most beautiful, the reports agreed, just before dawn. Some experts believed that it was the same comet that had been seen in February, 1880 – the same body, that is, which 'appeared to be descending straight on the Waimate Plains' when Bryce, thirty months before, first sent his army over the river to confront Te Whiti.

Bryce himself was not a superstitious man, and if he even noticed the symmetry – a comet at the start of his military campaign and another, or the same one, at its conclusion – he is unlikely to have imagined it to be a compliment from the starry universe. And yet the photograph, even in its dismal condition (the plate was cracked and damaged before it was lost and the comet and the snows have been touched up by brush), is a kind of trophy, a manifest of Bryce's triumph. He, 'Sir' Bryce, Honest John, the friend of the settlers, had sent an army on to the plains, he had heard his name blackened, had been betrayed, but in the end he had won through, overawed and scattered the Maori people of the district and rid the colony of Te Whiti, who was now far away and as good as dead under silent house-arrest. Here, as evidence of his success, below the snowy mountain and that one brushstroke among the planets, stood the new Parihaka, dark, lifeless, half-dismantled and nearly deserted. Bryce alone had solved the insoluble problem of race and land in Taranaki.

'The West Coast dictator', a Wellington paper said, 'rode over the scene of his late triumph.'

Te Whiti, shut up in the house in Nelson, was also 'greatly concerned' with the comet, according to Ward, and the two men debated its nature. Te Whiti's usual metaphorical and optimistic flair seems to have deserted him. The comet, he thought, was a distant world in flames.

Bryce's triumph was not exactly shortlived, but it was not to last for very many more months either. Even while he was galloping over the cultivations, a reversal, an unpleasant surprise, was in store for him. In fact it was already in operation right beneath him, so to speak, beneath his horse's hooves, beneath the unweeded furrows of Parihaka's old gardens. There is no real riddle here: at the (more or less) exact antipodes of Taranaki, straight through the globe, a printing press was running in London. It was printing the parliamentary Blue Book, in which information tabled in the House is published.

In the latest edition of 1882, a large number of despatches from Sir Arthur Gordon was being prepared for publication. Gordon's role and position in New Zealand had been invidious. He had arrived with the highest ambitions, to prevent the brutality and exploitation which he knew took place everywhere under colonisation. He had failed, and his choice was to resign and leave or carry on in his constitutional role. He chose the latter; it was often a torment. Two or three days after the

312

invasion of Parihaka, for example, the former parliamentarian Wi Parata, who had been sitting on the *marae* under Bryce's guns, came to Wellington to see Gordon. He brought with him as his interpreter none other than Alexander McDonald, that picaresque hero (of sorts) who had shot the grey horse years before and gone to prison for his pains. Alexander was now greatly depressed by the kind of country New Zealand had turned into, and he laid most of the blame at the door of Sir William Fox. 'The curses of a free and generous, though uncivilized people are justly resting upon us,' he lamented in a letter to the press. 'The Maori people, as a people, now curse us in their hearts.'

Wi Parata described to Gordon exactly what had happened at Parihaka and 'earnestly entreated the Governor to advise him what course they should adopt'. The Governor, 'after listening to his words with marked attention, explained to him with much care and kindness of manner that he could not, with propriety, interfere in the matter at its present stage but must refer him to his Excellency's Responsible Advisers.' His Responsible Adviser in this case was John Bryce.

This was bitter gall for Gordon himself. One of his own heroes was his namesake, 'Chinese' Gordon. Everyone at that time knew how 'Chinese' Gordon had stood on a battlefield carrying only an officer's staff and saved China, and how he had then gone to the Sudan and almost single-handedly released thousands of slaves, not neglecting to have their Arab slave-masters stripped, lashed and turned out in the desert they had depopulated.

At one place on a road lined with the bones of dead Africans, Gordon pointed at a child's skull and said to a captured slaver:

'The owner of that globe has already told Allah what you have done.'

'It wasn't me,' the man whimpered.

Sir Arthur, by contrast, meeting Bryce, was required to bow

313

to him and, in his absence, refer to him as his Responsible Adviser.★

Gordon was to take his revenge for this. First, he did some (quite unconstitutional) sleuthing about Bryce-*kohuru* and passed on his findings to the historian Rusden. (This was later found out and it nearly cost him a peerage. His elevation to the House of Lords, his natural habitat, was delayed for some years.)

Secondly, however, and well within the propriety of his role, he turned his despatches to London into a carefully prepared indictment of the colonial government, which would eventually be laid before the House of Commons and thus the British people. There was one obstacle to the plan: Lord Kimberley and Gladstone did not sympathise with Gordon or the Maori. Kimberley refused to table the despatches and Gladstone supported him. It was Gladstone who in 1847 said 'as far as England was concerned there is not a more strictly and rigorously binding treaty in existence than that of Waitangi', and Gladstone who in the 1860s handed full control of Maori policy to the settlers, like Fox, who laughed at the treaty and said it was fit only for the dustbin. The historian Rusden, who in the 1880s seems to have been everywhere at once – in his library in Melbourne, walking with Maori chiefs over stolen land in the Waikato, at the Athenaeum Club firing off letters to all corners of the world – one day happened to see Gladstone crossing the quadrangle at the Colonial Office and accidentally run into a Maori deputation who had come to London seeking help.

He described Gladstone's face: 'I saw a furtive glance. I saw an expression more of aversion than of pity . . . I saw the leader of the House of Commons stride away as if he had been injured by

★ Even from the Middle East, 'Chinese' Gordon kept abreast of New Zealand affairs. He wrote to Rusden from Syria: 'Men like Bryce do things and never think of the true bearing of them, and are horrified when their actions are depicted . . . I do not in the least imagine that civilization has made man more compassionate in himself. He fears the criticism, but when that is wanting he is as ruthless as ever.'

having an opportunity of using his great gift of words in alleviating the sorrows for which he had made himself in some degree responsible.'

The colonial ministers in Wellington knew that Gordon's despatches were hostile but, with allies like Gladstone and Kimberley in the Commons, they felt reasonably secure they would not be exposed. But the Commons was not the colonial assembly where rules of procedure were torn up whenever it suited the ministry, and ministries were torn up whenever it suited a majority. Gordon too had friends in the House, and finally, after persistent demands, his despatches were 'extorted' from the Colonial Office and laid before the House. They were being printed in October and were published in Britain in November.

In January 1883, a single copy of the Blue Book reached Wellington.

There was consternation. The despatches were worse than anyone had feared. For there, under 'Correspondence respecting Native Affairs in New Zealand, and the Imprisonment of Certain Maoris', was not only Gordon's own memoranda but commentary and reports from the local press. To be scrupulously fair, or rather to give the appearance of fairness, Gordon had included copy from the pro-government *New Zealand Times*, but far more impressive was the array of thunder and lightning from the *Lyttleton Times*.

Many persons are beginning to wonder where Mr Bryce ends and the British Constitution begins. Both are at present 'mixed up' like Buttercup's Babies. Magna Carta says: 'No freeman shall be taken or imprisoned, or be dissesised of his freehold, or liberties, or free customs, or be outlawed, or exiled, or any otherwise damaged, nor will we pass upon him, nor send upon, but by lawful judgement of his peers, or by the law of the land.' Mr Bryce's will seems now to be 'the judgement of peers' and 'the law of the land'. He takes

315

and imprisons men, women and children at his sole discretion; and arbitrarily destroys their property and despoils them of their goods. He sorts out families as he would deal a pack of cards, and deports them wholesale to what he is pleased to call their homes. If a native does not voluntarily state his name, he is forthwith handcuffed and sent to prison . . .

Mr Bryce has a genius. In whatever he undertakes he contrives to make himself look ridiculous . . . Let him loose and he is sure to be absurd . . . After carefully collecting a huge force of soldiery from all parts of the Colony, he has to read the Riot Act to a peaceful population calmly seated in their own market-place.

We never heard before that the reading aloud of the Riot Act made, *de facto*, an orderly meeting riotous. Assuming for the sake of argument that the words of that Act, when uttered by the human voice have that miraculous efficacy, we are quite unable to understand how they could similarly operate on villages twenty or thirty miles off, and altogether out of hearing. What law justified imprisonment, plunder, and destruction of property at those villages? . . .

What law has made Mr Bryce the controller of human liberties and lives? He has no more lawful power to do these things at Parihaka than he has at Christchurch.

We are told that the Colonial Treasurer [Atkinson] was foremost into a hut in a village far from Parihaka . . . Fancy, as a matter of good taste, a Minister of the Crown heading an illegal foray and rushing into deserted cottages in search of spoil!

It is not the fault of the Government that Te Whiti and his followers have not been shot down like dogs. Every preparation was made for that . . . fighting was only averted by the wise counsels and influence of Te Whiti . . .

The behaviour of the Maoris at Parihaka is the most striking feature of the story of the last few days. Such completeness of

316

good temper under great provocation has never been paralleled in history.

And so on and so on. Pages of the Blue Book were filled with comment of this kind, disclosing events never revealed by the Colonial Office, or imagined in the House of Commons.

But the worst was yet to come. Gordon had also included in his despatches a series of eyewitness accounts – mostly Croumbie-Brown's – of the events that took place at Parihaka. This was devastating. Those other things, the editorials, the official memoranda, might be taken with a grain of salt – a Governor's rivalry with his ministers, an editor's easy rage against politicians. But there on the pages of a Blue Book were the actual sights and sounds that could not be explained away. The drafting of the crowds like sheep; the tearing down of houses; singing children; the baying of dogs and then a silence; the sound of a distant band approaching: 'When a body meets a body, coming through the rye'. And, through the latticed walls of a cooking hut, not an action escaped observation, not an order was unheard.

Te Whiti was ordered to come and stand in the presence of Mr Bryce in the graveyard . . .

Bryce, in a harsh voice: 'Make a good road, therefore, for the passage of my horse through your people.'

A woman was weeping and another one said: 'Why are you sorry? Look! he is smiling as he goes away with the Pakeha.'

The colonial ministers and the Chief Justice were terrified of coming under the scrutiny of the House of Commons. This may seem strange when they cared little about the views of the Colonial Office or even successive ministries in Britain. But in the 1880s, parliamentary power was at its height and the House of Commons had far more power to direct the executive than the compliant and well-whipped body of today. Bryce and Whitaker probably, also, exaggerated the power of the House of

317

Commons: their local experience was of a truly unbridled and tyrannical assembly, which trampled on the rights of a minority whenever it pleased. (Fox even argued on one occasion that whatever the colonial assembly did was not only legal, it was constitutional.)

Now various dark thoughts must have flashed through their minds. The repeal of confiscation? The repeal of indemnifying bills? The taking back of control of Maori affairs? Mr Justice Prendegast and other ministers rushed off letters explaining and denying and complaining, and asked them to be laid before the Commons as well. But Kimberley had gone. The Colonial Office replied coldly that the new correspondence was not 'of sufficient public interest to justify the communication of further papers to Parliament on the matter'.

Action was needed rather than words. There was already on the books a recent law granting amnesty to various, now ageing, chiefs who had taken up arms years before. Within a week or two the amnesty was proclaimed for them. But the real issue was still the detention without trial of two chiefs who, even Bryce once admitted, had never borne arms and kept the peace for years on the coast. There was nothing for it but to set Te Whiti and Tohu free.

On 8 March, a certain Mr Dive of the Native Office was sent to inform the prisoners of their release and to look sternly into their eyes. The government wanted to bury the past and let them go free, but it hoped they would 'cease raising strife' and hold no more meetings. Te Whiti replied evenly: 'If grasshoppers find good new grass, they will come. Nothing can prevent them.'

With this mild and unwelcome image ringing down the wires to Wellington, the two men were taken aboard the *Stella* for the one-hundred-and-thirty-mile night crossing to Taranaki. With them they had 'nearly £30 worth of clothing, etc. . . . a *tohu aroha* . . . a gift of loving forgiveness from the Government'. They set sail from Nelson at dusk.

318

In the early light the following morning, the silhouette of Mt. Taranaki could just be seen from the deck of the *Stella* which was still far out to sea. Tohu came up from below, chanting an ancient greeting to the mountain that rose darkly above their lowland home. Te Whiti 'was much agitated, but very silent'.

The two chiefs went back to Parihaka and spent the rest of their lives there. The town was rebuilt in a splendid new style, with immense verandaed and balconied meeting-houses in European style, small cottages and thatched *whare* of raupo (reed) all mixed together. The crowds returned every month. The bush was gradually felled and white farms lay all around Parihaka, but relations were friendly. The settlers' children came to listen to Te Whiti. ('We were drawn to him in a way that very few Maoris could influence us,' one old pioneer remembered seven decades later. 'There is always something good in those who attract young people.') A Prime Minister ('King Dick' Seddon) came to call and tried to make light of the past, but he was rebuked and retired discomfited. Sometimes trouble flared in other parts of the province, when Maori suddenly reappeared on confiscated land and were beaten back by farmers and policemen. Te Whiti was arrested again, taken to the High Court in Wellington, and sentenced to three months' gaol by the Chief Justice Prendegast.

All this and more will be described properly when a biographer of Te Whiti gathers the facts and the speeches from the Maori oral record, rather than from newspaper stories and official reports. In any case, the stream of newspaper stories and government reports dwindled away over the final years. The long arc of the story began in the early 1860s and continued until Te Whiti's death, but the core of it, the essential drama, took place between 1880 and 1882.

What are we to make of this episode? Most whites, and many Maori, saw it as a defeat for Te Whiti, but some of both races saw it as a victory. If so, it was a strange kind of victory. 'Mine is the land, mine the people, this is the struggle of this generation,' Te Whiti said – but he lost more of his land than any other Maori leader and his people were abused and scattered. Why, with a little more flexion of the knee, could he not accept the power of the whites, take what was offered, avoid the risk of massacre? What did he achieve?

The answer is hidden in the meaning of the word 'land'. For Te Whiti, 'land' – even his own ancestral territory – was not just a material plain, so to speak, dotted with hummocks and lit by the sun. He was surrounded by the revolutionary language of Darwin, irresistible and multivalent, and Darwin's image of a world of slow geological changes, over which species moved slowly and changed blindly, adapting to become 'fitter' in the struggle for life. Te Whiti's own vision was carefully counter-poised to that: there *was* a great landscape over which mankind moved slowly, but for man it was, simultaneously, a moral landscape in which the struggle was between justice and in-justice. And even that landscape underwent change: 'The world since Cain and Abel has been flooded by war again and again . . . Now war shall cease and no longer create dissension . . . The race of Adam has fallen over many precipices, but those pre-cipices have now disappeared by numerous landslips and we shall not fall over them again . . . The one precipice which has not been levelled is death, and we must all die.'

This was the struggle that Te Whiti caused to be played out on the plains and among the hillocks around Parihaka. 'He will neither fight nor submit,' Hall complained. 'It is costing us a fortune.' To fight was to fall back into the past; to submit was to give into the fear of war, which amounted to the same thing. Te Whiti refused both. His genius was to convince his people that they were engaged in an unprecedented contest, as exciting and dangerous as hunting and killing the shark. The contest began with the arrival of armed men on the Waimate Plains and ended when it was clear that, with a little help from a gentleman wearing a shark's tooth breast-pin, Te Whiti had to be set free. Between them came the ploughing, the fencing, the invasion of Parihaka, deportation and demolition. Each of these battles, against war itself, he and his people won.

The beginning and the end of the period were marked by comets, and as I reached the end of this story it seemed to me, perhaps because I had already filled this book with quotations – some readers may think too many, but the voices quoted tell the story better than I could – that these 'long-haired stars', as the Greeks called them, took on the appearance of quotation marks, of apostrophes, of *commas* (no relation). Between these two great markers in the sky, suspended above a period of thirty months, what should be written?

There are almost too many candidates: there are the thunders from the *Lyttleton Times*; the prophecies heard in Parliament of shame in future generations; settlers' cries for 'extermination as a law of nature'; Bryce's calling 'from the vasty deep'.

Te Whiti alone, in thirty or forty speeches during that time, supplies many more.

'If war comes, we can only look on and laugh.'
'I am for peace. One day, when children are asked who made the peace, they will answer "Te Whiti".'
'All things made upon the face of the earth were created with affection and love. Therefore our affairs should continue by love.'
'Many generations in the past have tried to attain patience under tribulation and forbearance under suffering, but none have succeeded. You are the first.'

Perhaps it would be simpler to look for a single word, remembering that quotation marks have ambivalent powers: they rescue from the mass, they lift out to examine and admire; but they also possess a tendency to reduce and disempower. A single word, even the most powerful word, becomes ill at ease, unsure of itself, when it is suspended between quotation marks. Looking back over those thirty months, which began with the arrival of Bryce's armed men on the plains, one small word comes to mind. It could be written that Te Whiti achieved something that had never been done before. A great danger had approached and he had reduced it, made it look abashed, unsure of itself, even ridiculous. He turned war into 'war'.

Epilogue

Te Whiti o Rongomai died on 18 November 1907 after being taken ill on the night following the monthly meeting at Parihaka, which he had addressed as usual. He was said to be in despondent mood on the final evening of his life: Tohu had died less than a month before, and the crowds at the meeting earlier that day were much smaller than usual – 'not a single Maori from outside the village and only two pakeha visitors'. At least that was the report in the *Taranaki Herald* and it is not entirely reliable; in the week after Te Whiti's death, the *Herald* still could not make up its mind whether there were some 'fine traits in his character' or whether he was 'a wonderful old impostor'.

After the crowd dispersed that day, Te Whiti went along the veranda of his son-in-law's house where he now lived (his wife had died years before, while he was in jail for the second time) and attended to his pet pigeons. Pigeon-keeping was one of the customs of the Pakeha which had taken Te Whiti's fancy while he was in Christchurch; and for many years his own flock took off and wheeled above the rooftops of Parihaka. That night, Te Whiti sat alone in his sitting room, 'coughing and somewhat restless' and, perhaps, despondent. At midnight he was taken ill; by 3 a.m. he was partly conscious but speechless; he died at five in the morning not long before first light.

If the *Taranaki Herald* was ambivalent about the man, so was

Maoridom. The news of his death flashed across the country; thousands came to Parihaka – but not as many thousands as were expected. For two or three days most speakers lamented over the dead leader, but some denounced him. Tohu's son-in-law was one of the latter: 'What is the result of their work? Has the land come back to you? The land is gone. Talk about words! Wind! What is the use of their predictions? They have all come wrong. You have been duped. These men, Te Whiti and Tohu, were masters in word-painting, that is all. You have been deceived.'

One woman was still more bitter: 'Te Whiti was a swindler,' she shrieked. 'Tohu was a swindler. No more Te Whitis! No more swindles!'

Sometimes when a silence fell between the orations an accordion could be heard in the distance; some of the fashionable young people were seen 'gaily cakewalking in the back-ranks' of the mourners.

Swarms of children raced about everywhere taking no notice of cakewalkers, or of the elderly orators and singers of *moteatea* (death-songs). 'Behold the star in the east is dimmed with clouds,' one woman sang. 'It is lost for a day, a night, a month, yet it returns. But thou, beloved one . . . thy star has set for ever. Now thy brow is chilled by the cold hand of death.'

Large numbers of whites also came to Parihaka – there were more whites than Maori present at the actual burial. But they were 'merely thoughtless gapers', said the *Herald* severely. 'In the large circle, whites and blacks were intermingled. Great was the contrast of the eager faces of the pakeha, straining to catch everything of interest, and the solemn faces of the Maori whose heads were bowed in sadness and in reverence . . .'

One group of whites saved the situation; surveyors, government agents, ex-officials, they had known Te Whiti for years and knew something of Maori custom at a *tangi*. A Mr Skinner, a Mr Gray, a Mr Jack, a Rev. Brocklehurst, a Captain Young and a Captain Hood advanced on to the *marae* together, stood with bowed heads near the body lying in state, then two of them made speeches: Te Whiti was *makarau* (man loved by a thousand), said Mr Gray, who welcomed the tribes on behalf of Europeans of the district. He had always looked forward to the day when there would be a union of the two races, how sad it should not take place until the day of his death, etc.

Skinner, chief draughtsman in the Survey Department, said that whatever Te Whiti's defects, he always worked for the best.

The demeanour of this party of white mourners, said a Dr Pomare, made up for all the other thoughtlessness. 'We have feelings, and conduct like that is deeply appreciated.' Pomare had been one of the children at the gate of Parihaka charged by the cavalry twenty-five years before. He was now a government officer with his eyes set on a political career. He made a speech which became famous and, in a sense, became the nation's official ideology of race for many years:

> The Pakeha is not a stranger; he is one blood with us. Back in the fabled past we had a common ancestor; then the Pakeha went westward and met other races and acquired arts and sciences which placed him in the leadership of civilised nations. Our Maori ancestors went towards the rising sun but had the misfortune not to strike the metal key which opens the vast door of knowledge. He clung to the stone, while his Pakeha brother was advancing with the metal. Ever brave and venturesome the Maori set out over the unknown waters while his brother clung to the land, journeying westward through Europe, fearing to cross the ocean in case he should tumble off the edge of a square world . . . But we have met again after many years, in a strange land under new skies, where neither of us are native . . . One of your ancestors, Tiriwa, two hundred years before the white man came said 'Shadowed behind the tattooed face the stranger waits. He is white. He owns the earth.' Now the Pakeha has come, the

325

metal has taken the place of the stone. The lightning flash of the Pakeha's wisdom [the telephone] speaks from near and far. The old order has changed; your ancestors said it would change. When the net is old and worn it is cast aside and the new net goes fishing. I do not want to cast discredit on the old net; it was good in its time and many fish were caught in it. But it is now worn with time and we must go fishing with the new net that our brother has brought to us . . .

This was all nonsense, another speaker said. Te Whiti's doctrine was not that New Zealand was for both races. It was for the Maori alone.

Others gave up any attempt to make sense of the new situation. 'Go, illustrious one. Depart, depart. He was the last of the great. The wind has fallen mercilessly on this garden. This is the last day of Maori wisdom; the Maori day has passed; the Maori sun is set, it is done, done for ever. I too am done with Parihaka. I spit out my defiance!'

The disputes continued until the moment came for the burial.

'There was great lamentation while the shrouded body was being lowered to its resting place. Taare Waitara, calling in a loud voice, said: "Cease this noise; let peace be upon the people." And immediately the wailing and movement ceased. The silence was singular.'

'It was the only moment,' said the *Hawera Star*, 'throughout the whole five days of *tangi* that the voiceless quiet of nature was unbroken.' The great crowd watched the body go out of view.

Sir William Fox had died fifteen years before, outliving Lady Fox by exactly a year. Almost the last sighting of him was his ascent of Mt. Taranaki. He set a record as the oldest (and slowest) person to achieve the feat. From the summit that day little could be seen; smoke from new farms and cleared forests was rising in all directions.

'That Sir W. Fox should have accomplished the trip at his advanced age was a great feat, a compliment to British pluck and determination,' his niece, Miss Halcombe, wrote. 'There were some grand peeps of the distant snow-covered peaks. No *clearly* distinct Panorama of the country was obtained as bush-fires obscured the scene. Sir W. Fox from the crater beheld a sight rarely if ever seen before. *Sunset*, and a most marvellous shadow, a distinct, violet-coloured repelequ [sic] of the mountain showed itself laid over the country; so perfect was the shadow that it had the appearance of a carefully cut out *velvet* pattern of the mountain, laid over the country beneath.'

On the way up the mountain, the party came upon a splendid forest tree which 'some ruffian had fired'.

'Sir William expressed himself strongly on the subject of rigid conservation.'

Fox was soon forgotten after his death. He is remembered now only for a number of his watercolours, and his role in setting up national parks. Although he spent a good deal of his last years in Taranaki, he and the other, no longer young William Fox, did not meet again. In his will, Sir William left money to a crèche in Stepney Causeway, to Dr Barnardo's in Stepney Causeway, to the Bowen Thompson Girls School in Beirut and 'for the suppression of the liquor traffic in New Zealand, if it still be in existence'. Fifteen years after his death, an Auckland paper noticed that his grave was quite neglected and overgrown.

Young William Fox came and went at Parihaka for many years. At one stage he had an office in Tohu's meeting-house, Rangi-Kapuia ('the Gathering of the Skies'), and he also paid for a field near Mawhitiwhiti which could be used as a campsite for people travelling to Parihaka and helped set up a Maori school nearby. He never went back to the law. He worked as a licensed interpreter (first grade) in Wanganui and in Hawera set up a business teaching Maori language:

Fox's Epistolary-Phono-Postal Method
of
teaching the Maori Language by Home Study
Prospectus posted free
on application to
Mr. W. Fox,
Matapu, Hawera,
Taranaki, NZ

At one time he thought of entering politics, and was described then in a national weekly as 'a cultured man and a notable figure in Taranaki', but then nothing came of his campaign. He never resumed close ties with his family and he never married. Whatever became of his Hinemoa, slipping over melon skins with him down the back lanes at Parihaka?

'Why didn't he get married?' I asked Miri Rangi.

'Oh, dear . . .' she said. 'I *wish* he had.' I thought that in her reply I could hear some diplomatic deflection and I did not pursue the question. Perhaps after those years as a child in a big silent house reading stories with his Pakeha mother, whom he always loved (he referred to her for the rest of his life as 'Mama'), he paid the penalty for his fate and was never able to be fully at home in either world. Perhaps that is what fate means – paying the penalty for what happens to you.

Once or twice he went back and walked over the field of the battle of The Beak of the Bird, and he was in correspondence with various old soldiers and local historians about the wars. He died quite young, in 1918, 'respected by both races', and was buried at Leppertown to the north of the mountain – the same place where another child, the blonde Caroline Perrett, was once snatched away by members of another race and, like him, had her life changed for ever.

Driving north through Leppertown one hot summer day in 1998, I stopped and looked for his grave but couldn't find it.

There were only a hundred or so headstones, bees were buzzing hopefully in some new flowers set in a jam jar at the base of one, the sun was beating down, tree shadows darkened the verges, but there was no sign of William Fox Omahuru. I had a notion that this bright, intelligent, and peaceable man, whose destiny it was to be fought over and never to belong, had packed up everything, even his gravestone, and had slipped, very quietly, away.

★   ★   ★

In 1998, I also visited Parihaka for the first time. It was very quiet, very hushed; apart from the sound of distant hammering, you might have thought you were in a ghost town. It was just a small village standing among green hillocks, with a great mountain on the north horizon. That day, the mountain was hidden by a high bank of grey cloud.

The source of the hammering became plain. Te Miringa came towards us, jauntily swinging a hammer. Te Miringa Hohaia is one of the leaders of the Parihaka community today. We remembered each other vaguely from student days. We stood there by Te Whiti's tomb and looked at modern Parihaka.

The biggest of the old balconied meeting-houses and dining halls had been burned down thirty or forty years ago, but here and there I could see an old gabled house or building familiar from the early photographs.

Two paradise ducks flew overhead calling with a strange shrill cry. We could see their strongly contrasted colours, the male with its dark head and neck, the female with hers pure white. 'The call-notes of the two sexes', according to Buller, 'differ remarkably; the drake utters a prolonged guttural note, "*tuk-o-o-o, tuk-o-o-o*"; and the duck responds with a shrill call, like the high note of a clarionet.'

'They mate for life,' Te Miringa said as we stood there by the tomb watching them as they dwindled against the cloud. Tohu's meeting-house, Rangi-Kapuia, 'The Gathering of the Skies', is still there, and opposite stands a school which has a witty name, I thought – the House of Ignorance, or perhaps the House for the Ignorant.

There are only about fifty dwellings now at Parihaka. Once a month hundreds of people come from further afield, and twice a year, I was told, that number swells to a thousand or more. To my wonder, I had noticed that the place is not on the map, not even in the most detailed book of road maps I could find, which indicates almost every farmhouse in the country by a black dot. As far as mapmakers are concerned, Parihaka does not exist. And nor officially was there ever such a person as Te Whiti O Rongomai. Most public figures mentioned in this story have been commemorated in some way; Fox has a small beach town named after him, and a glacier; Richmond, a town; McLean, an avenue of palms and a major sports ground; even John Bryce has a mountain named in his honour, or at least there is a Mt. Bryce, although it is safely tucked away in a group of remote snow-peaks in the south.

Buller received no name-honours, but he is remembered for his books. His 1888 *History of the Birds of New Zealand* was described to me once by an English natural historian as the finest book on birds ever written. Buller died with the whiff of a land-deal scandal still hanging over him. He continued, until the edge of the grave, to hanker after more strings of letters to add to those after his name. In 1896 it suddenly came to him that he should have been awarded a certain military medal in view of his attendance at a battle in 1865. He wrote to the long-retired Governor and Commander-in-Chief, who still had a say in these matters. 'I have discovered a new *Larus*, a lovely little sea-gull, on which I propose to bestow your name.'

Rolleston presides over central Christchurch with his statue

330

looking down New Zealand's finest street to the cathedral, half a mile away, which was consecrated in the same week that he held the halter of Bryce's white horse at Parihaka. When we were children living in Christchurch, we took a vague familial interest in this stone man under the deciduous trees on Rolleston Avenue: his daughter had been my father's godmother. On a recent trip back there, my sister and I stopped and had another look at him, wise and grave, among the Victorian neo-gothic buildings.

'The old hypocrite,' I said.

'Yes,' said my sister, looking up at him. 'He's even got a hypocrite's *hairdo*, if you see what I mean.' And I did, for he does, although it is a physical feature difficult to describe. But as to Te Whiti . . . there has never been a sign of recognition of his existence or achievement at national or even provincial level; not a stamp, not a road, not a rock. This shows not only the ineptitude of the official mind, but its grand inconsequence. For no one driving through Foxton, with its bacon factory, or walking over the moraine at the foot of the glacier actually summons Sir William to mind, and no one now likes to remember the cold and subtle Whitaker or the frightening figure of Bryce. Te Whiti, by contrast, has never been forgotten, and year by year his reputation quietly grows.

One day, a few months after visiting Parihaka, I was back in Taranaki with my brother-in-law, Dene, and we drove up the mountain taking the road to a famous waterfall named Dawson's Falls. This was a place I rememberd with complete clarity from my only other visit. It was 1951: we were, I think, in a rented car, and it was Christmas Day. When we reached the car park my father took me to the edge of the field and showed me the view. There was New Plymouth, the town we lived in, there the church steeple, the roof of my sister's school, the blue Pacific . . . Later we walked into the bush and saw the Falls, dropping with a grey roar through the trees; I remembered people standing far below us on a kind of winding stair.

Now in January 1999, Dene and I were driving back up through the National Park forest. I should have realised something was wrong long before we got there. We parked the car and I walked over the grass paddock to see the view my father had shown me decades before. It was only then that I saw my mistake. We were on completely the wrong side of the mountain. It was impossible for me ever to have seen New Plymouth, which is north of Mt. Taranaki, from where I now stood on the southern slopes.

For a minute or two I was puzzled and even pained by this strange and arbitrary trick that memory had played on me. I must have combined the Christmas Day trip with another (now quite forgotten) to the north slope of the mountain, and painted over a landscape which meant nothing to me with the features of one I knew.

But then, looking down at the disappointing plains, I saw where I was. The town in the distance was not New Plymouth but Hawera. Down there in the haze was a remnant of forest where a battle had once been fought. Over the low hills on the horizon, a road led to Wanganui where a child had once been photographed beside a table with a black spiral stand. Across the fields directly below us an angry old knight on horseback had gone chasing after his foster-son, a law clerk, and over to the west was another town where one day a band was heard approaching and then an army came around the road and was blocked by a line of singing children.

We were, in other words, standing above the landscape of this book. Memory, that wilful filing-clerk with no idea of accuracy or order had achieved a feat that I would never have thought of. It had stealthily produced a single, wrong and economical image of a place that had lasted in my mind for years, and I thought perhaps it had done this not because the

332

place had mattered to me, but because one day it was going to.

It was a hazy, blue morning and I stood on the worn rocks above the car park looking at the landscape of the book I was about to begin. And I also thought, as we came down and went in to see the Falls, that this, also, is where it could end.

Chronology

Approx AD 1000	Discovery of New Zealand by Polynesians
Approx 1300	Colonisation by Polynesians
1658	Discovery by Abel Tasman
1769	Discovery and landfall by Captain Cook
Oct 1769	Kidnappings in Hawke Bay and elsewhere
1840	British sovereignty established by Treaty of Waitangi
1860	War breaks out
1862	Wreck of the *Lord Worsley*
1862	Birth of Ngatau Omahuru
1863	Confiscation laws passed
1866	Hostilities die away
1867	Truce
May 1868	Titokowaru attacks, war resumed
Sept 1868	Battle of the Beak of the Bird
Jan 1869	William Fox junior sent to Wellington
Feb 1869	Titokowaru flees
June 1869	William Fox becomes Premier, peace returns
1875–6	Foxes travel the world
1878	Armed survey of Waimate Plains begins
1879	Te Whiti's ploughing protests
1880	The fencing protests
1881	Attack on Parihaka
1882	Te Whiti released
1907	Death of Te Whiti
1918	Death of William Fox Omahuru

A Note on Sources

While writing this book, which begins with a ghost story and ends with a recollection of childhood, it at first seemed absurd to dress it up as a proper history book, with footnotes, sources and bibliography. On the other hand, I realised that the reader is entitled to feel confidence in a writer's sources. I tried to overcome the difficulty by indicating in the text the provenance of the material I was relying on at that point. This did not always fit the case. This note is intended to give some account of the material which provided most information.

The main difficulty I encountered in researching the life of such a small figure as Ngatau Omahuru/William Fox was that the Native Department archives were largely destroyed by fire in 1907. But there were other problems. It seems typical of Sir William Fox, so garrulous and indiscreet in life, that he should be so silent in death. His papers at the Alexander Turnbull Library are extremely scanty. There is a tantalising reference in Rusden to a Fox diary, but no one now knows the whereabouts of this. The most crucial letters that I found regarding young Fox were in the Buller papers.

The main published texts relied on were James Belich's account of Titokowaru's war, *I Shall Not Die* (Wellington, 1989), and two books on Te Whiti and Parihaka: *Ask That Mountain*, by Dick Scott (Auckland, 1975), and an exhaustive political history, *Days of Darkness, Taranaki 1878–1884* by Hazel Riseborough (Wellington, 1989). I also found Rusden's *History of New Zealand* (Melbourne, 1889) and his *Auretanga; Groans of the Maoris*, London, 1888, and James Cowan's *The New Zealand Wars and the Pioneering Period* (Wellington, 1922–3) valuable and suggestive works. The principal unpublished sources were: Maori Affairs Department archives (NZ National Archives); Buller papers (Alexander Turnbull Library); McLean Correspondence (ATL); Fox papers, (ATL); Hadfield papers (ATL) and McDonald Reminiscences (ATL).

The following is a list of other source material used or quoted:

Appendices to the Journals of the House of Representatives, 1868–1884

Army Department archives, National Archives

Baucke, W., *Where The White Man Treads*, Auckland, 1928

Bell Papers (ATL)

Boreham, E. W., *George Augustus Selwyn*, London, 1889

Broughton, Ruka, *Ngaa Mahi Whakari a Titokowaru*, Wellington, 1993

Bryce v. Rusden: in the High Court of Justice, London, 1886

Buick, T., *Old Manawatu*, Palmerston North, 1903

Buller, W., *History of the Birds of New Zealand*, 1888

Bulley, E. A., *George Augustus Selwyn, First Bishop of New Zealand*, London, 1909

Butler, Samuel, *Erewhon*, London, 1872

Curteis, George H., *Bishop Selwyn of New Zealand*, London, 1889

Darwin, Charles Robert, *On the Origin of Species by means of Natural Selection, or the Preservation of Favoured Races in the Struggle for Life*, London, 1859

Dictionary of New Zealand Biography, edit. G. H. Scholefield, Wellington, 1940

Dilke, Charles, *Greater Britain*, London, 1868

Domett, Alfred, *Ranolf and Amohia, a South-Seas day dream*, London, 1872

Downes, T. W., *Old Whanganui*, Hawera, 1915

Fildes Collection, Victoria University of Wellington Library

Fox, Sarah, *To the Mothers of New Zealand*, Wellington, 1881

Fox, William, general papers held at ATL

Fox, William, *The War in New Zealand*, London, 1866

Galbreath, R., 'Sir Walter Buller, a Biographical Essay', 1982

Gisborne, W., *New Zealand Rulers and Statesmen 1840–1885*, London, 1886

Gordon, W. F., Notes taken during the Troublous Times (ATL)

Gordon, W. F., Battlesites in Taranaki, correspondence and newspaper articles (ATL)

Grey, George, Collection, Auckland Public Library

Gudgeon, T. W., *The Defenders of New Zealand*, Auckland, 1887

Hadfield, O., Papers (ATL)

Halcombe family, Letters (ATL)

Hall, John, Papers (ATL)

Hodgson, Terence, *Colonial Capital*, Auckland, 1990

Houston, John, Papers (ATL)

Jackson, *Annals of a New Zealand Family*, 1935

Leckie, F. M., *The Early History of Wellington College*, Auckland, 1934

Livingstone, James, Diaries, New Plymouth Public Library

MacMorran, George, *Some Schools and Schoolmasters of early Wellington*, Wellington, 1900

McCormick, E. H., Paintings of Sir William Fox

McDonnell Papers (ATL)

McLean, Sir Donald, Papers (ATL)

Main, W., *Through a Victorian Lens*, Wellington, 1972

Mantell Papers (ATL), 1884

Martin, Mary, Lady, *Our Maoris*, London, 1884

Milosz, Czeslaw, *Native Realm*, 1968

Newland Reminiscences, New Plymouth Public Library

Nicholas, J. L., *Narrative of a Voyage to New Zealand*, London, 1817

O'Brien, Diana, *Oeo through the Years*, Hawera, 1985

Richmond Letters (ATL)

The Richmond–Atkinson Papers, edit. G. H. Scholefield, Wellington, 1960

Roberts, C. J., *Centennial History of Hawera and the Waimate Plains*, Hawera, 1940

Rolleston family, Papers (ATL)

Rusden, G. W., Papers (ATL)

Stafford, E. W., Papers (ATL)

Taylor, R., *Te Ika a Maui, or New Zealand and its Inhabitants*, London, 1855

Tempsky, Gustav von, *Mitla*, London, 1858

Ward, E., *Early Wellington*, Auckland, 1909

Ward, John, *Wanderings with the Maori Prophets, Te Whiti and Tohu*, Nelson, 1883

Williams, T. C., *The Manawatu Purchase Completed; or the Treaty of Waitangi Broken*, London, 1868

Wilson, J. G., *Early Rangitikei*, Christchurch, 1914

Wilson, J. G., *History of Hawke's Bay*, Dunedin, 1939

Newspapers:

Bulls Roarer

Evening Post

Free Lance

Lyttleton Times

Marist Messenger

New Zealand Mail

Rangitikei Advocate

Taranaki Herald

Wairarapa Standard

Wanganui Evening Herald

Daily Advertiser

New Zealand Herald

Hawera Star

Maori Record

New Zealand Herald

Patea Mail

Taranaki Daily News

Under Canvas (Rahotu)

Wanganui Chronicle

Wellington Independent

Glossary

Note: The following definitions are confined to the meanings of the words as they are used in the text.

ake ake — for ever
aroha — love
haka — a dance of challenge
hapu — sub-tribe, clan
Hau Hau — adherent of Pai Marire movement
heitiki — a type of ornament
hongi — to greet by pressing noses
hui — gathering, meeting
huia — forest bird, now extinct
iwi — tribe
kahikatea — white pine
kahu — native hawk
kai — food
karaka — glossy-leaved tree
kauri — native pine
kohuru — murder, wickedness
kore — nothingness
korero — talk, discussion
kupapa — Maori supporter of British rule
ma — pale, white

mana – power, prestige, efficacy
manu – bird
Maori – indigenous people of New Zealand
mauri – life force
marae – assembly place in front of meeting-house
moa – huge flightless bird, now extinct
mokai – tamed animal, pet
morehu – remnant, survivor
nga – the (plural)
ngati – the (plural), those of, the many of
nikau – native palm
pa (or pah) – a fortified Maori position, a village
Pai Marire – a syncretic Maori-Judaeo-Christian spiritual movement
Pakeha – Maori name for Europeans
patupaiarehe – fairy, forest sprite
paua – abalone-like shellfish
pouri – gloomy, sad, melancholy
puhoro – type of tattoo
pukapuka – letter
pakaru – broken, ruined, shattered
puku – belly, vital parts
punga – tree-fern
puremu – adultery
rangatira – leading man, chief, noble
rape – type of tattoo
roia – lawyer
ruru – native owl
takoha – gift
taipo – demon, goblin
Tane Mahuta – god of the forest
tangi – funeral, lamentation
taonga – treasure
tapu – sacred, forbidden
taringa – the ear

tatarakihi – cicada
tauiwi – alien, stranger
taumaihi – bastions
te – the (singular)
tena koe – a greeting
tito – liar
toa – warrior
tohu – sign
tokotoko – chief's staff
totara – large forest-tree
totoia – to be dragged, hauled
tui – a songbird
turehu – fairy people
tutu (noun) – a plant with poisonous seeds
tutu (adj.) – mischievous
tutua – low born
Uenuku – god of the rainbow, associated with war
waiata – a song
weka – small, aggressive flightless bird
whare – house
wharenui – meeting-house
whenua – land

A Note on the Author

Peter Walker is a New Zealander who has lived in London since 1986. He worked for seven years on the *Independent* and for three on the *Independent on Sunday* where he was Foreign Editor. He has also written for the *Financial Times* and *Granta*. He is currently writing a novel.

A Note on the Type

The text of this book is set in Bembo. This type was first used in 1495 by the Venetian printer Aldus Manutius for Cardinal Bembo's *De Aetna*, and was cut for Manutius by Francesco Griffo. It was one of the types used by Claude Garamond (1480–1561) as a model for his Romain de L'Université, and so it was the forerunner of what became standard European type for the following two centuries. Its modern form follows the original types and was designed for Monotype in 1929.